LIBRARY OF HEBREW BIBLE/
OLD TESTAMENT STUDIES

725

Formerly Journal for the Study of the Old Testament Supplement Series

Editors
Laura Quick, Oxford University, UK
Jacqueline Vayntrub, Yale University, USA

Founding Editors
David J. A. Clines, Philip R. Davies and David M. Gunn

Editorial Board
Sonja Ammann, Alan Cooper, Steed Davidson, Susan Gillingham,
Rachelle Gilmour, John Goldingay, Rhiannon Graybill, Anne Katrine Gudme,
Norman K. Gottwald, James E. Harding, John Jarick, Tracy Lemos,
Carol Meyers, Eva Mroczek, Daniel L. Smith-Christopher,
Francesca Stavrakopoulou, James W. Watts

READING ESTHER INTERTEXTUALLY

Edited by
David G. Firth and Brittany N. Melton

LONDON • NEW YORK • OXFORD • NEW DELHI • SYDNEY

T&T CLARK

Bloomsbury Publishing Plc

50 Bedford Square, London, WC1B 3DP, UK
1385 Broadway, New York, NY 10018, USA
29 Earlsfort Terrace, Dublin 2, Ireland

BLOOMSBURY, T&T CLARK and the T&T Clark logo are trademarks of
Bloomsbury Publishing Plc

First published in Great Britain 2022
Paperback edition published 2024

Copyright © David G. Firth, Brittany N. Melton and contributors, 2022

David G. Firth and Brittany N. Melton have asserted their rights under the Copyright,
Designs and Patents Act, 1988, to be identified as Editors of this work.

All rights reserved. No part of this publication may be reproduced or transmitted in
any form or by any means, electronic or mechanical, including photocopying,
recording, or any information storage or retrieval system, without prior permission in
writing from the publishers.

Bloomsbury Publishing Plc does not have any control over, or responsibility for, any
third-party websites referred to or in this book. All internet addresses given in this
book were correct at the time of going to press. The author and publisher regret any
inconvenience caused if addresses have changed or sites have ceased to exist,
but can accept no responsibility for any such changes.

A catalogue record for this book is available from the British Library.

Library of Congress Control Number: 2022933775

ISBN: HB: 978-0-5677-0301-9
PB: 978-0-5677-0304-0
ePDF: 978-0-5677-0302-6

Series: Library of Hebrew Bible/Old Testament Studies, volume 725
ISSN 2513-8758

Typeset by Newgen KnowledgeWorks Pvt. Ltd., Chennai, India

To find out more about our authors and books visit www.bloomsbury.com
and sign up for our newsletters.

*In dedication to John Goldingay, beloved teacher, mentor, and friend,
on the occasion of his 80th birthday.*

CONTENTS

List of Tables	x
List of Contributors	xi
Preface	xii
List of Abbreviations	xiii

UNDER THE INTERTEXTUAL UMBRELLA: AN INTRODUCTION
   David G. Firth, Brittany N. Melton, and Heath A. Thomas   1

Part I
ESTHER IN DIALOGUE WITH THE TORAH

Chapter 1
FOREIGN AMBIVALENCE IN THE SCROLL: READING ESTHER'S
COURT ALONGSIDE JOSEPH AND DANIEL
   Gabriel F. Hornung   11

Chapter 2
THE BOOK OF ESTHER: EXODUS, PASSOVER, AND FOOD-LAWS
   J. Gordon McConville   23

Part II
ESTHER IN DIALOGUE WITH THE FORMER PROPHETS

Chapter 3
ESTHER AND JOSHUA: NEGOTIATING IDENTITY IN AND OUT
OF THE LAND
   David G. Firth   37

Chapter 4
EYES, HEARTS, AND DOING "WHAT SEEMS GOOD": READING JUDGES
AND ESTHER SIDE-BY-SIDE
   Isabelle Hamley   47

Chapter 5
OVERTURNING SOVEREIGNTY: ESTHER IN DIALOGUE WITH THE
BOOK OF SAMUEL
    Rachelle Gilmour   57

Part III
ESTHER IN DIALOGUE WITH THE LATTER PROPHETS

Chapter 6
AT THE TABLE: BANQUETS IN ESTHER AND ISAIAH IN
INTERTEXTUAL CONVERSATION
    Andrew T. Abernethy   71

Chapter 7
THE FRUIT OF MOURNING: ESTHER ENRICHED BY THE LATTER
PROPHETS
    Heath A. Thomas   83

Part IV
ESTHER IN DIALOGUE WITH THE WRITINGS

Chapter 8
IN A WORLD WITHOUT GOD: READING ESTHER ALONGSIDE PSALMS
    David G. Firth and Brittany N. Melton   99

Chapter 9
READING ESTHER WITH PROVERBS: COMPLEXIFYING CHARACTER,
THEME, AND IDEOLOGY
    Suzanna R. Millar   109

Part V
ESTHER IN DIALOGUE BEYOND THE HEBREW BIBLE

Chapter 10
TRAUMA, PURITY, AND DANGER IN THE LXX PRAYERS OF ESTHER
AND JUDITH
    Helen Efthimiadis-Keith (Keith-van Wyk)   123

Chapter 11
ESTHER IN DIALOGUE WITH THE QUMRAN COMMUNITY
    Seulgi L. Byun   135

Chapter 12
READING JOSEPHUS READING ESTHER
   Paul Spilsbury   147

Chapter 13
ESTHER IN DIALOGUE WITH MARK: POWER, VULNERABILITY, AND KINGSHIP
   Kara J. Lyons-Pardue   159

Chapter 14
READING ESTHER IN DIALOGUE WITH THE RABBIS
   Jonathan Grossman   169

Chapter 15
HUMAN NATURE AND POLITICS: A MODERN POLITICAL-THEORETICAL READING OF ESTHER
   Kyong-Jin Lee   183

Chapter 16
READING ESTHER INTERTEXTUALLY AFTER THE SHOAH
   Marvin A. Sweeney   195

Bibliography   207
Author Index   223
Biblical and Other Ancient Sources Index   227

TABLES

0.1	Intertextual Connections between Esther and the Hebrew Bible	3
6.1	Feasts in Esther	74
6.2	Feasting in Isaiah 25	76
6.3	Comparison of Feasts in Esther and Isaiah 25	77
7.1	Intertextual Connections between Esther and Joel	90
7.2	Intertextual Connections between Esther and Jonah	91
7.3	Intertextual Connections between Esther and Isaiah	92
10.1	Structure of Esther's and Judith's Prayers	125
13.1	Promised Favor in LXX Est. 5:3, 6; 7:2; 9:12 and Mk 6:22b, 23	162
14.1	Comparison of Moses and Mordecai	176

CONTRIBUTORS

Dr. **Andrew T. Abernethy**, Associate Professor of Old Testament, Wheaton College

Dr. **Seulgi L. Byun**, Chair and Associate Professor of Biblical and Religious Studies, Grove City College

Prof. **Helen Efthimiadis-Keith (aka Keith-van Wyk)**, Associate Professor in Biblical Hebrew and Hebrew Bible/Old Testament, University of Kwazulu Natal

Dr. **David G. Firth**, Old Testament Tutor, Trinity College Bristol; Research Associate, University of the Free State

Dr. **Rachelle Gilmour**, Lecturer in Old Testament, Trinity College Melbourne

Prof. Dr. **Jonathan Grossman**, Full Professor at Department of Bible. Bar-Ilan University

Rev. Dr. **Isabelle Hamley**, Chaplain to the Archbishop of Canterbury; Lambeth Palace; Visiting Research Fellow, King's College London

Dr. **Gabriel F. Hornung**, Assistant Professor of Religious Studies, Trinity College (CT, USA)

Dr. **Kyong-Jin Lee**, Associate Professor of Old Testament Studies, Fuller Theological Seminary

Dr. **Kara J. Lyons-Pardue**, Professor of New Testament, Point Loma Nazarene University

Prof. **J. Gordon McConville**, Professor Emeritus of Old Testament, University of Gloucestershire

Dr. **Brittany N. Melton**, Assistant Professor of Biblical and Theological Studies, Palm Beach Atlantic University; Research Fellow, University of the Free State

Dr. **Suzanna R. Millar**, Chancellor's Fellow in Hebrew Bible and Old Testament, University of Edinburgh

Dr. **Paul Spilsbury**, Academic Dean and Professor of New Testament, Regent College

Dr. **Marvin A. Sweeney**, Professor of Hebrew Bible, Claremont School of Theology

Dr. **Heath A. Thomas**, Professor of Old Testament and University President, Oklahoma Baptist University

PREFACE

We, the editors, are indebted to the fine work of Katharine Dell and Will Kynes on the previous *Reading Intertextually* volumes. They graciously entrusted the continuation of the series to us once the traditional wisdom books had been completed. We would also like to thank the contributors to the volume for their time and insights. We are grateful to Jacqueline Vayntrub and Laura Quick, the new coeditors for the LHBOTS series, for their enthusiasm to continue the series after the preceding volume, *Reading Lamentations Intertextually* (ed. Brittany N. Melton and Heath A. Thomas). Finally, special thanks should be given to Dylan Watson for his careful editing assistance and to Heath Thomas for enhancing the volume introduction. The book of Esther has engendered many responsive texts, those referred to within this book, those composed for this book, and, it is hoped, those produced as a result of reading this book.

David G. Firth
Brittany N. Melton

ABBREVIATIONS

AB	The Anchor Bible
AIL	Ancient Israel and Its Literature
AJSL	*American Journal of Semitic Languages and Literatures*
AJSR	*Association for Jewish Studies Review*
AOTC	Abingdon Old Testament Commentaries
ArsOr	*Ars Orientalis*
ATD	Das Alte Testament Deutsch
BBR	*Bulletin for Biblical Research*
BI	*Biblical Illustrator*
Bib	*Biblica*
BibInt	*Biblical Interpretation*
BibInt	Biblical Interpretation Series
BibOr	Biblica et Orientalia
BKAT	Biblischer Kommentar, Altes Testament
BL	*Bibel und Liturgie*
BN	*Biblische Notizen*
BRev	*Bible Review*
BSOAS	*Bulletin of the School of Oriental and African Studies*
BTB	*Biblical Theology Bulletin*
BZAW	Beihefte zur Zeitschrift für die alttestamentliche Wissenschaft
CahRB	Cahiers de la Revue biblique
CBET	Contributions to Biblical Exegesis and Theology
CBQ	*Catholic Biblical Quarterly*
CEJL	Commentaries on Early Jewish Literature
CurBR	*Currents in Biblical Research* (formerly *Currents in Research: Biblical Studies*)
CurBS	*Currents in Research: Biblical Studies*
DCLS	Deuterocanonical and Cognate Literature Studies
DSD	*Dead Sea Discoveries*
ECC	Eerdmans Critical Commentary
EJL	Early Judaism and Its Literature
ESV	English Standard Version
FAT	Forschungen zum Alten Testament
FOTL	Forms of the Old Testament Literature
GKC	*Gesenius' Hebrew Grammar*. Edited by Emil Kautzsch. Translated by Arther W. Cowley. 2nd ed. Oxford: Clarendon, 1910.
HCS	Hellenistic Culture and Society
HS	*Hebrew Studies*

IBC	Interpretation: A Bible Commentary for Teaching and Preaching
ICC	International Critical Commentary
IECOT	International Exegetical Commentary on the Old Testament
IrAnt	*Iranica Antiqua*
ITC	International Theological Commentary
JAAR	*Journal of the American Academy of Religion*
JANER	*Journal of Ancient Near Eastern Religions*
JBL	*Journal of Biblical Literature*
JCS	*Journal of Cuneiform Studies*
JES	*Journal of Ecumenical Studies*
JNES	*Journal of Near Eastern Studies*
JQR	*Jewish Quarterly Review*
JR	*Journal of Religion*
JSem	*Journal for Semitics*
JSJ	*Journal for the Study of Judaism in the Persian, Hellenistic, and Roman Periods*
JSOT	*Journal for the Study of the Old Testament*
JSOTSup	Journal for the Study of the Old Testament Supplement Series
JTS	*Journal of Theological Studies*
KJV	King James Version
LCL	Loeb Classical Library
LHBOTS	Library of Hebrew Bible/Old Testament Studies
NAC	New American Commentary
NIBCOT	New International Biblical Commentary on the Old Testament
NICOT	New International Commentary on the Old Testament
NIV	New International Version
NRSV	New Revised Standard Version
OTE	*Old Testament Essays*
OTL	Old Testament Library
OTS	Oudtestamentische Studiën/Old Testament Studies
POuT	De Prediking van het Oude Testament
RBS	Resources for Biblical Study
RevQ	*Revue de Qumran*
RTR	Reformed Theological Review
SBLDS	Society of Biblical Literature Dissertation Series
SBLMS	Society of Biblical Literature Monograph Series
SEÅ	*Svensk exegetisk årsbok*
SemeiaSt	Semeia Studies
SK	*Skrif en kerk*
SMSR	*Studi e materiali di storia delle religioni*
STDJ	Studies on the Texts of the Desert of Judah
TAPA	*Transactions of the American Philological Association*
Tarbiz	*Tarbiz*
TCSt	Text-Critical Studies
TSAJ	Texte und Studien zum antiken Judentum
TZ	*Theologische Zeitschrift*
VT	*Vetus Testamentum*
VTSup	Supplements to Vetus Testamentum

WBC	Word Biblical Commentary
WO	*Die Welt des Orients*
WUNT	Wissenschaftliche Untersuchungen zum Neuen Testament
ZAW	*Zeitschrift für die alttestamentliche Wissenschaft*

UNDER THE INTERTEXTUAL UMBRELLA: AN INTRODUCTION

David G. Firth, Brittany N. Melton, and Heath A. Thomas

"More than any other text in the Old Testament, Esther asks us to read it in the light of the canon of Scripture" (Firth 2010b, 33). Scholars of disparate methodological approaches recognize the fecundity of intertextual relationships between Esther and the Hebrew Bible, and beyond. However, intertextual investigation in Esther studies ranges widely. A sampling of previous intertextual approaches to Esther with various motivations, be they more historical or literary, diachronic or synchronic, will be surveyed first, in order to facilitate our discussion of the umbrella term "intertextuality," which is then demonstrated further by the contributions in this volume.

Some intertextual work explores the use of earlier textual traditions that inform the later book of Esther, which is a primarily historical investigation in source-paternity.[1] Adele Berlin's (2001, xxxiv–xli) work has been foundational in exploring the connections, as she identifies several links to the Joseph story in Genesis, the books of Exodus, Samuel, Kings, and Daniel, among other minor connections.[2] She argues the writer of Esther made explicit intertextual links to other biblical books so that the story of the diaspora community would find its morphological fit with the story of the people of Israel. In so doing, the author of Esther connects

---

I first used this language in my chapter in Dell and Kynes (2014), arguing that the term "resonance encompasses the whole of the 'synchronic–diachronic spectrum,' keeping both history and hermeneutics wedded under the umbrella of intertextuality" (Melton 2014, 132).

1. For the purposes of this volume, we have set aside the redactional conversation concerning the textual tradition of MT Esther and the two Greek versions (AT and LXX), which has been adequately debated elsewhere (see Clines 1984, 107–12; Fox 1991a; Jobes 1996; Lacocque 1999; De Troyer 2003), as well as broader studies of reception (see, e.g., Carruthers 2008).

2. For recent discussion of allusions to still more texts, see Grossman (2009) and Koller (2014).

the people of the past to the community in the present, continuing the identity and ideology of the people of God for their new day.

Some intertextual studies nod toward historical questions (such as asking what *previous* tradition was employed by the author of Esther), but others assess how Esther resonates with the literary presentation of earlier texts, thus creating fresh ways of reading the book of Esther. For instance, David Firth sees connections between 1–2 Samuel and the book of Esther through internal focalization. While Berlin identified connections between Samuel and Esther as well, Firth takes this basic insight further through a narrative reading of Esther that attends to intertextuality (see also Berger 2010). Firth finds intertextual resonance between terms, phrases, and narrative focalization, which enables the reader of Esther to recognize connections with 1–2 Samuel otherwise missed by previous scholars. This interchange, in turn, enables the theology of the book of Esther to emerge (Firth 2010a, 27).

Still along literary lines, Matthew Michael (2016) has more recently investigated shared storytelling features between Daniel and Esther, signifying their intertextual relationship. In Michael's understanding, the intentional intertextual interchange between the books presents two opposing viewpoints on the problem of Jewish identity: Esther is more accommodating to culture in constructing a Jewish identity while Daniel is more defiant in a contested culture, formulating Jewish identity as a counter-community.

The works of Berlin, Firth, and Michael alert one to the plethora of possibilities for reading Esther in light of other texts in the Hebrew Bible. At once, their readings frame for interpreters the range of intertextual readings possible, generate questions about how intertextuality may be related to questions of poetics and narratology, and exemplify how intertextuality can be positioned with great fluidity—whether repeated terms between corpora, repeated type-scenes that seem to echo one another, or even a plot-line from one book that was left hanging might be resumed in another biblical book (e.g., the story of Agag, the Amalekite, picked up in the story of Haman who is an Agagite). One notes the range and flexibility of intertextual resonances in Esther, especially when one charts the work schematically (see Table 0.1).[3]

Three significant observations emerge from previous research. First, scholarly interest centers upon intertextuality between narrative texts and Esther. This is due, in part, to the fact that Esther comprises a narrative and recognized intertextual relationships between Esther and the rest of the Hebrew Bible occur in terms of narrative focalization, storytelling techniques, reversals, and allusions. As a result, it is, in a sense, natural that scholarly focus would gravitate toward biblical narrative. Second, despite the interest in intertextuality and Esther, scholars have underexplored the interchange between the prophets and Esther. But recent work, even in the present volume, reveals potential intersections between Esther 4 and the Latter Prophets that cast a possible future where God will "show up" in the narrative world of Esther (see further Thomas' chapter). Third, it must be

---

3. Biblical quotations throughout follow the ESV.

Table 0.1 Intertextual Connections between Esther and the Hebrew Bible

Esther	Intertextual Connection	Explanation of Intertext
	Jacob Story	
Est. 3:4	Gen. 39:10	Speaking "day after day" and not listening
Est. 2:3-4	Gen. 41:34-37	Appointing officials; gathering food for storehouses // gathering women for a harem
Est. 6:11; 8:2	Gen. 41:42-43	Joseph/Mordecai dressed in honor; signet ring given to Joseph/Mordecai
Est. 4:16	Gen. 43:14	"If I perish, I perish" // "if I am bereaved …, I am bereaved" (using a similar grammatical construction)
Est. 8:6	Gen. 44:34	Interrogatives using similar constructions with איככה and איך, respectively
	Exodus[a]	
Est. 6:1	Exod. 12:42	Presuming Ahasuerus' sleepless night is on the "night of watching," which is the night of the Exodus from Egypt according to Jewish tradition
	The Book of Samuel[b]	
Est. 1:10; 5:9	1 Sam. 25:36-37; 2 Sam. 13:28	Ahasuerus, Nabal, and Amnon each display "heart"'s "merry" with wine (טוב לב) that foreshadows foolish action // Haman displays a "merry heart" (טוב לב) in Est. 5:9.
Est. 3:1, 10; 8:3, 5; 9:24	1 Sam. 15; 2 Sam. 1:1-16	Haman is an Agagite; Saul fails to destroy Agag, the Amalekite king. Thus, the Amalekite problem in the history of Israel is retold through the person of Haman when in Persia.
Est. 2:6	1 Sam. 9:1	Mordecai's genealogy links him to Saul; Saul's failure with the Amalekites is recast through Mordecai's victory over Haman.
	The Book of Kings	
Esth. 3:1	1 Kgs 1:5	"And he <u>exalted him</u> (וַיְנַשְׂאֵהוּ) and placed his authority over the princes who were with him." // "And Adonijah, son of Haggith, <u>exalted himself</u> (מִתְנַשֵּׂא), saying, 'I will be king.' And he prepared for himself chariots and horsemen, and fifty men running before him."
Esth. 5:3	1 Kgs 1:16	"the king [Ahasuerus] said to her, 'What do you want' (וַיֹּאמֶר לָהּ הַמֶּלֶךְ מַה־לָּךְ)." // "the king [David] said, 'What do you want' (וַיֹּאמֶר הַמֶּלֶךְ מַה־לָּךְ)."
Esth. 2:6	2 Kgs 24:11-15	Nebuchadnezzar of Babylon exiles Jerusalem and Judah during Jeconiah's reign and takes captives to Babylon.
	Daniel 1-6[c]	
Esth. 1:1-12	Dan. 5:1-4	Ahasuerus' banquet // Belshazzar's banquet
Esth. 2:1-18	Dan. 1:8-16	Beauty contest // body contest
Esth. 3:1-6	Dan. 3:1-30	Not bowing to Haman // not bowing to Nebuchadnezzar
Esth. 3:1-15	Dan. 6:1-24	Plots of royal administrators
Esth. 6:1-14	Dan. 2:1; 6:18	Sleepless kings

[a] Berlin (2001, xxxvii).
[b] Firth (2010a, 22–7).
[c] Berlin (2001, xxxiv–xli); Michael (2016, 124–7).

recognized that "intertextuality" has been used as an umbrella term for a vast range of motivations and methodological deployments. This third observation will be explored further, before introducing the volume chapters.

Although Kristeva's original concern was with the ways in which all texts relate to each other, the concept of intertextuality has moved considerably since her foundational work (see Raj 2015, 77–9). This is perhaps inevitable, because her work was largely concerned with the existence of intertextuality. Although her work also led scholars to reflect on how intertextuality might function in any given instance, not all have accepted her more minimal approach to authors (see further Schmid 2010, 40–51). Thus, John Barton (2013), in his introductory chapter to the first LHBOTS *Reading Intertextually* volume on Job, rightly questioned whether intertextuality properly understood is more of a theory than a method, while at the same time recognizing that it is diversely understood and applied within biblical studies. In the wisdom volumes edited by Katharine Dell and Will Kynes, *Reading Job Intertextually* (2013), *Reading Ecclesiastes Intertextually* (2014), and *Reading Proverbs Intertextually* (2018), along with the subsequent *Reading Lamentations Intertextually* (2021, edited by Melton and Thomas), this diverse application is aptly demonstrated. As with the previous volumes, contributors to the present volume were free to adopt or formulate their own conception of intertextuality in relation to two or more texts.

Of course, scholars taxonomize intertextuality variously, classically delineating diachronic and synchronic studies.[4] Diachronic studies of intertextuality, by definition, are an outworking of the recognition that one text must be earlier than the other; and are thus concerned with a source text and its receptor. Whether consciously or not, a receptor text engages with its source text, and may do so for a range of reasons. For instance, one receptor text might use a source text to affirm it or reject it, to claim it as evidence in support of its perspectives, or simply to recognize that the engagement adds depth to the reading experience.[5] Synchronic studies, by contrast, do not work from the assumption that either text is a source for the other. Rather, they read one text in light of the other, exploring ways in which curating a relationship between one text and another enriches the reading experience. However, as editors we suggested previously a move away from the binary evaluation of intertextuality into strictly synchronic and diachronic approaches, offering instead a tripartite categorization: historical relationships, canonical relationships, and readerly interests (Melton and Thomas 2021).

---

4. Recognizing that these are not mutually exclusive, many have integrated both into their methodology (e.g., Kynes 2012).

5. Garrett (2020, 272–90) treats all such material as allusions, though a wider typology is helpful in considering the function of any one allusion. Garrett is concerned only with intentional allusions, though Kristeva's wider insight suggests that authors may not always be aware of every allusion. Hays's (1989, 14–32) famous model serves as a good example of a diachronic model.

In the present volume, our aim is to extend this work by highlighting underlying questions that uphold the intertextual approaches offered here. In other words, intertextuality exceeds defined "methods" one might find in the scholarly toolbox of biblical studies, such as form or redaction criticism, such that intertextuality should be conceived of as an umbrella concept under which particular deployments of scholarly study ensue. Each of these studies is interested in questions that inform their activation of intertextuality, whether these questions are historical, literary, canonical, or otherwise. On this understanding, intertextuality serves interests that interpreters bring to the biblical text. The biblical scholar must, then, situate oneself more distinctly under this broad umbrella concept of intertextuality, in terms of the kinds of questions the interpreter is asking and why.

Diachronic approaches to Esther can consider it either as a source or receptor text. Those treating it as a receptor text are interested in the use that Esther makes of earlier works. For the purposes of this volume, this interest is focused on works from the Hebrew Bible, though consideration of other works is possible. Studies that are concerned with diachronic approaches where Esther is a receptor text are found in Parts I and II of this volume, which place Esther in dialogue with the Pentateuch and the Former Prophets. It should be noted that although Hornung's chapter engages with parts of the Pentateuch, his is a self-consciously synchronic work, demonstrating that a chronological relationship does not require a diachronic approach to intertextuality. Each of these chapters (by McConville, Firth, Hamley, and Gilmour) identifies relevant texts from the Pentateuch or Former Prophets as antecedent to Esther. As becomes apparent from reading these chapters, the fact that these chapters share a common diachronic model does not result in a flattened approach to intertextuality. For example, Rachelle Gilmour, in exploring the dialogue between Samuel and Esther, finds that Esther largely parodies the earlier material. By contrast, both David Firth (exploring the dialogue between Joshua and Esther) and Isabelle Hamley (exploring the dialogue between Judges and Esther) argue that the links to Joshua and Judges aid a constructive exploration of the issue of Jewish identity within the diaspora. All three chapters understand diachronic intertextuality to be theologically formative for reading Esther, with each enriching our understanding of Esther as a result. That diachronic intertextual work does not thereby resolve the interpretative issues of Esther, and may in fact contribute to them, is a central contribution of Gordon McConville's chapter as he explores the significance of Exodus, Passover, and food-laws for our reading of Esther. Esther's use of antecedent texts is theologically important, but it is allusive and therefore its meaning can be elusive.

Works considering Esther as a source text are not only diachronic but also concerned with the use that later texts make of Esther, that is, these are studies in reception. Although the relationship to Esther differs, methodologically these approaches are closely aligned. Studies that are concerned with diachronic approaches where Esther is a source text are found in Part V of this volume, which place Esther in dialogue with various sources beyond the Hebrew Bible. In this section, it should be noted that Kyong-Jin Lee's exploration of political readings of Esther is also synchronic, as is Helen Efthimiadis-Keith's reading of LXX Esther alongside Judith. Once again, this demonstrates that the presence of a recognizable chronological relationship does not constrain the deployment of intertextuality, even if it might incline some scholars toward a diachronic approach. Due to the wider range of possible points of reception, these chapters address various possible settings within Judaism and Christianity. Kara Lyons-Pardue provides a chapter on the reception of Esther in the New Testament, exploring the themes of power, vulnerability, and kingship in the gospel of Mark, finding echoes of Esther in its presentation of Herod through whom Mark draws a marked contrast with Jesus. The other chapters that work with Esther as a source text are all concerned with how various Jewish sources engaged with it. So, Seulgi Byun examines the place of Esther at Qumran, finding that despite the lack of manuscripts of the book in the recovered scrolls, and contrary to the scholarly consensus, it was known there. Paul Spilsbury examines Josephus and his reading of Esther. Spilsbury shows that the challenges faced by the Jews in Esther continued to be a real lived experience for Josephus and his readers, drawing on Esther to help his readers offer a positive model for Jewish experience in diaspora. Jonathan Grossman looks at how rabbinic materials read Esther, highlighting the range of ways in which they engage with the text, with no one approach determinative. His phrase about the text "winking at the reader" is particularly illuminating as he demonstrates how "the argument quite frequently depends precisely on the part of the verse that is not cited explicitly." Finally, Marvin Sweeney examines Esther in light of the Shoah, arguing that it reveals that G-d might not come to the aid of the Jewish people; rather, all humans have a responsibility to resist evil, and this is the book's key theological concern.

Synchronic intertextual studies make no claim about the chronological relationship between texts. Neither is therefore the source or receptor for the other. Rather, these texts may illumine one another when one is read alongside the other. Sometimes features within the text encourage this (e.g., genre similarities), but this is not necessary. Synchronic studies are scattered throughout this volume, though they are particularly clustered in Parts III and IV, in part resulting from the mismatch of the genre of Esther with non-narrative works and in part because these are texts with no clear chronological relationship; though relatively contemporaneous production to the book of Esther would explain why the diachronic relationship is easier to establish with other Parts containing texts that appeared well before and much after. In other words, either the author of Esther likely knew of the other text or a later text is reflecting upon the book or story of Esther. Yet chronology alone does not lead to a synchronic approach. This can be seen outside of these Parts where Gabriel Hornung takes a deliberately synchronic approach to reading Esther in comparison to the court narratives of Joseph and Daniel. Aware that others have approached this diachronically, Hornung argues that we see a more multilayered reading of the text through a synchronic approach. Both chapters in Part III place Esther in dialogue with prophetic texts. Andrew Abernethy puts Esther in conversation with Isaiah, finding that shared motifs (such as feasting) enable a broader canonical vision that enables better understanding of the competition for power in the world. Heath Thomas also considers Esther in dialogue with Isaiah, but extends this to consider the Book of the Twelve. He finds extensive linguistic and thematic connections that help to situate the theme of mourning in each, enabling us to see Esther's moral vision more clearly. Both chapters in Part IV are also synchronic as they put Esther in dialogue with other parts of the Writings. Firth and Melton explore the theme of the absence of God in Psalms 9–14 and Esther, arguing that when read together they become an important resource for addressing the issue of theodicy. Suzanna Millar looks at Esther and Proverbs, in order to show that the character of Esther herself is far more complex than sometimes suggested, as are key themes within the books and their ideologies. It is the intertextual reading that demonstrates this. Helen Efthimiadis-Keith's study of the prayers in LXX Esther and Judith sees both as a response to trauma. Nevertheless, although there are similarities between the prayers, the intertextual reading shows how differently each responds to the trauma because of their underlying ideologies. Finally, Kyong-Jin Lee offers a theological and political reading of Esther, engaging with works of contemporary political theory to understand how law functions in the book and in modern society, as well as how the book of Esther critiques certain views of power. Synchronic readings may take other works from the Bible as an obvious dialogue partner, but they are not restricted to this.

Therefore, the essays in this volume operate within this synchronic–diachronic taxonomy, but as the discussion above reveals, they exceed the strictures of the taxonomy itself. We suggest rather than continuing to domesticate intertextuality in biblical studies according to a strict taxonomy or appropriating it as a particular "method," it would be more profitable to explain what kinds of questions interpreters are trying to answer via intertextuality. Simply weighing the strength of intertextual connections, in terms of quotation, allusion, echo, or the like, does not go far enough in helping interpreters understand what questions are being put to the text(s). Instead, upon acknowledging Kristeva's intertextual phenomenon, interpreters must be clear about which lines they are tracing and why, letting the evidence speak for itself. It is hoped readers of this volume will find insight in the essays that operate under the vast umbrella that is intertextuality.

Part I

ESTHER IN DIALOGUE WITH THE TORAH

Chapter 1

FOREIGN AMBIVALENCE IN THE SCROLL: READING ESTHER'S COURT ALONGSIDE JOSEPH AND DANIEL

Gabriel F. Hornung

Amidst the sprawl of Scroll scholarship, two threads have occasionally bubbled to the surface. If influential twentieth-century criticism tended to orient itself around the genre considerations that stem from Esther's setting, then a number of recent intertextual studies reflect the growing interest in inner-biblical allusion and interpretation.[1] Though both of these fascinating trains of thought have earned well-deserved attention on their own terms, the present essay will seek to explore their dynamic intersection—how certain critical connections to the Joseph story (Genesis 37–50) and Daniel 1–6 narratives depend on all three tales occurring in nonnative courts.[2] The points of departure for this two-pronged analysis are well-known: despite important differences of detail, these texts employ similar phrases to tell of good-looking Israelites rising in governments outside their own; moreover, as such actions repeat, Jewish heroes defy all odds to deliver themselves and their people from threats both acute and oblique.[3]

1. In a series of penetrating articles from the 1970s, Meinhold (1975, 1976) argued that Joseph and Esther represent the outline of a *Diasporanovelle*; pointing to over ten similar plot stages, Meinhold sought to explain the striking correspondences in formal terms. More recently Craig (1995) has invoked Bakhtin in an effort to place the Megillah alongside certain European analogues; and, in similar fashion, Berlin (2001) has sought to read Esther in light of ancient Greek comedies. On the intertextual side Grossman's (2011) book stands out: arguing for a series of intentional allusions to a plethora of biblical texts, the Bar-Ilan professor concludes that Esther's penchant for invoking other ancient Israelite literature brings God, the Law, and more orthodox biblical norms into the text; along such lines, Berger's (2010) article argues that Esther repeatedly invokes the David story in order to reclaim the greatness of Saul's heritage.

2. Though Daniel and Esther have particularly interesting and important Greek witnesses, this analysis will limit its focus to the Hebrew versions.

3. In brilliantly concise fashion, Rosenthal (1895) outlined a number of these similarities from a philological perspective. Assuming that Esther was composed at a time when classical Hebrew was losing its vitality, Rosenthal argued that the author of the Scroll modeled his

While these suggestive links have often been used to offer insight into the date, provenance, and literary form of the Scroll and its biblical analogues,[4] this synchronic reading will demonstrate how certain points of contact to Joseph and Daniel evince Esther's dramatic ambivalence toward the foreign.[5] For as the repetition of the uncommon phrase כי כן ימלאו ימי (Est. 2:12 and Gen. 50:3) will begin to articulate, customs alien to biblical norms both imperil and elevate key Israelite figures in outside lands; and, as the parallels between a decree of Persian murder and the heat of a Babylonian furnace will then determine, edicts intended to devastate the Israelites flip to engender their most improbable victories. Bolstering those conclusions that have situated the Megillah inside a larger conversation interested in the maintenance of Israelite identity amidst the allure of outside authority, this analysis will underline the function of the foreign in Esther by placing it in conversation with the analogies found in Joseph and Daniel.[6]

Foreign Rites in Jacob's Death and Esther's Rise

This first example of Esther's striking ambivalence will place the last patriarch's final breaths next to the vibrancy of a young Jewish woman's stunning rise; and, as

work off of Joseph out of linguistic necessity. Extending this thread to include overlapped literary motifs, Gan (1961) demonstrated how both Esther and Joseph change courses at banquets and tell of Jewish courtiers rising to second-in-command. And, in her monograph about Esther, Berg (1979) suggests that the similarities Rosenthal and Gan lay out indicate that the Scroll may have been an interpretation of certain aspects of the Joseph story.

4. Though Moore (1971) bases his late-Persian or early-Hellenistic dating of Esther on a number of factors, the relationship the Scroll shows to other biblical texts is primary among them; and, in a different but ultimately related context, Collins (1975) has argued that the settings of Daniel 1–6 offer overwhelming evidence that these tales were authored in a diaspora environment.

5. In other contexts, I have firmly advocated for an author-oriented approach to Esther's relationship to Joseph (see, e.g., my essay (Hornung 2020)). In this essay, however, I employ a synchronic intertextual method in order to shift focus onto the role of the foreign. While the argument forwarded here does not consider the direction of influence, its conclusion, which suggests Esther ought to be seen as part of a larger cultural context interested in exploring the posture taken toward the nonnative, can still be relevant for historically minded criticism.

6. Suggesting that the sources behind MT Esther can be identified and then isolated, Wills (1990) has argued that this literary-critical work shows that the earliest version of the Hebrew Scroll was a court conflict between Mordecai and Haman. Though the present analysis defers from carving the final biblical text, it will second aspects of Wills's project. For as his work conclusively demonstrates, as long as Esther is to be understood in its current state, the Scroll must be read in light of its connections to other texts that tell of courtiers rising in foreign governments.

the language these disparate movements share will indicate, foreign rites signify both the unique problems the nonnative presents as well as the rescue it alone can offer. When Jacob finally completes his blessing and succumbs to the inevitabilities of old age (Gen. 49:33), his presence in Egypt represents a final twist in a story that has otherwise found a set of miraculous resolutions. For as the disparate but still intertwined cycles of Genesis make clear, God's promise brings the paradox of great peril: though Abraham is to father a great nation, his wife cannot bear even one child (Gen. 11:30, 12:2); if Isaac is to carry on his father's promise (Gen. 21:12), Abraham's own hand brings his favored son within an inch of death (Gen. 22:10); and, if Jacob is to overtake his elder brother's status (Gen. 25:23), then his own children's rivalries (Gen. 37:20) drag him to the depth of despair (Gen. 37:33-35). That so much of this action reaches improbable resting points—Sarah is visited by a divine emissary (Gen. 18:9-15), the angel appears to Abraham at the very last moment (Gen. 22:11-12), and Judah risks his own incarceration to bring about familial reunification (Gen. 44:18-34)—makes Israel's death in Egypt all the more ironic.

Though this terminal event brings Genesis to its close, the underlying Egyptian tension remains productive throughout the entire Joseph story. For after the younger but favored brother is thrown to the bottom of a pit (Gen. 37:24), Joseph's sojourn in a foreign land signals yet another twist of these opposing poles. If his descent to Egypt brings about his own enslavement, then his oppressive surroundings also represent an improbable rescue from an otherwise sure death. As Joseph then navigates his way to the uppermost echelon of a plentiful Egypt (Gen. 41:38-46) while the promised land languishes under devastating famine (Gen. 43:1), this curious alternation extends.

When the brothers approach the vizier with their desperate arms out for a second time (Gen. 43:26), the counterintuitive balance between the safety of Egypt and risk of Israel begins to tilt uncompromisingly toward the foreign. Allowing him to implement the next phase of his extended probe, Joseph's position in the Pharaoh's court, which saw him in the first instance store the very grain that his brothers have come to seek (Gen. 41:47-49), now presents him with an opening for reunification. After the goblet is furtively placed in Benjamin's bag (Gen. 44:2) and the unwitting brothers sent back home with their deep-seated fears ostensibly averted (Gen. 44:3), a twisted sense of déjà vu strikes when the vizier's underling overtakes (Gen. 44:4-6). Though Joseph's favor had previously so enraged his brothers, Judah now seeks to flip the script by offering to sacrifice himself for the sake of Rachel's only remaining son (Gen. 44:18-34).[7] If this tectonic shift in the brothers' character brings about long-lost reunification, then the peculiar role of Egypt as refuge remains the same: much as Joseph was sold south into a bondage

---

7. Of course, this is the driving tension of the story: though the reader knows that Judah is addressing Rachel's other son, Judah and his brothers remain entirely in the dark at this juncture.

of forced deliverance, so does his brothers' arrival in the best of Pharaoh's land (Gen. 47:11) signal the rescue for which they had so desperately begged.

That Jacob finally reaches peace in this foreign setting thus recalls this past movement while also foreshadowing the next and most prolonged sequence of threats—slavery, exodus, and conquest. As the patriarchal cycles close with the Israelites outside the land once promised to them, Joseph requests that the Pharaoh allow him to bring his father's body home (Gen. 50:4-6). Israel's remains thus embody this foreign pivot: first his corpse must go through Egyptian rites, and only then can his beloved son bring his father to his ancestral home (Gen. 50:2-7).

Though much of the language is formulaic, the phrase כי כן ימלאו ימי ("for such is the full period" Gen. 50:3[8]) stands out: these four words are also found in this exact order in the Esther book (Est. 2:12). While the immediate context in the Scroll appears unrelated to Genesis—if the great Israel is leaving this earth, then the young Esther is being forced into an amorous encounter with the foolish Persian king—attention to this shared language will uncover how similar court settings betray a consistent ambivalence toward the foreign.

On the one hand, the beautiful Esther is trapped so precariously precisely because of her presence in Persia. Though Haman has not even yet been introduced, the looming trouble has already rumbled. Ahasuerus, so utterly incompetent that maintaining the thinnest of order at a drinking party slips out of his stunningly weak grasp, strikes Vashti from the palace for the most understandable of personal slights: as opposed to presenting herself for her intoxicated husband and his inebriated friends to admire, she chooses to remain at her own women's party (Est. 1:12). Thrown into a violent rage, the king tips his hat to the sorts of swings that will come to imperil the Jews: if Vashti failed to listen to her husband, all women of the empire must always obey theirs (Est. 1:20). When this idiocy then culminates in a nationwide search for the deposed queen's successor (Est. 2:2-4), Esther's required presence in the royal harem feels anything but salvific.

On the other hand, however, much as Joseph's unenviable position at the bottom of a pit twisted into a most unexpected relief, so too will Esther's unorthodox beginnings catapult her toward the Persian throne. If that unusual phrase, כי כן ימלאו ימי, marked the end of the productive foreign theme in Genesis, in Esther it will jump-start much of the movement. Once again, these words mark a custom that occurs outside of Israel:

> When each girl's turn came to go to Ahasuerus at the end of twelve months' treatment prescribed for women (for that was the period spent on beautifying them (כי כן ימלאו ימי מרוקיהן): six months with oil of myrrh and six months with perfumes and women's cosmetics, and it was after that that the girl would go to the king) ... When the turn came for Esther daughter of Abihail—the uncle of Mordecai, who had adopted her as his own daughter—to go to the king, she did

---

8. All biblical translations come from the 1985 JPS Edition.

not ask for anything but what Hegai, the king's eunuch, guardian of the women, advised. (Est. 2:12-15)

When Esther then finds miraculous favor (Est. 2:17), the peril of the king's impetuousness flips to elevate the young Israelite. Enthroned in Vashti's stead, Esther rises only to confront the next challenge: promoted to prime minister for utterly no reason at all (Est. 3:1), the wicked Haman enters to turn the tables yet again. If the completion of such markedly foreign customs had brought about Esther's gain, now the instability of the Persian court twists to imperil all the Jews.

That Mordecai must seek relief from the highest ranks of the very government persecuting him (Est. 4:1) articulates a similar version of the ambivalence seen in Joseph. In both cases the foreign settings stand as source of and solution to the clear and present dangers. Though the differences are not to be overlooked—if false accusations threatened Joseph in Egypt, then Haman imperils all the Jews of Persia—the outlines of a coherent discourse maintain. As Joseph's unanticipated Egyptian status orchestrates familial reunification, and Esther's improbable royal perch affords her the inside track with the king, the instabilities of the foreign court repeatedly constitute the only antidote to the very menace they pose.[9]

Edicts Reversed in Esther and Daniel

In her exceedingly learned tome on court collections of the Ancient Near East, Tawny Holm (2013) has convincingly demonstrated the importance of considering non-Israelite texts when thinking about this literary genre. Through a tireless examination of analogues mainly from ancient Egypt, her work demonstrates both direct and indirect lines of influence between the Bible and its neighboring cultures.[10] Though Holm's historical point must certainly be

9. In his influential 1973 article, Humphreys argued that MT Esther's final form has done palpable violence to the original Esther and Mordecai tale. For as Humphreys sees it, the earlier sources, which saw the two Jewish heroes navigating their way to the top of the Persian summit without any reference to Purim, advocated a doubled lifestyle: success in the foreign court can come for those who remain true to their own roots. With the addition of the particularistic holiday, however, Humphreys feels an original universalism undercut. Though the current synchronic focus once again refrains from jumping into the source critical fray, the conclusions pursued do present a contrast to Humphreys's exegetical stance. Instead of viewing the Scroll as a winding but still pragmatic road map to Jewish life in the diaspora, Esther's connections to Joseph and Daniel reveal how the Megillah tells a fictitious tale to reflect on a thornier and far less tangible truth: much as the foreign brings threat, so too does it provide tantalizing glimpses of promise.

10. Demonstrating the breadth and depth of her work, Holm (2013, 32) turns to Chaucer criticism to distinguish between source and analogy. If sources represent those texts that a later author purposefully invoked, then the category of analogy can be broken down further: "hard" analogies indicate those that had near-source status, "if the work

saluted—the biblical authors' influences must not be limited to only those texts that happened to find their way into the same later collection—the intertextual analysis followed here will show the exegetical merit of retaining narrow focus on the three most salient canonical takes on the foreign court. For as the admirable breadth of Holm's work identifies the import of cross-cultural comparison,[11] this concentrated investigation will bring the particular biblical ambivalence into closer grip.

If Esther's foreign perspective was first illuminated through a linguistic link to Joseph, then a comparison with Daniel 3 will underline how the design of state-imposed danger also includes paralleled motifs. For in both stories, foreign rulers' unbridled hubris expresses itself through heavily satirized edicts that demand prostration from all adherents; and, in both cases, as this persistent vainglory mixes with a stout Jewish determination, the decrees themselves twist to exalt those who had originally been targeted.

Though the Megillah sees this decisive action repeat (Est. 5:9-10), the basic outlines of the conflict come directly after Haman is promoted (Est. 3:1-2).[12] Enraged by Mordecai's refusal, Haman recalls his king's governing style to turn

---

would have been available to the compiler and has striking narrative resemblances," while "soft … denotes a work that could scarcely have been known because of date or remoteness of parallels." While Holm employs all sorts of these influences and borrowings to argue that Daniel is best understood as an ancient story-collection, the present essay seeks to demonstrate how similar kinds of parallels indicate a larger discussion around the danger and promise of the foreign.

11. She writes in summary fashion, "The building blocks of Daniel's story-collection, the generic conventions and stylistic devices, are evident in the many Near Eastern court tales and cycles of court tales, in addition to the story-collections. The fact that the same characters, themes, and sometimes whole stories appear in both independent tales as well as story-collections demonstrates the existence of a large common well of traditions and sources from which an ancient author-compiler could work … One important conclusion of this study is that Egypt, because it has an abundance of court tales that have often been overlooked, ought to be included in the search for sources for and analogues to Daniel" (485–6).

12. As has long been noted, two factors make Mordecai's refusal particularly peculiar. As the brothers' behavior in the Joseph story clearly illustrates, Israelites can and did bow to foreign leaders without second thought or punishment (Gen. 42:6, 43:26); moreover, since Mordecai's behavior throughout the Megillah indicates a clear-headed and forward-thinking wisdom, his incendiary actions here stand out all the more. Though a number of intriguing suggestions have been brought to make sense of this curious moment—the most compelling, at least in my view, being Haman's adversarial heritage (Est. 3:1)—the advent of this conflict may also be picking up on the problem of the foreign: for in ironic fashion, Mordecai can only scale the Persian ladder after he has inexplicably disrespected those in positions of authority. (For more on Esther's wisdom, see Talmon (1963); on Joseph's

personal slight into outrageous policy. "There is a certain people," Haman shrewdly begins, "scattered and dispersed among the other peoples in all the provinces of your realm, whose laws are different from those of any other people who do not obey the king's laws; and it is not in Your Majesty's interest to tolerate them" (Est. 3:8). The king assents to Haman's proposed annihilation and the pogrom seems well on track.

The Daniel episode will also revolve around official decrees, servants bowing, and Jews refusing. If Haman's embarrassing insecurity could not cope with a group displaying loyalties other than to him, then Nebuchadnezzar's arrogance will grow so outsized as to require physical form.

> King Nebuchadnezzar made a statue of gold sixty cubits high and six cubits broad. He set it up in the plain of Dura in the province of Babylon. King Nebuchadnezzar then sent word to gather the satraps, prefects, governors, counselors, treasurers, judges, officers, and all the provincial officials to attend the dedication of the statue that King Nebuchadnezzar had set up … As they stood before the statue that King Nebuchadnezzar had set up, the herald proclaimed in a loud voice, "You are commanded, O peoples and nations of every language, when you hear the sound of the horn, pipe, zither, lyre, psaltery, bagpipe, and all other types of instruments, to fall down and worship the statue of gold that King Nebuchadnezzar has set up." (Dan. 3:1-5)

As the pomp of the Babylonian court rivals the excess of Ahasuerus' unending party (Est. 1:3-8),[13] these matching literary devices also record important differences. If the prime minister sought homage in the Scroll (Est. 3:2), here the king hungers for constant adulation (Dan. 3:4-6); if Haman himself endured the impossibility of Mordecai's disrespect (Est. 3:5, 5:9), then certain Chaldeans report the intolerable Jewish offense to their insatiable ruler (Dan. 3:12).[14] In Esther this sordid mess begins to climax when Haman approaches the king with his motive sealed. As Ahasuerus contemplates honoring the very man Haman is seeking to kill, the dramatic turn—"'Quick!' the king exclaimed to Haman, 'get the garb and the horse, as you have said, and do this to Mordecai the Jew!'" (Est. 6:10)—becomes

---

potential inclusion in this proposed genre of narrative wisdom, see von Rad (1953); and for a subtle but incisive critique of von Rad's proposal, see Fox (2012).)

13. As the ostentatious wealth of each monarch lines up, so does the universality of the decrees: both Haman and Nebuchadnezzar's edicts are to be publicized in all the languages of the empire (Est. 3:12 and Dan. 3:7). (For the role multiple languages play in wisdom accounts, see Talmon (1963, 436–7).)

14. As is often the case with such complex literary parallels, this difference also yields an underlying similarity: in both cases, the kings have to be convinced by underlings in response to Jewish disobedience. As Mordecai compels the king to his own edict while the Chaldeans goad Nebuchadnezzar into enforcing his, these paralleled but still twisting designs sharpen into focus.

a harbinger of things to come: Haman's fall deepens and Mordecai ascends all the higher.

In Daniel 3 the action also pivots on a visit to the king, but this time by the offending Jews themselves. Much as Haman lost all control when Mordecai declined to bow, so too does Shadrach, Meshach, and Abed-nego's uncompromising principle push Nebuchadnezzar over the ledge.

> In raging fury Nebuchadnezzar ordered Shadrach, Meshach, and Abed-nego to be brought ... "Is it true ... that you do not serve my god or worship the statue of gold that I have set up? Now if you are ready to fall down and worship the statue that I have made when you hear the sound of the horn, pipe, zither, lyre, psaltery, and bagpipe, and all other types of instrument, [well and good]; but if you will not worship, you shall at once be thrown into a burning fiery furnace, and what god is there that can save you from my power?" (Dan. 3:13-15)

If Haman's pernicious aim needed to be fully unearthed before the Jewish courtier could scale the Persian government (Est. 7:5-10), then the switch in Daniel is as swift as it is complete. For when Nebuchadnezzar sees four moving figures in a furnace that should only have the charred remains of three (Dan. 3:24-25), the previously established order is reversed for the benefit of the once-imperiled Jews. Celebrating the men for doing exactly what he had previously outlawed, Nebuchadnezzar, and his stunning shift in stance, clarifies the foreign swing. "Blessed be the God of Shadrach, Meshach, and Abed-nego," the humbled king cries, "who sent His angel to save His servants who, trusting in him, flouted the king's decree at the risk of their lives rather than serve or worship any god but their own" (Dan. 3:28).

If refusal to comply with the Babylonian decree results in its inversion, then the Jewish queen in Persia will employ her unique status to upend Haman's evil edict. As Ahasuerus remains entirely unaware of his handpicked prime minister's sinister scheme, Esther outs Haman to position Mordecai for the gain. And once again the exact opposite of what had been planned occurs: on the very same day Haman had been impaled on Mordecai's stake, "King Ahasuerus gave the property of Haman, the enemy of the Jews, to Queen Esther. Mordecai presented himself to the king, for Esther had revealed how he was related to her. The king slipped off his ring, which he had taken back from Haman, and gave it to Mordecai; and Esther put Mordecai in charge of Haman's property" (Est. 8:1-2).

In strikingly similar sequence, directly after Nebuchadnezzar realizes that his fire has no power to scald God's people, the Babylonian king raises those whom he had sent to die. "I hereby give an order," he begins, preparing once again to contravene his earlier decree, "that [anyone of] any people or nation of whatever language who blasphemes the God of Shadrach, Meshach, and Abed-nego will be torn limb from limb, and his house confiscated, for there is no other God who is able to save in this way" (Dan. 3:29).

Though Daniel brings God to the fore while Esther leaves any divine trace beyond direct expression, their similar motifs still depend on the postures both stories take toward the foreign. And for this second time, the two tales pivot on the precariousness of a doubled edge: if Mordecai found danger due to Haman's heinous order, then Esther flips the very government oppressing her people to establish Jewish victory; and, in similar fashion, much as Babylonian law threw Shadrach, Meshach, and Abed-nego into a burning cauldron, then so does the all-powerful Nebuchadnezzar upend his own policy by declaring Jewish promotion.

Conclusion: Foreign Ambivalence

Once such analogies have been considered, these overlapped approaches to the foreign point toward a set of important divergences. The first centers around the foreign rulers themselves. While the Joseph story and Daniel 3 both present one supreme leader, the Scroll introduces two; and, as the interplay between the king and his prime minister proves increasingly decisive (Est. 6:6-10 and 7:5-10 in particular), both Ahasuerus' and Haman's characters become all the more distinct. On the one hand, the Persian king is far less hubristic than his Babylonian counterpart, but on the other he is exceedingly more inept than his Egyptian; and, though Haman and Nebuchadnezzar frequently function along parallel tracks, their obvious distinction in rank—second to Ahasuerus as opposed to commander of the entire empire—helps to generate the key conflicts in both stories.

If the doubled rulers of the Scroll begin to mark its particular take on the biblical version of the Jew in the foreign court, then so will Esther's two heroes, and the dramatic interactions that develop between them, further demonstrate the unique perspective of the Scroll. For even though Daniel 3 also narrates multiple Jewish victors, Shadrach, Meshach, and Abed-nego's unflagging commitment to act as a block prevents any dynamic space from separating them.[15] This sort of discontinuity is also found with respect to Joseph: though the story hinges on the Egyptian vizier's relationship with his family, its plot development depends on these characters standing on opposing sides instead of the same.[16] The third and most well-known divergence arises from the second. In both the Joseph story and

---

15. Even at the threat of horrific death, the three protagonists remain in perfect unison: "We have no need to answer you in this matter," they calmly respond to Nebuchadnezzar, "for if so it must be, our God whom we serve is able to save us from the burning fiery furnace, and He will save us from your power, O king. But even if He does not, be it known to you, O king, that we will not serve your god or worship the statue of gold that you have set up" (Dan. 3:16-18).

16. Lest we see these patterns as entirely incongruous, it should be recalled that Mordecai also had to convince Esther of the immediacy of Haman's threat and the necessity of her own action. Much as the Joseph story reaches its apex when Judah's speech breaks through Joseph's defenses (Gen. 45:1), so does the Scroll pivot after Esther reverses her previous course by agreeing to take up Mordecai and her people's mantel (Est. 4:16).

Daniel, since the protagonists are for the most part left to deal with overwhelming challenges without the aid of direct human associates, the divine comes to shift the otherwise immovable earthly landscapes. In the Megillah, however, since the divine is never expressly invoked, Esther's own characters must combine to effectuate the result that God helps to bring in Joseph and Daniel.

In thought-provoking fashion, Matthew Rindge (2010) has suggested that this sort of restyling signifies an intentional hierarchy.[17] If Joseph, Rindge contends, simply made sense of the Pharaoh's dreams (Gen. 41:25-32), then Daniel divined what the foreign ruler's night visions actually were (Dan. 2:29-45); and, if Joseph seems to embrace his newfound Egyptian identity (Gen. 41:41-42, 45, 50-52), then Daniel openly maintains his proud Israelite heritage (Dan. 2:27-28, 47). Concluding that the author of Daniel 2 knew Genesis 41 and consistently sought to one-up it, Rindge reads Daniel 2 as rejecting Joseph's assimilation by demanding a firmer fidelity to the customs of home.[18]

While appreciating Rindge's effort to achieve diachronic specificity, the present synchronic approach prefers a multilayered tone. Instead of finding that single pitch that pits one text against another, the process of reading Esther alongside its biblical counterparts reveals the natural variance that characterizes wide-ranging cultural efforts to grapple with complex themes.[19] For in all three books, the two-sidedness of the other finds articulation through a series of opposing poles: on the one hand, Persia, Egypt, and Babylon all represent the instability of nonnative customs and the threat of aggressive rule; on the other, however, much as these rites catapult the Israelite characters to positions of unexpected prominence, so too do the threatening leaders contravene their own edicts to deliver the Jews from the

---

17. For more on the relationship between Daniel 2 and Genesis 41, see Segal's (2009) essay, in which he argues that the same sorts of intertextual connections indicate the secondary nature of Dan. 2:15-24a.

18. After arguing that Daniel 2 exceeds Joseph in both interpretive abilities and piety, Rindge (2010) concludes his piece by suggesting that the Babylonian Jew's relation to the foreign empire is also preferred to the Egyptian's: "Considering Joseph to be an unfortunate example of extreme assimilation, the author of Daniel 2 offers Daniel as a model of 'moderate resistance'" (95). He thus sums up his position: "In his ability to interpret dreams, his piety, and his resistance to foreign imperial rule, Daniel is consistently presented as a 'new and improved' version of Joseph" (98).

19. Though Rindge (2010) is entirely correct to harp on the differences he astutely notes, his impressively detailed method overlooks how Daniel 2 also pivots on a decidedly ambivalent understanding of the foreign. For there a strikingly similar pattern to the one traced here surfaces: if the king's troubling night visions endangered all (Dan. 2:13), then so does Nebuchadnezzar's demonstrable show of favor to Daniel (Dan. 2:46) elevate all the Jews to otherwise unattainable positions (Dan. 2:48-49). Instead of subordinating all other themes to this persistent through-line, this analysis suggests that dramatic variations of this motif indicate differing expressions of a similar idea as opposed to pointed criticism of one previous story.

danger they had once posed. Thus, after these critical through-lines are perceived, the position of the Scroll inside this discourse clarifies. Addressing a productive channel concerned with the role of Israelite norms amidst the pull of outside influences, Esther's parallels to Joseph and Daniel underline how the Megillah reflects on the penchant of the foreign to present both opportunity and peril.

Chapter 2

THE BOOK OF ESTHER: EXODUS, PASSOVER, AND FOOD-LAWS

J. Gordon McConville

Esther and the Old Testament Tradition

One of the curiosities of the Old Testament book of Esther is that, in its defense of the distinctiveness of the Jewish people in diaspora, it draws in no explicit way on the hallmarks of Jewish identity: the traditions of exodus and covenant, the land of Israel, the temple in Jerusalem, the dietary laws, nor even that epicenter of Jewish memory, the Passover. And lying over all of these is the absence in the book of any overt reference to God.

Esther's omissions mark the book out from all its Old Testament comparators. In the Christian canon, it keeps close company with Ezra and Nehemiah, which, however, differ sharply from it because of their central concerns with law, covenant, temple, and land. The Hebrew Bible aligns it with the mixed bag of the *megilloth*, placing it after Ruth, Song of Songs, Qoheleth, and Lamentations, and before Daniel. Of these it is perhaps closest to Qoheleth, which also shows little interest in the traditional marks of Israel's distinctiveness. Esther, however, differs conspicuously from Qoheleth, because it is crucially interested in Jewish identity and cannot be assigned simply to the category of wisdom literature.

Modern scholarship has discerned a further set of family resemblances for Esther, in those parts of the Old Testament and Apocrypha that address the condition of Jews living in exile. These include the story of Joseph (Gen. 37–50), Daniel 1–6, and the apocryphal book of Judith. Along with these, the LXX Additions to the Book of Esther may be considered, because those additions evidently aim to compensate for what their author saw as deficiencies in the MT form of the book. While this category of diaspora literature is illuminating, here the distinctiveness of Esther stands out. Daniel has in common with Mordecai the figure of the pious Jew who wins favor under imperial rule, while maintaining his Jewish identity. Daniel, however, achieves this while pointedly refusing to compromise, by declining the food offered by the king (Dan. 1), by attributing his gift of interpreting dreams to God (Dan. 2), and by defying royal commands to worship Nebuchadnezzar's golden statue (Dan. 3) or Darius himself (Dan.

6). Joseph is like Daniel in attributing his power of interpretation to God (Gen. 41:16). In resisting the seduction of Potiphar's wife, he declares that he will not sin against God (Gen. 39:9).[1] The *Greek* Esther, in obedience to Mordecai, strictly maintains her Jewish way of life even when married to the king (2:19-20 LXX), whereas in MT, Mordecai merely instructs her to keep her Jewish identity secret (2:20). Mordecai also enjoins *Greek* Esther to pray to God (4:8 LXX), the narrator tells of the Lord's overruling of events (6:1 LXX), and, in a final addition, Mordecai makes appeal to the historic deliverance of Israel by their God (10:4-13 LXX). The Esther literature also includes the so-called Alpha Text, which though less explicit than LXX features both prayer and celebration to God. In proto-AT, Mordecai entreats Esther to call on God, before speaking to the king to ask for her people's deliverance (iv:5-6). Similarly, in viii:33-38, he urges the people to hold a celebration to God (Fox 2001, 259-61).[2]

The most striking contrastive parallel with the story of Esther, however, is that of Judith. Judith too is a Jewish woman who uses her beauty to overcome a powerful enemy of the Jews and delivers her people from destruction. But the differences between the two narratives and their heroines help accentuate the remarkable silences of Esther. In Judith, the threat to Israel comes from the invading army of King Nebuchadnezzar, under the command of its general, Holofernes.[3] The scene-setting includes a report to Holofernes by the "Ammonite" Achior, which tells the history of Israel from the origin of their ancestors in Chaldea (5:7), alluding to Abram's home in Ur (Gen. 11:27-32), to the destruction of the temple, and their return from Babylonian exile (5:18b-19). Achior also knows that it was Israel's sin against their God that led to their punishment (5:17-18). Judith herself is both devout and theologically articulate, taking the lead in strengthening the people of her besieged city and urging them to prayer in faith that God will deliver them (8:11-17), before taking decisive action herself. Her plan to assassinate Holofernes in his camp, using her feminine charm (10:1-5), entails some agonizing over the compromises she may have to make by entering the Gentile environment of the enemy camp, and indeed the bedroom of the general. The narrative is at pains to show how she protects herself against these dangers. She expressly refrains from the enemy's unclean food, and during a three-day stay, she withdraws each night to bathe and purify herself

---

1. For Joseph and Esther as examples of the form of "Diaspora Novella," see A. Meinhold (1976, 72-93).

2. (Fox uses roman numerals for chapters in AT.) For the complicated history of the Esther literature, see Fox (2001, 254-73), "Three Books of Esther." The three "books" are the Alpha Text (a Greek translation of an original Hebrew), MT, and LXX; but the full story involves a hypothetical proto-Esther, which unfolds on separate tracks through proto-AT, AT, and MT (diagram on 255). Clines (1984, 139-74) finds five different Esther stories. There is no relationship of direct dependence between AT and MT; Fox (2001, 259) describes proto-AT as a "collateral version" of the story, alongside MT or, alternatively, as its "cousin."

3. The story lacks historical verisimilitude, not least in the portrayal of Nebuchadnezzar as "the king of the Assyrians" (Judg. 4:1).

(12:1-9). Having done the bloody deed, she expressly affirms that she had no sexual relations with Holofernes: "it was my face that seduced him to his destruction ... he committed no sin with me, to defile and shame me" (13:16, NRSV).[4]

All of this is in sharp contrast to the book of Esther, which declines to locate itself in the history of Israel. Esther, like Judith, is beautified to enter the presence of a foreign lord, King Ahasuerus, and indeed becomes his wife, without any explicit agonizing over the compromises she may have to make, nor any defense of her chastity. She takes no initiative to save her people from the mortal danger arising from Haman's plot against them but yields only to Mordecai's moral coercion (Est. 4:9-17). Though she fasts, she utters no prayer (4:16). While feasting plays an important part in both stories, no concern is expressed about her consumption of unclean food. Indeed, it is probably to be assumed that in her adoption of Persian royal lifestyle, and particularly in the two banquets at which she hosts the king and Haman, she consumes the food of the king.

Esther thus differs from all the Old Testament and apocryphal literature with which it has affinities, and consequently may be said to be unique, or, as some have it, the only true Old Testament book of exile.[5]

Esther and the Feasts: Food-Laws, Passover, and Purim

In spite of the silences of Esther outlined above, it remains an unmistakably Jewish book. The distinctiveness of the Jews from all the other nations in the Persian Empire is essential to the book's action, and the very point of Haman's attack on them:

> There is a certain people scattered and separated among all the peoples in all the provinces of your kingdom; their laws are different from those of every other people, and they do not keep the king's laws, so that it is not appropriate for the king to tolerate them. (Est. 3:8)

Haman's tantalizing reference to the Jewish "laws" is not an allusion to Mosaic laws.[6] Rather, it is the observation of an outsider on the Jews' divergence from all others in their customs and way of life. It is paradoxical that this Jewish distinctiveness lies at the heart of the book, both as the cause of hostility and that which must be preserved, yet so little is disclosed about what constitutes that distinctiveness. This does not mean that our author has no interest in the constituents of the Jewish heritage. There is something in the avoidance of naming them that seems

---

4. For a full comparison between Esther and Judith, see Crawford (2003). See also Craghan (1982). English translations are from NRSV unless otherwise stated.

5. This is attributed to Goitein (1957), via Levenson's (1976, 446) translation, as cited by Laniak (2003a, 79).

6. The word is דָּתֵיהֶם, "their laws," a general word for law, that is applied by Haman in the same sentence to the king's laws, דָּתֵי הַמֶּלֶךְ.

deliberate, as if to pose the question to the attentive reader, an impression that is reinforced by comparison with the overtness of the other exilic literature sketched above. It is also borne out by certain features of the narrative, which suggest a kind of knowing allusion to the elements of Jewish identity that do not appear in it.

Chief among these features is the system of dating that runs through the story. An interest in times and dates is evident from the beginning of the narrative, in the description of the great feast given by Ahasuerus for his officials (ch. 1). Indeed, it is part of the author's meticulousness about facts and figures generally, for he does not tire of numbers and lists, as in the enumeration of the king's provinces, and in the fastidious distinctions between kinds of officer (1:1-4). This aspect of the narrative's style is an important part of its structure and strategy, contributing to its atmosphere of legality and procedural inevitability that becomes essential to its dramatic tension.

In the first month, Nisan, Haman has lots cast פּוּר to determine the date of a pogrom to destroy the Jews (3:7). On the thirteenth day of the first month, the edict is sent out to all the provinces of Persia, ordering the annihilation of the Jews on the day identified, namely the thirteenth of the twelfth month, Adar (3:12-15). These dates are intriguing, because of their close relationship to the date of Passover, which falls on the fourteenth day of the first month (Lev. 23:5). The edict, therefore, is promulgated on the day before Passover, and the pogrom is scheduled to take place a month and a day before Passover the following year. The action in chs 3–5 is then compressed into a few days. On the day of the edict (the thirteenth of the first), Esther is persuaded by Mordecai to approach the king and commands a three-day fast to be held by all the Jews in Susa (4:16). Assuming that the first day of the fast is the thirteenth itself, the three days of fasting span the date of the Passover, the fourteenth. Esther and the Jews are fasting, therefore, precisely at the time when Jews would normally be celebrating the Passover feast.

The crucial events that follow are also dated. The "third day" (5:1) is presumably the third day of the fast, namely the fifteenth of the first month or, in the festal calendar, the first day of Unleavened Bread (Lev. 23:6). Esther holds the first banquet on that day, thus ending her fast (5:4—"come *today* to a banquet that I have prepared for the king"). The second banquet follows on the sixteenth (5:8) and extends to a second day (7:2), that is, the seventeenth, on which also Haman is hanged (7:10). The decisive events recounted in chs 4–7 fall within the week of Passover and Unleavened Bread.

With Haman's plot uncovered and punished, attention turns to the defense of the Jews against the pogrom, which remains in force and incapable of being repealed. The device adopted to achieve this is a counter-edict, whose inscription is also dated, namely on the twenty-third day of the third month, Sivan (8:9-12). This date does not fall readily into the festal calendar, and its significance, if any, is obscure.[7] The decree, however, is greeted by the Jews of Susa with a joyful festival and holiday (8:15-17).

---

7. Levenson (1997, 110), noting that the date falls two months and ten days after Haman's decree, which is now reversed by 8:9-15, suggests that there may be a connection with "the symbolic number seventy," citing Gen. 46:27; Judg. 9:2, 4; Jer. 29:10; Ps. 90:10.

The action now moves to the thirteenth of the twelfth month, Adar, the date set for the pogrom, and also for the Jews' actions in self-defense, permitted "on a single day" (8:12). On that day, the Jews in Susa succeed in striking down their enemies (9:5-10). Armed with fresh royal permission, they continue on the fourteenth, on which also they execute the ten sons of Haman (9:13-14). The Jews in the provinces accomplish their self-defense on the thirteenth alone. In both cases, the end of the slaughter, and so of the threat against them, is celebrated with joyful feasting, on the fourteenth in the provinces, and on the fifteenth in Susa (9:16-19). Once again, the dates hint at those of the Passover, which falls, in this case, one month later.

Veiled Allusion?

If there is a system for all the dates in the book of Esther, it has not yet been discovered.[8] However, the hints of Passover we have noted above look assured.

The point is reinforced when we notice other kinds of veiled allusion in the story. Levenson (1997, 14) draws attention to analogies between the stories of Esther and Exodus: in Esther, "one can hear overtones of the struggle in Exodus between the God of Israel and Pharaoh, who first oppresses the Israelites and slights their God (Exod. 1:8-22; 5:2), but later submits to them—and to God." He has also pointed out an echo in 5:2 of Exod. 12:36, in the phrase "grace, or favor (חן), in the eyes of" (Levenson 1997, 89); Esther finds favor in the eyes of the king in response to her request, just as the Israelites of the Exodus found favor in the eyes of the Egyptians in response to theirs. The resonance is significant because the Exodus text comes in the immediate wake of Moses' instructions for Passover.

Still in Exodus, Mordecai's ceremonial attire, in which he appears following the writing of the counter-decree (Est. 8:15-17, cf., 6:6-11), though described as "royal," has been likened to that of Aaron the priest at the dedication of the tabernacle in Exodus 28. The honor bestowed by Ahasuerus on Mordecai is evidently intended to suggest his closeness to the king, not least in the crown on his head, implying quasi-royal status. But there are unmistakable echoes of the priestly adornments in the gold, blue, and purple, and the fine linen in which Mordecai is arrayed (8:15, cf., Exod. 28:5, and throughout that chapter). Levenson (1997, 116), noting the overlap between the offices of king and priest in ancient Israel, follows Bardtke (1963, 374) in thinking that Mordecai is here presented as a kind of "secular priest."[9] The term "secular" raises a question to which we shall return. But in Mordecai's quasi-sacral role, there seems to be another example of the narrative's veiled allusion to Israel's foundational events.

---

8. Fox (2001, 97–8) writes, "The factors underlying the choice of dates may lie in the realm of calendar or astrology, but are at present unknown."

9. Levenson (1997, 18) does not accept the concept of secularizing as a general explanation for the peculiarities of Esther, however.

The motif of feasting too strikes a chord with Israel's traditions. As in Deuteronomy's festal calendar deliverance from slavery in Egypt was to be celebrated with joy, at the Feast of Weeks and the Feast of Tabernacles (Deut. 16:11-12, 14), so the Jews of Persia celebrated both the issuing of the counter-decree and their actual escape from the threat of the pogrom with feasting and rejoicing (Est. 9:16-17; 10:17-19). The gifts to the poor (9:22) carry a further echo of Deuteronomy's characteristic inclusion of the marginalized in the festal aspects of Israel's worship (Deut. 16:11, 14, cf., 12:12, 18; 14:22-29; cf., Tob. 2:2).

These insistent evocations of Deuteronomic feasting, converging with the hints of the date of Passover, strongly suggest deliberate allusion to the ancient traditions. It is striking too, that the keeping of Purim is "adopted as a custom" by the Jews. Thus, just as the narrative of the events of the first Passover (Exod. 12) is at the same time an authoritative mandate for the perpetual observance of the feast, so the narrative of the first Purim in Esther is precisely such a mandate for the perpetual celebration of that feast. As the plot of Esther is sustained by the writing of edicts, the keeping of Purim is finally enjoined by the authoritative written decree of Mordecai (9:20-23): "they adopted it as a custom, *as Mordecai had written to them*" (9:23). Significantly too, the Deuteronomic language of "observing" and "remembering," through every generation, is deployed at this formal inauguration of Purim.[10] To Mordecai's priestly traits, therefore, may be added a resonance of Moses as lawgiver. Moses himself, indeed, across the Pentateuchal traditions, had combined these two roles (see Exod. 24:3-8).

All these features imply a definite aesthetic strategy in the book. It is often noted how carefully the narrative carries the action by means of a series of coincidences and reversals. It so happens that Queen Vashti defies the king and so creates an opportunity for Esther to become queen. Likewise, Mordecai overhears the plot against the king's life, and through Esther can act to thwart it. This crucial element[11] is then stored up by the narrator to be recovered at the moment when the king happens to have a sleepless night, and as a consequence Mordecai is elevated to the highest rank in preference to Haman. The technique of reversal is also employed with great skill. Haman's plot for his own rise and Mordecai's fall is precisely reversed, as is the plan for the enemies of the Jews to slaughter them. The perfectly executed swivel-point is in ch. 6, where Haman happens to be in the king's outer court just at the moment when the king has been informed of the foiled plot against his life, and Haman, thinking he is about to be honored himself, has to endure the realization that it is his enemy who is to be elevated.[12]

---

10. Bechtel (2011, 83), citing Deut. 6:12, 20-25, notes this couching of the Purim command: "In language that sounds very like Deuteronomy's plea to remember the passover."

11. In LXX, it is the first thing that is told, heralded in Mordecai's consciousness by a dream. This opening account also tells briefly of Mordecai's reward and Haman's discomfiture; Est. Add. 11–12.

12. For a detailed account of the literary strategy of reversal in the book, see Grossman (2011, 12–14).

The self-consciousness of this art is apparent in the words of Mordecai to Esther in 4:14, which are the closest the narrative comes to an interpretation of the events it tells:

> Who knows? Perhaps you have come to the royal dignity for just such a time as this.

The narrative's studied reserve is present even here, in the rhetorical "Who knows?"[13] Yet, unmistakably, it draws attention to the remarkable way in which events conspire to bring about a resolution to the crisis in favor of the Jews.

These features of coincidence and reversal by no means exhaust the reach of the book's narrative art. One of the most problematic aspects of the story is the obliteration of Esther's Jewish identity when she becomes wife to the Persian king. The point is illustrated by the motif of clothing. Esther the queen is appalled by the appearance of Mordecai at the king's gate dressed in sackcloth and ashes, and sends him proper clothing, which he refuses to wear (4:1-4). While the wearing of such symbolic garb attracts criticism from certain prophets for its supposed superficiality,[14] the narrative here suggests that Esther's motive has more to do with keeping up decent appearances. Grossman (2011, 113 n. 7) finds a note of strong criticism of Esther in this scene, citing the unusual verb used to express her deep agitation at the sight of Mordecai.[15] The clothing motif continues in ch. 5, in which she dons her royal robes in order to approach the king (5:1). This in itself may just be the force of necessity (Judith did the same). Yet the narrative artistry extends further to emphasizing the extent to which Esther's movement from the Jewish sphere into the Persian court raises questions about her identity. In the banqueting scene in ch. 7, she is twice described simply as "the queen" (7:6, 8), in a way that suggests complete assimilation into Persian identity.[16]

It follows that the aesthetic strategy of Esther is not a straightforward solution to the troubling questions posed by the book. Rather, it accentuates some of its ambivalence.

Explaining the Silences

Even so, as David Clines (1984, 154–5) has put it, "no Jewish author could have told the Esther story without a consciousness that the exodus story lay in the background as a prototype." The observations made above confirm this in my view. But the question remains, why has the author told the story in the form in which

---

13. Grossman (2011) notes an echo of Joel 2:14, "Who knows whether he [God] will not turn and relent?"

14. See Joel 2:12-14; Isa. 58:5; cf., Grossman (2011, 113).

15. The verbal form *wattithalkal* occurs here only in the Old Testament; Grossman (2011, 114).

16. As Grossman (2011, 114) puts it, "the narrator indicates that Esther's identity had become assimilated with her role as queen, at the expense of her Jewishness."

we have it in MT? Do the silences tend toward the diminishment of the activity of God, the Passover, and the food-laws in Diaspora Israel? Or, on the contrary, do the unmistakable hints about these convey to the knowing reader that these things remain very important? There have been various answers to the question.

Not surprisingly, perhaps, the lack of overt features of Israel's religion led some to think of it as "secular." G. Gerleman (1973, 21–3) proposed that Esther detheologized the exodus story, perhaps intending to replace Passover with Purim. A variation on the secular idea is that Esther is nationalistic. That is, the book is so fixed on the politics of Jewish survival that it simply leaves God out of account.[17] Such approaches have not found favor, partly because the idea of the secular is anachronistic, as is that of nationalism. The story of the nation Israel is elsewhere always bound up with Israel's relationship with Yahweh, and Yahweh's actions in history. As we have seen, these things are true even of the Old Testament literature that most resembles Esther. Our questions are not answered, therefore, by positing such purposes for the book. At best they pose them in a different way: where would the author of Esther get the idea that a secular or nationalistic idea best served the interests of the nation Israel?

Others have looked for answers to the conundrum in terms of inner-Israelite religious issues. Grossman (2011, 24–5) suggests that the book may be motivated by a contention between those exilic Jews who returned to the land following the exile and the Jews of Susa, who had not; the descriptions of the rich royal palace and lifestyle are, ironically, "a condemnation of the Jews of Shushan who luxuriate in the lavish royal feast instead of helping their brothers and sisters who have returned to their land." Somewhat related to this is the idea that Esther can be explained in terms of honor and shame. Timothy S. Laniak argues that diaspora is a "shame-state," citing the typical occurrence of exile in lists of curses in ANE treaties and covenants. While Ezra and Nehemiah, and other Old Testament literature, find an end to the shame of exile in return to the land, Esther offers no such relief:

> To be separated from land, temple and monarchy in the ancient world was to be separated from one's source of identity as a people. (Lanmiak 1998, 172–3)

Mordecai and Esther have even been regarded as apostate, idolaters from Babylon, who defied the Jewish law.[18]

The problem with views of this sort is that the events of Esther are portrayed as the foundation of a feast that came to take its place in the mainstream of Jewish life. The book of Esther is unapologetic about maintaining Jewish identity

---

17. Rodriguez (1995, 84, 140) cites H. Ringgren, R. Pfeiffer, and O. Eissfeldt for these approaches.

18. Hoschander (1923, 103, 112), cited by Rodriguez (1995, 86). Rodriguez (1995, 86–7, 141) also cites Whitcomb (1979, 26), who thought that Mordecai and Esther failed to support "God's theocratic program" by refusing to return to the land of Israel.

apart from king, land, and temple. On the contrary, it can be seen as a positive program for the "transformation of the *exile* into the *Diaspora*" (Levenson 1997, 15).

Also unconvincing is the idea that Esther is a "wisdom" tale, and as such leaves God out of account.[19] In Proverbs and Job, wisdom is pursued in overtly religious contexts. And while the idea might have some traction in relation to Qoheleth, we have already noticed important differences between Esther and that book.

These objections have in common attempts to explain why the author of Esther might have wished to sideline God in his view of the historical reality of Israel. Yet this impulse fails to do justice to the implicit allusions to God's action in history that we have observed above. Clines (1984, 155–6) even disputes the idea that God's action in history is "veiled," finding it to be assumed, given the context of the narrative.[20] Levenson, similarly, argues that the story is not about whether God works in history, but how. For him, the providential hand of God is opposed in it to the pagan notion of fate represented by the casting of lots.

Fox finds the question more difficult to answer, however, and declares that he has "gone back and forth" on it over the years. For him, it is inherently difficult to resolve the question whether the confidence expressed by Mordecai in Est. 4:14a arises from faith in the covenant God or from the Jews' "inner strength and potential for self-help" (Fox 2001, 244).[21] He goes on to urge that the question of God's absence or presence in Esther "cannot be decided." Rather, "the author is carefully creating and maintaining uncertainty." He does so in an appeal to faith that honestly acknowledges such uncertainty (Fox 2001, 246-7).[22] Fox's position is not a "secular" one, still less deconstructive.[23] Rather, it belongs within a religious orientation to the text.

Fox's view finds echoes in the work of others. For Sandra Berg, the text's silence about God is explained by the narrative's intention to accentuate human responsibility in the shaping of history. Yet she places this human responsibility in a "dialectical" relationship with Yahweh's control of history. She does not appeal,

---

19. The point is argued by Talmon (1963), see Clines (1984, 157). Clines (1984) also cites Humphreys (1973). Clines thinks that Humphreys sees the story as "merely a tale of human wisdom and cunning," though he grants that this may not have been Humphreys's intention (1973). See also Rodriguez (1995, 83).

20. For Clines it is "*unexpressed*, but it is unmistakable"; *contra* Loader (1978, 418).

21. Intriguingly he cites (on pp. 244–5) a phrase in 1 Sam. 15:29: נֵצַח יִשְׂרָאֵל לֹא יְשַׁקֵּר, which, when spoken by religious Jews, means: "The Eternal One of Israel will not deceive," but when used by non-religious Jews means: "the eternity of Israel will not deceive" (or "fail"), that is, "the inner resources of the Jewish people will guarantee its existence."

22. This careful creedal statement is perhaps too readily dismissed by Levenson (1997, 19).

23. He expressly disowns such a move, on the grounds that the uncertainty in the text derives from the author's intention (2011, 246 n. 23).

therefore, to the concept of uncertainty, but rather thinks Esther entrusts the future of the Jews to "both God and humanity" (1980, 118).[24]

A Theological Perspective

It remains to ask whether a theological motivation can be discerned for the aesthetic decision to refrain from naming God in the narrative, as well as for the silences concerning Passover and food-laws. We have seen enough, I think, to be clear that the author of Esther wanted subtly to draw attention to the traditions of Israel. The silences are loud with implication. If the Passover is not named, it is precisely the Passover that is not named. If Esther, queen of Persia, feasts with the king and his highest official, the Mosaic food-laws call out to be noticed. It follows that the silences about the history of Yahweh with Israel are hardly mere omissions. One possibility is that they conspicuously draw attention to silence itself. The Old Testament authors are familiar with the concept of God hiding his face from his people. Rodriguez proposes an intriguing twist on this topic, suggesting that Esther addresses a people who had no prophetic ministry for guidance on the meaning of events. They had become accustomed to events being decided by human authorities. Esther is an aesthetic means of addressing this apparent absence of God, and so of challenging the serious threat it poses to faith:

> The perceived absence of the Divine from salvation history—in fact the perceived end of salvation history—is used by the author to communicate a message of comfort and faith. (Rodriguez 1995, 96)

Be that as it may, it does not by itself account for the exotic setting of the story in Persia. This setting is unlikely to be analogous to Shakespeare's choice of far places (Venice, Verona) as a dramatic device of defamiliarization, since the spread of a postexilic diaspora was a real historical fact that was bound to raise serious religious questions for the Jews. As we have seen, Esther does not address some of the obvious questions that did indeed arise for Jews in diaspora, in consequence of their dislocation from temple and land. Yet one might interpret the implicit allusions to exodus and Passover as a key to reading the events reported: "The same Power is present in both stories, bringing deliverance to God's people" (Rodriguez 1995, 110).

Even so, it is difficult to think of Esther merely as a lightly veiled reprise of the exodus story. There is a glimpse of a more specific theological interest in its orientation to the world of empire. Significantly, what is at stake in the threat to the Jews from the pogrom plot affects all Jews wherever they are. That perspective must include those who have returned to Judah and rebuilt the temple, under the aegis of the same Persian empire that is the subject of Esther. For Esther, there is

---

24. Rodriguez (1995, 83) attributes similar views to a range of authors, including R. K. Harrison, J. A. Loader, W. Lee Humphreys, and Arndt Meinhold.

no in-principle distinction between those who returned and those who did not. Furthermore, its narrative locates events decisive for the salvation of all Jews, not in the furtherance and protection of the project to repopulate Judah and rebuild temple and walls, as in Ezra-Nehemiah, but at the heart of empire, far removed from the historic land. In an additional tweak to this broad perspective, Esther quietly signals an openness to non-Jews joining the Jewish community (8:17; 9:27). These two texts hint at a completely new way of seeing the Jewish community. The latter in particular has suggestive overtones of the vision of the renewed community in Isaiah 56, in which the "foreigner" who "joins" it is welcomed into full membership. The verb "join" in Est. 9:27 is the same one found twice in Isaiah 56 (at vv. 3, 6).[25] In 8:17, the unique form מִתְיַהֲדִים is based on the word "Jewish" (*yəhûdî[t]*), that is, foreigners were "becoming Jewish."[26] In this "newly-defined Israel,"[27] Jews and Gentiles throughout the world are becoming a single unified people, under Yahweh. In such a program, it is understandable that the memories of exodus and Passover might be treated *sotto voce*. Passover is about leaving a tyranny and a territory in order to enter another space under another rule (that of both Yahweh and the Mosaic Torah, as administered by duly appointed human agents). Esther, in contrast, has no place for "next year in Jerusalem." Purim is about maintaining Jewish identity without radical displacement, and without a revolution in human rule. As Levenson (1997, 14) has it, Ahasuerus, unlike Pharaoh, "continues to rule the Jews." As to divine rule, that is probably intact, but conceived in a novel way.

All such interpretative attempts must remain tentative. The elephant in the essay is that we know very little about either the authorship or the intended first audience of the book. While we believe we have been able to see significance in some of the data, some are indigestible, such as the date of the counter-edict on the twenty-third day of Sivan (Est. 8:9-12). This leaves us with the uncomfortable (but unsurprising) feeling that there are things going on here that we simply cannot see.

It is clear enough that our author has woven intertextual signals into the narrative. We have observed other kinds of intertextuality by comparing Esther with certain Old Testament and apocryphal literature with which it shares features. While such echoes can be fairly confidently identified, they leave the work of interpretation to be done. Indeed, they belong intrinsically to the interpretative puzzle of the book.

---

25. The form in Est. 9:27 is הַנִּלְוִים, as also in Isa. 56:6; Isa. 56:3 has the singular form הַנִּלְוָה .

26. Arguably, it means they were pretending to be Jewish. But in the light of 9:27, "becoming Jewish" is probably to be preferred.

27. See Levenson (1976, 451); Rodriguez (1995, 107).

Part II

ESTHER IN DIALOGUE WITH THE FORMER PROPHETS

Chapter 3

ESTHER AND JOSHUA: NEGOTIATING IDENTITY IN AND OUT OF THE LAND

David G. Firth

Introduction

As might be expected for a relatively late work in the canon of the Hebrew Bible, Esther is a work that is full of references and allusions to earlier texts. Indeed, I have argued elsewhere that a key mechanism by which Esther develops its theology is through interaction with other parts of the Hebrew Bible, inviting readers to explore the events recounted in Esther in light of other texts.[1] In a work that famously does not mention God, theology is not something that is expressed directly. Yet the book does at least hint at a theology, and this theology exists in its interaction with other texts that have this more explicitly displayed. One area where this is important is concerned with the issue of the land. Although Esther is perhaps most famous for its lack of reference to God, it is also notable for the fact that, apart from Job, it is the only book of the Hebrew Bible that does not mention the land. Given its setting in the heart of the Persian empire this might not seem entirely surprising. But this is in fact typical of Esther's concern with a life that continues in an emerging diaspora rather than being focused on life in the land. Yet, a lack of concern for the land is part of a wider pattern where Esther also shows no interest in either the temple or the covenant, even though these are motifs that receive considerable attention in most of the other books in the Hebrew Bible. As Lau (2013, 100–2) has argued, these absences are crucial to the ways in which Esther constructs Jewish identity, so that rather than focusing on these traditional motifs, those who are truly Jewish demonstrate their loyalty to their fellow Jews, though it is likely that this also implies loyalty to their God.[2]

If Esther constructs its theology through interaction with other texts, then one interesting option is to read Esther in light of the book of Joshua. One reason for this is the clear contrast between these two books on the issue of the land—where Esther shows no interest in the land, for Joshua the land is of pivotal importance.

---

1. Firth (2010a, 15–28, 2010b, 33–5).
2. See also Kissling (2013, 106).

If for no other reason, this would suggest that there is value in reading these texts alongside one another. But we will also note that for both Joshua and Esther the identity of Israel is a matter that is under negotiation, and that reading one in light of the other particularly sheds light on Esther. Moreover, it will be argued that Est. 9:2[3] alludes directly to Josh. 1:5, 21:44, and 23:9, so that as the book moves toward its close it develops a strong link with Joshua. Since this indicates that Joshua is the older work, we can most effectively read Esther in light of Joshua rather than the other way around.[4] The presence of this clear verbal link also suggests that there is value in exploring other points where the echoes of Joshua are not as pronounced and yet may still be important for an enriched reading of Esther. In particular, as well as exploring the inability of Israel's opponents to resist them in Esther 9, we will note possible links between the story of Rahab in Joshua 2 and 6 and Esther's integration into the royal court in Persia. In both instances we will see that the links with Joshua show how Esther constructs Jewish identity more broadly than might have been expected had the traditional focus points of land, temple, and covenant been retained.

Esther and Rahab

At first sight, Esther and Rahab might seem to be characters with little in common—one is a Canaanite prostitute in Jericho, the other a Jewish woman in the diaspora. Apart from their sex, there would appear to be few reasons for reading one in light of the other. Yet, there are important parallels in their presentation, which encourage us to read them this way, especially as Esther herself is introduced to the narrative. As Grossman (2011, 58–62) has noted, Esther 2 is full of allusions to other stories in the Hebrew Bible, and these elements point to a depth of meaning that may not be apparent on the surface. Although he does not point to connections with Rahab's introduction in Joshua 2, there are several key factors which suggest that Esther's introduction here can be understood, in part, through the connections made with Rahab.

At a fairly general level, we can note that both Rahab and Esther are presented as outsiders. Although Rahab dwells in Jericho, as a prostitute she is a marginal member of her society.[5] In particular, she is someone under the control of men who must yet take control of her situation. Esther, likewise, is introduced as someone who is under the control of men—she is Mordecai's ward and is taken to the king where she is simply made a part of his harem, a gathering of women who exist

---

3. Although it is possible that an early form of AT Esther does not include Esther 9, this essay is concerned only with MT Esther which has always included Esther 9. For a brief summary of the issues with Esther's textual variants, see Fox (2001, 9–10).

4. Hence, the reading is shaped by the criteria outlined by Hays (1989, 29–32).

5. Coote (1998, 592–6), makes this central to his reading. Arguably, his approach goes beyond the text, but the issues he highlights are real.

solely for his sexual gratification. There can be no doubt on the suggestion that this was the purpose of gathering all the "beautiful virgins" in the realm for Ahasuerus since the one who "pleased" the king (תִּיטַב בְּעֵינֵי הַמֶּלֶךְ) was to be assessed on the basis of the night they spent with him (Est. 2:4). As a prostitute, Rahab is also understood as someone who exists for male sexual gratification, something that is particularly evident when we note the extent to which the language of Joshua 2 is full of double entendre.[6]

Beyond these more general links, there is also the intriguing point that both Joshua 2 and Esther 2 make significant use of the word חֶסֶד. This is a theologically significant word across the Hebrew Bible as a whole, but it occurs in only two verses in Joshua, both in the Rahab story (Josh. 2:12 [×2], 14). The word, likewise, only occurs twice in the book of Esther, both times in the account of Esther's entry to the harem and ascent to being queen (Est. 2:9, 17). Moreover, although its function is different in each account, it occurs at crucial points in both narratives. Although not necessarily the central intertext in Esther 2, these factors indicate that Joshua 2 is a significant echo that readers attuned to the wider Hebrew Bible may pick up.

In noting these connections, we can also observe that Joshua 2 is itself full of intertextual allusions and echoes. Perhaps the most important is triggered by mention of Joshua secretly sending his scouts to Jericho from Shittim. This place-name evokes memories of the story in Num. 25:1-5,[7] an account where Israel had prostituted themselves as they had encountered foreign women. Yet in Joshua 2, Rahab reverses the role played by those foreign women, and even though as a prostitute we might have expected that she would engage in inappropriate sexual activity, the account here is notable for the fact that nothing of the sort is recorded. It is impossible to know how much Esther 2 is intended to be read with the whole intertextual background of Joshua 2, but given Esther's rich engagement with other texts some wider awareness is certainly possible.

But attention to Joshua 2 also points to significant contrasts between Rahab and Esther, and it is in the interplay of the similarities and differences that we appreciate the richness of Esther. Some elements are seemingly minor, and yet may have potential for enriching our reading. So, we may note that Joshua had sent his scouts in secret,[8] whereas Ahasuerus was entirely open about his actions. As is typical of each book, Joshua is presented as someone who was quite decisive, whereas Ahasuerus only ever acts at the suggestion of another. Perhaps more importantly, where Rahab did not have a sexual relationship with the scouts, it is evident that Esther and Ahasuerus did. Yet even though this contrast is present, we can note that both Joshua 2 and Esther 2 use language that points to sexual activity though without ever actually describing it, preferring double entendre.

6. See, e.g., Nelson (1997, 43–4).
7. See Krause (2015, 416–27).
8. Presumably in secret relative to Israel since this would not be noted in regard to Jericho. See Krause (2012, 454–6).

Nevertheless, Esther could only become queen because she "pleased" the king sexually.

Is this difference between them fatal to an intertextual reading? No, because as will be seen, we need to understand the actions of both Rahab and Esther through the grid of חֶסֶד; and when we do this it becomes evident that each needs to express this in rather different ways, in both cases at great risk to themselves.

In Rahab's case, the theme of חֶסֶד first appears in the midst of her confession of faith to the scouts (Josh. 2:12). This confession begins in v. 9, where she notes that she knows that Yahweh has given Israel the land. She points to key events in the wilderness wanderings as evidence for this, with the crossing of the Sea of Reeds and the defeat of Sihon and Og effectively creating a bookend for the events before Israel had reached the plains of Moab.[9] Having confessed faith in vv. 9-11, Rahab then puts her request to the scouts, asking that just as she has shown חֶסֶד, so also they might show חֶסֶד to her. The clear implication is that she has taken a significant risk for them in not handing them over to the king of Jericho's officers, and accordingly she asks that they do the same for her. In response, the scouts swear an oath in which they commit themselves to practice חֶסֶד for her too, putting their own lives at risk should they fail to do so. Readers of the Joshua story may feel some discomfort at the oath sworn by the scouts given the seeming prohibition of such agreements in Deut. 7:1-2. In Joshua 2 it is not possible to know whether or not this oath is valid since the narrator there avoids providing information that would help readers to resolve this dilemma.[10] However, following Rahab's exclusion from the ban at Jericho (Josh. 6:17, 22-23), readers have good reason to believe that the oath was valid. Certainly, the note in Josh. 6:25 would suggest that Rahab's act of hiding the scouts was understood as good reason for enabling her to live within Israel. Indeed, within Joshua she becomes the paradigm figure for Israel's entry to the land, the one who understands what Yahweh is doing and who commits herself to it. In this she is clearly contrasted with Achan (Josh. 7), who is the Israelite who becomes (in effect) a Canaanite as he is excluded because he put his own desires before those of Yahweh.[11] Rahab has shown חֶסֶד and this provides the basis for her continued existence within Israel, modeling a pattern that permits those who are not Israelite to join the nation. Indeed, through the contrast with Achan, we see a pattern that demonstrates that the true Israel is made up of those who commit themselves to Yahweh's purposes and not simply those who can claim a genealogical connection.

When we turn to Esther 2, there is an immediate difference that should be noted. Where Rahab had demonstrated חֶסֶד through her commitment to the scouts, Esther is never said to have practiced חֶסֶד. Rather, Esther finds favor, first with the keeper of the women (Hegai, v. 9) and then with the king after her night

---

9. Her confession is clearly written up from an Israelite perspective, and this probably explains the links to other parts of the Pentateuch noted by Berman (2016, 344–9).

10. On the narrative techniques employed, see Firth (2017b, 413–30).

11. On this, see Firth (2017a, 71–88).

with him (v. 17). In this latter text, it is noted that along with חֶסֶד she also found חֵן. The idiom used here (חסד + נשא) does not occur elsewhere in the Hebrew Bible, but the implication appears to be that though Esther has not particularly sought to gain חֶסֶד,[12] it still has come to her. Indeed, to this point Esther has consistently been reported as having done what Mordecai and Hegai have told her. Unlike Rahab, who demonstrated חֶסֶד through the initiative she has taken, Esther has gained it with no evidence of an activity to merit it.

At this point in the narrative, the mention of חֶסֶד serves largely to show the distinction between Esther and Rahab, even if recurrence of the term along with various double entendre encourages us to read one in light of the other. But as the story progresses, these points of contrast between Esther and Rahab are gradually reduced as Esther must also take risks for the Jews. That is, the introduction of Esther highlights some connections to Rahab along with key differences. Although these key differences are not completely removed, the balance of the narrative shows them being greatly reduced as Esther takes risks for the Jews while she herself is under threat.

Rahab's actions are those of someone under threat, specifically because of her ethnicity. Her actions effectively mean she rejects her ethnic connections to commit herself to Israel. In Esther 2, it is not yet clear that Esther is under any particular threat, or at least no more than any beautiful virgin girl in an empire where the desire of the king to bed as many as possible dominates. That is, she faces personal peril due to extraordinary sexism, but not yet an ethnic one, though the possibility of this as a point of threat is introduced through Mordecai's command to her that she should not reveal her ethnicity (Est. 2:10). But the reality of that threat is only made clear in Esther 3 where, in response to Mordecai's refusal to bow before him, Haman determined to destroy all the Jews in the empire (Est. 3:6). Such language of destruction, even though avoiding mention of חֵרֶם, perhaps because this is too overtly theological, uses terms that are otherwise important in Joshua, starting with שׁמד, a term used to describe the destruction of at least some of the inhabitants of the land (e.g., Josh. 11:14, 20).[13] Once the edict supporting this is published (Est. 3:12-14), Esther is at risk because of her ethnicity, thus placing her in the same position as Rahab.

The decree authorizing the pogrom against the Jews means that Esther is then in a position like that of Rahab—she is a woman who expects to be killed because of her ethnicity. Like Rahab, she needs to act. But where Rahab acts by effectively joining Israel, Esther needs to take a different path. This is in part because she lives within the Persian empire and in many ways is indistinguishable from other women in it. She is clearly Jewish, but not recognized as such by all. In her

---

12. Day (2005, 48) interprets the language here as indicating astute political acts by Esther, but nothing in the story indicates any obvious activity on her part apart from doing what others have told her to do.

13. Interestingly, in Josh. 23:15 the term is used as a threat against Israel should they fail to remain faithful to Yahweh.

dialogue with Mordecai in Esther 4 there is a hint that she might have thought herself sufficiently indistinguishable from the majority population that she would be secure, though Mordecai is quick to disabuse her of this (Est. 4:13). Instead, he insists that she needs to go to the king and intercede for the Jews, even though he suggests that if she does not, then help would arise from another place (Est. 4:14). Whether or not this is a reference to God need not detain us at this point, but more importantly for our purposes, Mordecai refers to the possibility of the destruction of both Esther and her "father's house." This may seem an odd phrase,[14] but it may draw on more than just the traditional language of the family. In the Hebrew Bible such destruction happens to one family—that of Achan following his sin at Jericho (Josh. 7). In that Achan is the key contrast to Rahab in Joshua,[15] an echo of his story is important, for this is definitely not the path that Esther needs to take. Rather, like Rahab Esther will need to take a risky path to commit herself to the Jews in the empire, showing that she truly is a Jew and not simply a Persian.

Esther's response to this is her famous declaration that she would go before the king, even though she knew it could result in the loss of her life (Est. 4:17). But just as Rahab had to be clever in her dealings with Jericho's king, so also Esther would need to be astute in her dealings with Ahasuerus. For Rahab, this involved misdirection, playing on his messengers' expectations of what a prostitute would do in order to protect the scouts (Josh. 2:3-4). Esther, likewise, will need a degree of misdirection as she goes through a process of preparing two banquets for the king, only revealing her actual purposes at the second. It is only at this point that she reveals her ethnicity (Est. 7:3-6), leading to the overthrow of Haman as he is impaled on the stake he had earlier erected for Mordecai. But, as the events of Esther 8 also demonstrate, Esther could not simply save her own family; she and Mordecai also needed to develop a scheme to deliver all the Jews.

Esther's own journey within the book of Esther thus gains richness when read against the story of Rahab in Joshua, a story that Esther seems to echo at key points. Both are notable for their experience of חֶסֶד, but in this they are both joined and yet also initially separated. Rahab acts in Joshua 2 to demonstrate her חֶסֶד, but in Esther 2 it is something Esther experiences but does not obviously demonstrate. Yet in the combination of חֶסֶד and ethnicity we see that their stories are gradually brought together. Rahab is the Canaanite who becomes part of Israel through her commitment to Israel, a commitment that requires astuteness on her part. Esther is a Jew who initially looks more like a Persian and yet who progressively demonstrates her commitment to the other Jews, with the result that the חֶסֶד she had initially received is now shown. For both, this is a commitment that involves risk, and both show variability in their ethnicity. In Joshua, Rahab becomes prototypical of other foreigners who join Israel (such as the Gibeonites), while in Esther it is Esther's emergence as someone truly Jewish who prepares the

---

14. Berlin (2001, 49) notes that the phrase appears "deficient in logic," though she goes on to note its rhetorical function here.

15. See Firth (2019, 24–7).

way for the many who associate themselves with the Jews (Est. 8:17). In Joshua, association with Israel means life in the land, but in Esther the life the Jews live is now scattered throughout the empire, showing that the value of joining Israel that was once associated with a particular place can now be experienced in any place.

Unable to Resist Israel

Although Esther's actions had created a context in which the Jews could continue to exist within the Persian empire, the nature of the king's edict against them meant that it could not simply be canceled (Est. 1:19, 8:8). It is this challenge that the Jews face in Est. 9:1-19; and although the echoes of Rahab's story fade, other links to Joshua are made. Once again, these links show the possibility of life for the Jews outside the land, demonstrating that the promises that had once shaped Israel's life in the land continue to provide hope outside it.

The context of Est. 9:1-19 has been established by the counter-decree initiated by Mordecai, which allowed the Jews to gather to defend themselves (Est. 8:11-12). The content of this decree is sometimes understood as allowing the Jews to initiate further attacks against the women and children associated with those who attack them, but it seems more likely that the wording of his decree is intended as an exact reversal of Haman's original decree and that the women and children are among those attacking. If so, the decree is purely defensive in its orientation. Its main focus would then be to deter would-be attackers who now know the Jews can organize themselves in defense. The language of both Haman's decree and Mordecai's counter-decree certainly evokes the חֵרֶם described in Joshua, though in the strictest application of this principle at Jericho the taking of plunder was not permitted. Perhaps more importantly, the situation presumed here is similar to the one presented in Josh. 9:1-2, 10:1-5, and 11:1-5, where the Canaanite forces gathered to attack Israel. That is, although it is common to refer to these chapters in Joshua under the rubric of "conquest," as Joshua presents the various battle reports which dominate Joshua 10–11 they are primarily defensive—Israel gains land because their enemies attack them and are unable to overcome them. Likewise, Esther presents the Jews as responding by defending themselves against their attackers in language that evokes the campaigns reported by Joshua.[16]

These links might be regarded as fairly general; though given the other connections to Joshua already noted, there is good reason to think they are significant. But there is also the strong verbal link that is established through the note in Est. 9:2, וְאִישׁ לֹא־עָמַד לִפְנֵיהֶם. The inability of Israel's enemies to resist them is a significant theme in Joshua, established as early as Josh. 1:5. Although there is a change of the verb, the phrasing here is otherwise quite similar to that of Est. 9:2, as Joshua was promised לֹא־יִתְיַצֵּב אִישׁ לְפָנֶיךָ. The importance of this promise for the book as a whole is evident from its inclusion in the narrator's summary statement

---

16. Similarly, Kissling (2013, 107–8).

of Yahweh's faithfulness in Josh. 21:44, this time in language that is closer again to the statement in Esther, וְלֹא־עָמַד אִישׁ בִּפְנֵיהֶם. In Joshua's address in Josh. 23:9, this motif is again taken up, once more in language very close to that of Esther (לֹא־עָמַד אִישׁ בִּפְנֵיכֶם). The presence of language that has evoked the type of destruction expected in the חֵרֶם along with these close verbal parallels all encourage a reading of Est. 9:1-19, which is informed by the book of Joshua. In effect, Est. 9:2 claims that the inability of those attacking the Jews needs to be read as parallel to the inability of Israel's enemies to resist them within Joshua. If so, then although Esther characteristically does not mention God, there is good reason to treat וְנַהֲפוֹךְ (Est. 9:1) as a divine passive. In the same way that Yahweh had ensured that no one could resist Israel as they entered the land in Joshua, so also, they are protected from their enemies as they live outside the land across the Persian empire. The life that had been made possible within the land is now possible in the diaspora.

But there is a major shift that also happens in Est. 9:1-19, which needs to be read against the background provided by Joshua. Although Mordecai's decree, in mirroring Haman's, had permitted the Jews to take the plunder from those who attacked them, and even though Est. 9:1-10 reports a comprehensive victory, it is expressly noted in Est. 9:10 that the Jews did not take the plunder. Although it is not expected in terms of Mordecai's original decree, Esther is said to have gained royal approval for the Jews to organize themselves for defense on a second day (Est. 9:11-15). Although this too resulted in comprehensive victory, once again it is reported that the Jews did not take any plunder. The motif of not taking any plunder is repeated in the summary statement (Est. 9:16), which prepares for Purim to be celebrated over two days. Clearly, three mentions of this point in so short a passage make clear its importance. If we are correct in reading the victories of the Jews in light of Israel's victories in Joshua, then this suggests another important point of contact between these books. Most notably, Joshua takes a flexible approach to the taking of items under the חֵרֶם. Only at Jericho is the taking of plunder prohibited (Josh. 6:18), since taking of the plunder would place Israel under the ban. The Achan story demonstrates with tragic clarity what happened to an Israelite who took any plunder there. But elsewhere in Joshua, the taking of plunder is permitted—and in Achan's case the tragedy of this is made clear when Yahweh permitted Israel to take plunder at Ai (Josh. 8:2). Unlike the events in Est. 9:1-19, not only was the taking of plunder permitted, Josh. 8:27 specifies that it was in fact taken.

The background from Joshua shows that the rule of חֵרֶם could be applied with varying degrees of strictness, but an absolute prohibition on taking plunder was possible in the strictest form it could take. The Jews in Est. 9:1-19 thus treat the battles in which they found themselves along the pattern of the strictest form of חֵרֶם. In that we have previously noted a possible connection to Achan, it may be that his story also lies in the background here; so that rather than risking a situation in which they might be like Israel at Ai (Josh. 7:4-5), the Jews do not take any plunder and thus avoid the risk of being placed under divine judgment. Life is possible outside the land, but the Jews still need to be faithful for this to happen, especially in a world where they are a minority under threat.

Conclusion

Although Joshua and Esther may seem rather disparate works within the Hebrew Bible (and their very real differences must also be noted), it is also the case that the book of Joshua provides important background material that enriches the reading of Esther and that seems to contribute to Esther's theology. Esther does not make this theology explicit but nonetheless by making direct references to Joshua it does suggest a theological reading of its themes. In particular, attention to the links with Joshua, both similarities and differences, makes much clearer the possibility of Jewish life in the empire, showing that such a life is possible outside the land.[17] That life is one that is open to the possibility of others joining the Jews, just as Rahab became a part of Israel. Participation in the life of the Jews is thus marked by a commitment to them, even when this is at risk to oneself, as can be seen in the parallels and differences between Rahab and Esther. This openness does not ignore the continued threat that existed in the diaspora. Instead, again drawing on background in Joshua, Esther also shows that even if some aspects of Jewish life (such as kosher food) might be treated more lightly, there was still a requirement to work out how life could be lived faithfully. This faithfulness was not only the commitment to the rest of the Jews that Esther herself had shown, it was also a commitment not to act against foes in a way that exceeded their actions against the Jews. Lived this way, this life could well be one that enjoyed the promises of God, just as is seen in Joshua.

---

17. The importance of Esther for life in the diaspora was particularly established by Humphreys (1973, 211–23). As his work does not consider the issues addressed here, this study can be seen as supplementing his work.

Chapter 4

EYES, HEARTS, AND DOING "WHAT SEEMS GOOD": READING JUDGES AND ESTHER SIDE-BY-SIDE

Isabelle Hamley

Judges and Esther sit toward opposite ends of the story of Israel—in Judges, a people is slowly coming together, while in Esther, the same people have moved from autonomy to life in dispersion. Both are, however, concerned with the identity of a nation how this identity is preserved in a strange land; how it is shaped, owned, and told in adversity; and how a nation processes traumatic memories through telling its story. There are no overt parallels between these texts, despite the effort of the writer(s) of Esther to stress continuity with the biblical story of Israel. There are clear thematic and verbal references to Genesis, Kings, and Samuel, for instance (Berlin 2001, xxii), but no generally accepted parallels to Judges.[1] A lack of obvious intertextual markers, however, does not mean these texts do not relate in deeper ways, which reveal shared concerns and suggest joint avenues for exploration. These may form a common pre-text, to use the words of Mieke Bal (1988, 254), which sheds light on Jewish writers' and redactors' shared focus on the construction of communal identity. Read together, these texts may also prompt the readers to ask deeper questions of the surface narrative. The texts share surprising similarities in motifs and narrative technique: both narrators remain unobtrusive, and moral judgment is invited through the telling of ironic, complex tales. Both texts, on the surface, tell simple stories of poetic justice and unbridled violence, yet in both, the heavy use of irony and the marginalization of Yahweh form a deeper disturbing ethical and theological subtext. In addition, both books use similar motifs and themes: sexual politics, women as tricksters, what happens when leaders encourage/allow their followers to do what is right in their own eyes, the delineation of ethnic self, and others. These parallels suggest that Judges and Esther share some similar goals and functions. Both contribute to the construction of national identity through a clear differentiation between self and other, through lampooning and caricaturing the nonself, and attempts at

---

1. Morgenstern (2009) stands alone in arguing a clear intertextual link based on the idea of the production of texts, though her argument stretches the meaning of "texts" quite thin, as well as the metaphor of the concubine's body as text in Judges 19.

eradication (or at least subjugation) of the other—whether this other is an ethnic other or a gendered other. This chapter will therefore lay both texts side-by-side and explore what questions emerge from a synchronic reading, without assuming any deliberate relationship, allusions, or dependence between them.

Common Words, Motifs, and Stylistics

Common words and motifs are relatively few between Esther and Judges. Some of the strongest resonances echo the second half of Judges, in particular the story of Samson—with repeated feasts and a female trickster—and the final three chapters—the story of the Levite's concubine and the civil war with Benjamin. Mordecai is identified as a Benjaminite (2:5).[2] The end of Judges, followed by the tragic kingship of Saul in Samuel, forms an initially negative background to this identification. The echo of Saul is reinforced with Haman being an Agagite, given that Saul's conflict with King Agag led to the loss of his kingship (Beal 1999, 25). It is not entirely clear how this marker is meant to function: Is it a negative omen about Mordecai? Is it a chance for redemption? Or is it a qualification of Mordecai's hero status, prompting readers to delve deeper? The text does not identify Mordecai coherently; he is often said to be a Judahite or Judean. The word may have come to apply to anyone of Hebrew descent, or it may be focalized through the eyes of outsiders to whom tribe distinctions mean little, so that difference within the Jewish community is erased by outsiders, yet contested by the text (Beal 1999, 26). The sense of fluidity as to markers of who forms Israel is reminiscent of Judges and the constant reconfiguration of tribes named as forming the nation.

The next nexus of concepts resonating between the books surrounds feasts (מִשְׁתֶּה), drinking, and making merry. The book of Esther opens with a series of feasts, with excess of wine and difficult relationships with women, as in the Samson story. In 3:15, the king and Haman sit together to drink while destruction is ordered in the city, just as the Levite and the old man in Judg. 19:22 eat and drink while disaster approaches in Gibeah. Further feasts ensue at Esther's instigation, where she plays the role of trickster toward Haman, much as Delilah plays trickster to Samson. The configuration of partners differs, but overall, feasts and drinking form part of the same tapestry of warning. These scenes contain frequent references to the "heart" in Judg. 19, with repeated injunctions to "strengthen" and "do good to" the heart (19:5, 6, 8, 9, 22). In Esther, the focus is on Haman's heart, particularly as the place where he conceives evil (6:6; 7:6). Feasts, drinking, and the heart are all fairly common motifs. However, a further common motif joins these three together and strengthens the parallel with deeper meaning. The epilogue of Judges is bookended by the refrain, "every man did what was right in his own *eyes*" (17:6; 21:25), while the rest of the book repeats, "the Israelites did what was wrong in the *eyes* of the Lord." A similar motif emerges in Esther, though

---

2. All biblical quotations and references were taken from the NRSV.

in slightly different words. In 1:8, every man does as he desires; in 1:21, the "thing seems good to the king's eyes"; 2:4 mentions twice "what is good in the king's eyes"; in 3:11, Haman's decree tells the people to do with the silver and the Jews "what seems good in their own eyes"; in 8:5, Esther tells the king, "if I am good in the eyes of the king"; in 8:8, the king tells Esther and Mordecai to write "what seems good in your eyes," with the final result, in 9:5, that the Jews did "as they pleased" to their enemies. In both texts, we find a subtext of individualism and personal decision-making unrelated to Yahweh or the law, with an outcome of unbridled violence. In Judges, it is internecine war in Israel; in Esther, the slaughter of non-Jews. Reading the texts together may prompt an evaluation of all the characters in Esther: it is not just Haman who is condemned but the king in his foolishness, and Esther's and Haman's actions are at least questionable within a wider moral framework. Overall, this then fits with a wider scriptural trajectory of examining leadership in the real world: its pitfalls, problems, and the inevitable compromises it entails.

Esther and Judges not only share themes and motifs, but they draw on similar narrative techniques. Both texts have an unobtrusive, almost absent narrator, who leaves readers to think for themselves rather than make overt moral judgments. More saliently, both texts use humor and irony: humor, in setting up a contrast between self and laughable other, and irony as a narrative device that draws attention to questions of justice. If we take humor first, the obvious parallel is with the story of Ehud, in Judg. 3:15-30. Esther on its own could be described as slapstick comedy, even farce (Berlin 2001, xix): we find exaggerated caricatures of the king and his aides, unlikely situations, physical and verbal humor. Berlin argues that nothing is to be taken seriously, that there is no real threat and no real satire, because it is carnivalesque comedy (xxiii). Political humor aimed at those considered oppressors is rarely gratuitous. Underneath, we find the tragedy of an empire that cares more about feasts and domesticity than the welfare of an entire people; there is the bitter edge of a people in the diaspora asserting their own worth over and against the all-powerful empire. In this sense, Esther shares much with the story of Ehud. Ehud is also an unlikely hero: where Esther is a woman, he is left-handed (but both belong to Benjamin). In both texts, the enemy is lampooned and portrayed as stupid, unable to anticipate what is coming, because of the arrogance of power. Both texts play with sexual innuendo (Ehud's concealed sword which penetrates Eglon, Haman's unfortunate pleading with Esther). Both texts move from caricaturing the enemy to annihilating the enemy through exaggerated violence. While both texts may function as a release of emotion for an oppressed people, the setting of the Ehud story within the wider narrative of Judges, and its spiraling account of violence that finally damages Israel itself, guides an interpretation of the story as tragi-comic and draws out the darker shadows of the narrative. While Esther, on its own, may stand as a burlesque or carnivalesque tale (Berlin 2001, xx), reading it within the wider story, and in parallel with a narrative with similar features, draws us into asking more searching questions.

Humor in Esther is closely linked to irony: in the fall of Haman, who never considered that Esther could be an opponent, in the king's repeated lapses of judgment (he had allowed Haman to do whatever he wanted to the Jews, which then allows Esther and Mordecai to do whatever they want to their enemies), in the glaring inconsistencies (affirming that a decree from the king cannot be rescinded, when the previous one clearly has been), and in the "poetic justice" of Haman dying on the gallows he had erected for Mordecai, and his own people being the victims at the hands of those he had sought to eradicate. Irony is equally central to the book of Judges, as Klein (1989) powerfully demonstrated. Situational irony occurs, for instance, with Jael, a liminal figure, just like Esther, in between Israel and its enemies, never seen as a danger by the powerful men around her (4:11-23), along with Sisera's mother, dreaming of victory while her son was slain (4:28-30). Here, irony serves the wider purpose of underlining the difference between Israel/the Jews and the ethnic other, portrayed as the oppressor, and justifying Israel's actions in response to oppression. Irony takes a darker turn when it is used to portray "poetic justice," in Esther, with Haman, in Judges, as a recurring motif: Abimelech, the man who killed his brothers on a stone, killed by a millstone; Samson, led astray by his wandering eyes, having eyes gauged out; the concubine (פילגש), an "unfaithful" woman, dying from an excess of unlawful sexual behavior. Initially, in Judges, irony brings the reader on the side of the Israelites, in cheering against evil. As the book progresses however, this poetic justice gets darker and more questionable: Is Samson's punishment proportionate to his crimes? Can we possibly justify the rape of the Levite's concubine on grounds of what she may or may not have done? At which point does this concept of natural justice become warped and draw the readers into acquiescing to disquieting and unjustifiable behavior? The logic of Judges invites readers, by the end of the book, to go back to the beginning and examine the judgments they made (Hamley 2019, 211). Reading Judges together with Esther prompts readers to ask the same questions of Esther: is the "poetic justice" of the book really justice? Or does it tip into something far less ethically defensible?

Gender and Sexuality

Both Judges and Esther showcase women as main actors. The book of Esther opens with the story of Vashti, before moving on to Esther herself. Judges contains the highest number of individual female characters, especially named characters, in an Old Testament book (Klein 1993, 24–6). While the contexts are radically different, both books have as a subtext questions about how women are treated and perceived and a complex construction of gender identity. Both books use types and antitypes, which the narration both reinforces and undermines. Judges displays a breathtaking breadth of female characters: Achsah as daughter, wife, and independent woman; Deborah as prophetess, judge, and poet; Jael as trickster and dangerous seductress; Jephthah's daughter, innocent and virginal victim; the wife of Manoah, mother of Samson; Samson's wife, burnt alive; another Samson interest, a prostitute; Delilah, seductress and trickster; the Levites' concubine, allegedly unfaithful wife, another victim of male violence, pretext for civil war; the women of Jabesh-Gilead, and Shiloh, virgins to be married, and gateways out of civil war.

The book of Esther focuses on two women, yet between them, they cumulate several typical roles. Vashti is the disobedient, difficult spouse (the shrew?)—often the description of women of independent will and action. Esther is an interesting fusion of types: the innocent, virginal daughter (niece) who does as she is told; the woman sold into a form of sexual slavery, along with all the other women selected for their beauty alone; the intelligent, loyal spouse; the trickster; the seductress who uses the king's attraction to her advantage; the woman of independent mind who saves her people; and finally, the warrior queen who dictates the extermination of her enemies. The framework that supports these portrayals is radically different. In Judges, we start with positive portrayals of women (Achsah and Deborah), who act in their own right and are secure and respected within the nation. As the nation slowly disintegrates, as everyone does "what seems right in their own eyes," the fate of women grows progressively darker, with women hurt and abused, who gradually lose their individuality, and become nameless victims. The treatment of women is an indicator of the spiritual, political, and social (ill-)health of the nation. Reading Judges and Esther together, one might ask: what is the health of Israel and of the Persian empire, as reflected in the treatment of women?

In both stories, women are used as part of political wrangling; women are treated as sex objects, but they subvert this role by turning it to their advantage (as Jael and Delilah do, and Esther uses her position with the king). Both stories give a complex account of a woman's position with regard to private and public spaces. In the story of the concubine, as with Vashti, women are excluded from men's drinking feasts. In both stories, women are placed in an impossible position by being asked/made to do simultaneously contradictory things. When Vashti is invited into the world of men, things go wrong: she must behave as a woman by obeying her husband, and as a not-woman (or at least a non-wife, more like a prostitute) by trespassing on a male-only scene. The concubine trespasses onto male space by leaving her husband in Judg. 19:1; in Gibeah, she is thrown to the men surrounding the crowd: she has to be woman by obeying her husband, being outside the house, yet this simultaneously makes her a non-wife by being forced into sex with multiple other men. Both stories open a window onto the ambiguity of gender roles and the impossibility for women to fulfil the different roles they are expected to embody. Both stories also link the domestic and the national, sexual politics and national politics. The link is made explicitly in Est. 1:13-22, with the farcical, exaggerated response of the sages to Vashti's refusal to be treated as a mere sex object for consumption by the male gaze (which, interestingly, will be the focus of the search for a new wife, as Esther initially fulfils the male fantasy of the beautiful wife which Vashti challenged). In Judg. 20:3-11, the Levite's speech turns the events of Gibeah into a pretext for civil war against the whole of Benjamin. Something deeper is at stake than domestic politics. Philosopher Luce Irigaray is helpful here. She argues that, in many cultures and languages, women are a mirror for the construction of male identity. "Woman" is not an independent concept, not allowed to be truly "other" to man, but instead is non-man, and needs to reflect to men the image they need to see of themselves (Irigaray 1974, 123). In both texts, women acting independently—Vashti's refusal and the concubine's leaving—triggers a deep challenge to masculinity, which is therefore threatening to all men, rather than individual husbands. If masculinity is challenged in one area, its construction may be challenged in another. A man challenged by a woman is seen to be vulnerable in battle, and therefore in the political life of the nation, as the stories of Jael and Sisera (Judg. 4) and the story of Abimelech (Judg. 9) exemplify. Esther may be more light-hearted, but the same deep uneasiness about the potential of women to threaten masculinity emerges, with similar extreme consequences. The outrageous levels of violence in both texts can be seen as a challenge, however: is this really worth it? Is it right? Can such violence ever be justified?

The story of Esther has other uncomfortable parallels with Judges, which dampen its light-heartedness. Esther is described with the same word as Jephthah's daughter—בתולה. Both young women are resourceful, yet work strictly within the confines of the patriarchal order. Both inaugurate a new festival. Yet one is killed, whereas the other turns killer. Which fate is worse? Why is one remembered, her festival honored, and the other not? Is it because Esther, while working within patriarchy, takes on the values of the men around her and champions its violence, whereas Jephthah's daughter quietly challenges it by exposing its consequences and retreats to the world of female companionship? The parallel prompts a difficult evaluation of Esther. Is she a triumphant heroine or victim? Two additional details reinforce the question. The girls taken into the harem are called נערה (2:13), like the Levite's concubine (Judg. 19:3-9); once they have gone to the king, they are transferred to the keeper of the concubines—פילשם. Given that every narrative portrayal of a concubine is a text with overtones of sexual abuse and extreme violence (Hamley 2018, 415–34),[3] the combined use of these two terms at least raises concerns about the treatment of Esther.

Esther, however, does not conform fully to any type. In the feast scene with the king roles are reversed, and Esther becomes host (normally a male role) and trickster. As host who turns her domestic space into an opportunity to dispose of her enemy, she is reminiscent of Jael. As trickster who uses the fact that she is "pleasing in the king's eyes," she is reminiscent of both Jael and Delilah, while the king and Haman appear more like Sisera and Samson—men whose disregard for women leads them to underestimate what they are capable of. In all three stories, sexuality is used as the weapon of a weaker partner (in gender and ethnicity) against a perceived oppressor. Esther also embodies a woman of strength and resourcefulness. She enables the writing of decrees that lead to massacre as Deborah writes a song of incredible violence. She shows herself as strong as Vashti, yet politically more astute. Esther does not simply behave as the object of men's gazes and machination; she takes up the role of subject. Yet her subjectivity is tightly bound, as she remains at all times confined to the domestic sphere and it is Mordecai who gains direct political power. Her subjectivity, therefore, does

---

3. See my 2018 article, "Dis(re)membered and Unaccounted For: Concubines in the Hebrew Bible," for a detailed study of relevant texts.

not lead her to challenge or undermine the status quo (unlike Vashti); rather, she enters the men's game and plays within its rules, much like Deborah, and unlike Jephthah's daughter or the Levite's concubine. As a result, she lives, rather than being killed as a victim. But whether this is a triumph is questionable, when we lay her story alongside others. What is clear is that the construction of gender in Esther is ambiguous and highly unstable. Therefore, this text, just as Judges, contains the seeds that enable women as subjects to emerge in the fault lines of a strict patriarchal context.

Collective Identity, Otherness, and Violence

Just as the text of Esther raises interesting questions about the construction of gender, it also presents an account of the construction of ethnic and national identity that can be read helpfully against that of Judges. Both texts present ethnic conflict between Israel/the Jews and Canaan/the Persian empire. The balance of power is not equal in both texts, however. Esther chronicles the institutionalization of oppression: Haman's accusations start with truth (the Jews are scattered and dispersed), then moves to half-truth (they have different laws and customs), then to lies (they do not observe imperial laws). The process charts the birth of anti-Semitism and racial discrimination, starting in personal vendetta and widened to an entire ethnic group (Berlin 2001, 38). The process is then reversed at the end, when the Jews kill "all their enemies." These enemies are not singled out primarily on ethnic grounds, though it is fair to assume that all of them are non-Jews. On the surface, the story has much stronger parallels with Exodus than with Judges. Judges, covering a much longer period, shows several swings of the pendulum between Israel being the attacker and the attacked in a land into which Israel is seeking to settle. The ethnic basis for violence is most clearly seen in ch. 19, when the Levite refuses to stay in Jebus, because it is a "city of foreigners, who do not belong to Israel" (19:12). The text then takes an unexpected turn and proceeds to show the men of Benjamin behaving in ways that are considered utterly un-Israelite (19:30); this is followed by the whole of Israel descending into civil war, directing *herem* toward Israel itself, and behaving toward the daughters of Shiloh and Jabesh-Gilead in ways no better than the men of Benjamin. The epilogue of Judges chronicles the "canaanization" of Israel (Block 1999, 57) and collapses the ethnic and religious boundaries that had been the basis for violence in the rest of the book. This uncomfortable ending, read together with Esther, should prompt us to question how far the Jewish community is behaving distinctively: they visit equal violence on the Persians; the decree that goes out from Esther and Mordecai parallels closely Haman's plans; they do not mention Yahweh or the law; indeed, 10:1-3 tells us that the "fear of Mordecai has fallen upon the people," not the fear of Yahweh. Has Israel in Esther become *Persianized*?

These texts not only reflect but also shape the construction of identity and of collective memory.[4] How we read the text, and the identity it seeks to mold, is

---

4. For a detailed consideration of the biblical texts as the construction of collective memory, see Cataldo (2019).

therefore crucial to what is formed in primary and secondary readers. The function of texts like Judges and Esther is not simply to tell a story of what (may have) happened but to tell this story in a way that enables trauma to be processed and integrated into a new understanding of the community's history and identity. The vilification of the "other" is, partly, an attempt to tell the story in ways that enable Israel to understand why they were subjected to what they suffer and justify the acts they committed (trauma can be induced by what one does, as well as what is done to one). The importance of Esther in constructing memory is seen in the book's institution of Purim, a new, post-Torah festival of national importance (Berlin 2001, xvi). Unlike the festival of the daughter of Jephthah, Purim gains momentum and is fully established as a festival of all Israel. Just like the festival of Jephthah's daughter, however, and in contrast to Torah festivals, there is no mention of Yahweh and of the way it fits within the wider set of festivals and laws that undergird Israelite religious identity. At one level, Esther, just like Judges, lacks any focus on cultus and spiritual practices. There is a general lack of clarity on what being Jewish is about: it is not obviously about behavior, since Esther's Jewish identity is not known until it is disclosed (Beal 1999, 105). It is interesting to see which laws Mordecai chooses to obey: he will not bow despite the royal decree (an obvious political statement, as much as religious) but seems to think little of marrying his niece to a foreigner. Being Israelite does not seem to rest on recounting the story of salvation or explicit allegiance to Yahweh, just as, in Judges, the people write Yahweh out of the Exodus story (19:30). Yet, when read in the overall canon, this lack of precision may be helpful. It reminds the diaspora of the many other stories that also show that they do not need to be in Jerusalem for God to act, or be ritually perfect, or need a royal figure (Laniak 2003b, 187). God instead reaches out in grace (as he does in Judges, when the people fail to repent and mend their ways, yet God still delivers) and brings up unexpected deliverers: a woman, like Esther, Jael, or Deborah; younger sons, left-handed men, men of questionable parentage, and a whole host of others. As such, Esther is a story of grace and hope, which fits alongside many other.

However helpful, this way of constructing collective identity comes at a cost. Constructing the other as the nonself (whether gendered or ethnic other) leads to violence as surely in Esther as in Judges. Jews and Persians construct national identity in similar ways. Because Vashti disobeyed, therefore, all women are a threat to all men and must be brought into line. Because Mordecai refused to bow, all Jews are seen as a threat and must be exterminated. Because Haman as an enemy threatened Mordecai, all those who are perceived as enemies present an equal threat to all Jews and must be exterminated. In Judg. 20, because some men in Benjamin hurt a couple, all Benjaminites must be a threat to the integrity and safety of Israel and must be exterminated. And so it continues. This dualized approach to identity erases important differences. Haman, for instance, argues that there is one people, the Jews, scattered throughout the empire, while Persia is cast as homogenous. Jewish identity is conflated into one, with uncertainty about Mordecai the Benjaminite and Judahite, while the enormous diversity of the Persian empire is equally reduced to a theoretical unity. The same process is at work in reverse with Mordecai and Esther's decree. In both cases, the "other" is defined solely by being the nonself. The other is vilified (Haman), or lampooned (the King), as in Judges, for instance, with the story of Ehud, casting Eglon of Moab as stupid and physically laughable. While laughter and derision are often one of the only weapons of the oppressed and a way to claim dignity over and against oppressors, the dark shadows of both books suggest that this is also a dangerous strategy. What does ethnic hatred lead to? And if this process is applied to one group, can it easily slide into being applied to another? In Judges, the hatred of the Canaanites, vilified and caricatured, relocates itself into the nation's attitude toward Benjaminites, while oppressive otherness is increasingly applied to women and leads to their objectification and abuse in the latter parts of the book. In Esther, we start with two "others": Vashti as the other, woman, and Mordecai as the other, Jew. Esther, of course, is both (Beal 1999, xiv). Both concepts of otherness lead to threats and violence: not only for Vashti herself but also for Esther, a young girl taken (whether she wants it or not) into the harem of the king; for the Jews, threatened by Haman. Esther uses her double otherness to her advantage, by confounding stereotypes to surprise her oppressors. We may cheer at this, but has the Esther of the end of the book simply reversed the polarity of oppression, without challenging its underlying principles?

Conclusion

How we interpret the ending of Esther depends on our judgment of its exaggerated violence. Parallels with the end of Judges are instructive. Haman's command in 3:13 is very similar to the *herem* decreed on Jabesh-Gilead in Judg. 21:10, with the specific mention of women and little ones, and chillingly reflected in Esther and Mordecai's decree in Est. 8:11. The mention of children takes the story beyond the realm of self-defense. The parallel also suggests alarm bells in the text of Esther. In Judges, the people of Israel became increasingly fragmented, by doing what seemed right in their own eyes, to the point that Israel subdivided and treated itself as the enemy, the nonself. Their quest for "justice" for the Levite's concubine became so entangled with politics of identity that, in the end, any sense of justice and proportionality collapsed. Are the people of Israel in Esther at risk of the same fate? Have they, just like the people of Judges, let go of an identity founded in Yahweh and Torah, in order to pursue *what seems right in their own eyes*, including unbridled violence? If they have, then they risk the same fate: the dissolution of community structures, the loss of a common vision for the good of the nation, and, paradoxically, the loss of individuals as worthy of care and protection by the wider community.

Reading Judges and Esther together helps bring difficult questions to the text of Esther concerning the way in which identity is constructed in similar ways by Jewish and Persian characters: in simple binaries, in opposition to one another, rather than based on a distinctive, positive foundation in Yahweh. As such, the book Esther is more than a comedy or an explanation for Purim: it interrogates the foundations on which the community builds its life together and its relationship to those that surround it.

Chapter 5

OVERTURNING SOVEREIGNTY: ESTHER IN DIALOGUE WITH THE BOOK OF SAMUEL

Rachelle Gilmour

The absence of God as a "character" in the book of *Esther*[1] is one of the story's most well-known and discussed features.[2] Among modern scholars, interpretations of the literary absence of God range widely: some assert the theological absence of God in the book's message;[3] others argue for God's hiddenness instead of absence, and a subsequent emphasis on human action;[4] others see God's action as central to the plot through coincidence or "chance," although human action also plays an important role;[5] and it has been suggested the book of *Esther* is deliberately indeterminable, raising but not resolving a question of divine presence and absence.[6]

This essay will examine the literary absence of the character of God in the story of *Esther*, and the wider issue of divine sovereignty, in dialogue with *Samuel*

This essay was written with the aid of a grant from the Centre for PaCT, Charles Sturt University.

1. Unless otherwise stated, all reference to the book of *Esther* in this essay will refer to the Masoretic Text. The Septuagint and AT attestations of *Esther* will not be discussed here and, as is well known, feature the literary character of God differently from the MT.

2. Note Josephus' interpretation (*Antiquities* 11.227) that "from another place" in Est. 4:14 is a veiled reference to God.

3. E.g., Sweeney (2000, 264–75); Beal (1999, xx). See also Talmon (1963, 419–55); Koller (2014, esp. 90–106).

4. E.g., Crawford (1989, 161–77); Berg (1979, esp. 173–84); Grossman (2011, 243–4); Levenson (1997, 12–23); Tomasino (2019, 118–19).

5. E.g., Clines (1984, 155–7) sees God as providing opportunity for human action (cf., Tomasino above). Loader (1978, 417–21) delineates human and divine action as different levels of meaning.

6. E.g., Fox (2001, esp. 235–47). See also Fox's more detailed overview of positions on the literary absence of God (235–44). Melton (2018, 67–9, 72–4) suggests literary absence of the divine does not rule out hope of hidden providence, thus both God's presence and absence are viable interpretive options.

as intertext. It will be argued that divine sovereignty is not literarily absent in the story of *Esther* at all, even though the character of God is. Instead, divine sovereignty is embodied in the Persian king, Ahasuerus. This new locus for power is not designed to legitimize or promote obedience to the power of the Persian king, instead to satirize it, and describe (not prescribe) the contemporary situation of the diaspora. The satirization is via parody of the system of sovereignty in the book of *Samuel*, in a type of parody that uses the intertext as weapon, not target.

The shift in sovereignty between the *Samuel* intertext, and the *Esther* text, will be demonstrated in three sets of character parallels between texts and within texts: Vashti-Mordecai-Saul, Esther-David-Saul, and, finally, Ahasuerus-God. Although not all of these parallels and connections have been discussed previously, the intentionality of many allusions in *Esther* to the book of *Samuel* is well established (Berlin 2001, xxxviii-xxxix; Firth 2010a, 22-3), giving a strong foundation for identifying further connections and opening a dialogue between the two texts.[7] The allusions invite a more extensive intertextual reading of these two books in the Hebrew canon.

Mordecai-Vashti-Saul

Mordecai is linked to King Saul and the book of *Samuel* through his genealogy in Est. 2:5, "Mordecai son of Jair, son of Shimei, son of Kish, a Benjaminite." According to 1 Sam. 9:1, Kish is also the name of the father of the Benjaminite King Saul and is named nowhere else in the Hebrew Bible. The most notable Benjaminite Shimei is also found in the book of *Samuel*. Although called "son of Gera" (2 Sam. 19:16, 18), not son of Kish, he curses David in 2 Sam. 16:5-13 and is forgiven by David in 2 Sam. 19:16-23, and he seems to be a supporter of the house of Saul.

Beyond the genealogical connection between Mordecai and Saul, they are paralleled through the identity of their enemies. Haman is identified as an Agagite (Est. 3:1), evoking Agag the Amalekite whom Saul fails to destroy immediately in 1 Samuel 15. Comparison turns to contrast when Mordecai's Agagite enemy is hung and the Jews have no restraint in destroying their enemies and take no spoil (Est. 9:5-16), whereas Saul took animals and King Agag alive from the spoil (1 Sam. 15:19, 21).[8] Yet the parallel returns when Haman hopes he will be spared when he begs Esther (Est. 7:7), and Agag believes he has been spared, before Samuel hacks him to pieces ("Surely the bitterness of death has turned aside,"[9] 1 Sam. 15:32).

---

7. Firth (2010a) has demonstrated availability of *Samuel* for the book of *Esther*, and drawn on the criteria for intertextual allusion in Hays (1989, 29-32). A wide range of studies, notably Berger (2010), have demonstrated volume and recurrence of allusions to *Samuel* in *Esther*.

8. Cf., McKane (1961), who points out that a true reversal would have seen Mordecai and the Jews devote their enemies to destruction.

9. All translations are my own.

Mordecai has succeeded in gaining power where Saul failed and lost his kingship; but in fact, the fate of their enemies is the same when Haman and Agag are each killed at the conclusion of the story, and both at the direct instigation of another agent, Esther and Samuel.

There is a pointed allusion to 1 Samuel 15 in Est. 1:19, where Memucan advises the king—"let the king give [Vashti's] royal position to a neighbour who is better than she" (ומלכותה יתן המלך לרעותה הטובה ממנה)—reformulating Samuel's words to Saul in 1 Sam. 15:28: "[the LORD] has given [the kingdom of Israel] to your neighbor who is better than you" (ונתנה לרעך הטוב ממך).[10] The use of the term "kingdom" (מלכות) to denote Vashti's royal position as queen is unusual, and so also increases the saliency of the allusion to 1 Samuel 15. Thus, Vashti's rejection is cast in similar terms to Saul's rejection.

Both parallels, the opposition between a descendent of Kish and Agag(ite), and the rejection from kingship for one who is preferable, invite 1 Samuel 15 as intertext. However, the parallels between the characters in *Esther* and the *Samuel* story are inconsistent, with both Vashti and Mordecai traceable to Saul. This points to a further dynamic within *Esther*, where Vashti and Mordecai are paralleled *within* the text. They each refuse the king's command before the king (1:10-12) and Haman (3:3) respectively; this results in the proposal that Vashti be banished (1:13-20) and that the Jews be killed (3:8-9); and the king accepts each proposal (1:21-22; 3:10-11), as indeed he accepts all proposals made to him throughout the book (Beal 1997, 54–5; Levenson 1997, 8–9).

A Saul–Vashti–Mordecai complex of parallels is evoked, where the dual comparison to Saul strengthens the identification of Vashti with Mordecai. However, there is also contrast when Mordecai succeeds where both Saul and Vashti, the rejected or disobedient "rulers," failed.

Esther–Saul–David

Once a *Samuel* intertext has been introduced, parallels in plot and character description between *Esther* and *Samuel* emerge. Berger (2010) has found that these parallels and connections are largely between Esther and Saul, as much as between Mordecai and Saul. Indeed, the parallels and contrasts between Mordecai and Saul also relate to Esther and Saul: they have the same Agagite enemy, Haman; Esther is also an agent in the revenge for the Jews (Est. 9:13), and the restraint from spoil is at the hands of the "Jews," not Mordecai or Esther personally; and by virtue of being Mordecai's paternal cousin, Esther is also descended from Kish. Just as Kish is introduced in 1 Sam. 9:1, before his son Saul in 9:2, the central character in the ongoing plot, so also Mordecai is introduced in Est. 2:5 immediately prior to Esther his cousin in 2:7, who will dominate the plot in the proceeding chapters.[11]

---

10. Noted also in *Esther Rabbah* 4:9.

11. On Esther as the main character, see Tomasino (2019, 116–18); Crawford (1989, 166–72).

According to Berger (2010, 628–31), the connections between Esther and Saul extend beyond those found between Mordecai and Saul. Alongside their introductions, both Saul and Esther are described as good-looking (1 Sam. 9:2; Est. 2:7), in common with David (1 Sam. 16:12) but in contrast to Mordecai. Both Saul and Esther are initially reticent in their roles: Saul does not tell his uncle that he has been chosen as king, and he remains silent when he is mocked (1 Sam. 10:16, 27); Esther remains silent about her ancestral people and is reminded again that if she is silent, help will come from elsewhere (Est. 2:10-11).

Developing Berger's argument, although Mordecai will gain a prominent role in the kingdom, only Esther is said to have royal rule (2:17; וימליכה "he made her queen"; Est. 4:14 הגעת למלכות "you have come to the kingship") just as Saul is king (מלך). Saul brings "deliverance" (ויצל; 1 Sam. 14:48) for the people from the Amalekites; and so also Esther is implicitly charged to bring relief and "deliverance" (והצלה; 4:14) for the diaspora people. Both Saul and Esther are selected through a trial and error process: in 1 Sam. 10:17-24, although Samuel has already anointed Saul, the people go through a process where each tribe, family, and then man is brought forward in a selection process of Saul; and so also Esther is chosen by Ahasuerus after a selection process in which the women are taken turn by turn to spend the night with him. Finally, whereas Mordecai is promoted *after* he has brought about the end of Haman and their enemies, Esther uses her position to bring deliverance, just as Saul defeats the Amalekites when he has already been made king. Indeed, if the primary parallel were between Mordecai and Saul, then an enemy such as the Ammonites, who are part of Saul's *rise* to power in 1 Samuel 11, might potentially be expected, rather than an Agagite, recalling the battle with the Amalekites after Saul's kingship is established. Once again the intertextual parallel highlights the chief divergence: although both Saul and Esther bring deliverance for the people, Esther succeeds where Saul failed, by retaining her royal position.

There is another set of intertextual links that have not received the same attention as those between Esther and Saul: links between Esther and David. These connections are to some degree a product of parallels between Saul and David internal to the book of *Samuel* (Gilmour 2011, 116–30), creating a triangulation similar to that of Saul–Vashti–Mordecai. The midrash suggests a parallel between Mordecai, Moses, Saul, and David, on the basis of their delayed appearance. However, the framing of Mordecai is as follows:

> And let the maiden who pleases Your majesty ...—who would be worthy of this description? Mordecai: "In the fortress Shushan lived a Jew by the name of Mordecai."[12]

Although the midrash names Mordecai, Esther is the maiden who is pleasing to the king, and her appearance is also delayed in parallel with the delayed appearance of Moses, Saul and David.

---

12. *Esther Rabbah 5:4*, translation taken from Grossman (2011, 69).

A number of links between Esther and David can be found within the narratives.[13] As with Saul, the description of Esther as having "royal rule" and a "kingdom" draws a parallel to David as "king." Just as both Saul and Esther are chosen through a process of trial-and-error selection, so also David is chosen in 1 Sam. 16:1-13 after each of his brothers has already been brought forward turn by turn before Samuel. Moreover, unlike Saul who is a rejected ruler like Vashti, Esther and David share the position of replacement to the rejected ruler. Both Esther and David will retain their positions. Even Esther and Mordecai's ancestors potentially allude to David, because Shimei is also the name of David's brother (2 Sam. 21:21), and, although Benjaminite, Mordecai and Esther are described as "Judahites," a term related to David's tribe, Judah.

Crucially, in David's story in *Samuel*, he also faces the Amalekites as an enemy and overcomes them just as Esther overcomes Haman. In 1 Sam. 30:1-3, the Amalekites have attacked Ziklag and taken the wives, sons, and daughters of David and his men. David counter-attacks, killing all but four hundred men (1 Sam. 30:17) and recovering everything that they have taken. Moreover, spoil features prominently in this story when David insists that those who did not join battle also receive a share of the spoil. In 2 Sam. 1:15, David will have a lone Amalekite executed, as Haman is executed. The literary significance of this repeated Amalekite encounter within the book of *Samuel* is that David succeeds where Saul has failed.

Therefore, another triangulation of parallels is created between Saul–David–Esther. Moreover, one character in the triangle is a point of contrast as well as parallel: Saul's fate is linked to that of David and Esther but ultimately diverges from them.

Parody of the Israelite Royal Court

The significance of these connections between *Esther* and *Samuel*, and the meaning of the success of a Benjaminite line in *Esther* in contrast to *Samuel*, is debated among modern interpreters. Any straightforward parallel between Vashti–Saul and Esther–David is complicated by Esther and Mordecai's descent from Kish. Davies (2013, 138) suggests that for Benjaminites in the Persian period, the downfall of Saul still needed to be avenged, this vengeance performed by Mordecai and Esther against Haman the Agagite (Davies 2013, 138). In this argument, Esther and Mordecai rehabilitate the Benjaminite royalty through succeeding where Saul failed. In the notice in Est. 2:6, that Kish or Mordecai[14] was exiled with

---

13. Cf., Berger's (2010, 635) observation that the death of ten sons of Haman, Esther's enemy, is similar to the death of ten sons of Saul, David's enemy.

14. Note the ambiguity in this verse whether Mordecai or Kish was exiled. Mordecai is the more natural referent, but this would make him 110 years old during the reign of Xerxes. See Fox (2001, 29).

King Jeconiah of Judah, the implication is that two lines of kings have been exiled but now the line from Kish is preeminent.

Alternatively, A. Koller has suggested that the Saulide focus does not foreground the Benjaminites so much as it points to a polemic against hopes for the resurrection of the Davidic dynasty (Berg 1979, 68–70; Koller 2014, 88). He writes, "In all, the use of the Saul imagery allows the author of Esther to claim that redemption, thought by some to be possible only in the land of Israel and with a Davidic king on the throne, will actually be realized by the anti-David, in the land of exile" (Koller 2014, 88). In Koller's reading, the Jewish people take responsibility to bring about salvation, formerly the role of the divine king, or the Israelite king.

Both Davies' and Koller's positions point to a message of hope for the audience, either through Benjaminite leadership or some other leadership or human action that is *not* Davidic. However, hope is not warranted by this story. The positions of power at the conclusion of the story are temporary, for the lifetimes of Esther and Mordecai. Even though Mordecai is presented as a quasi-royal figure when he receives the king's garb in 6:11 (Berg 1979, 62–4), there is no indication that he has an heir who will take up his position of power after him. Haman is removed, but Ahasuerus remains on the throne and it is Ahasuerus' propensity to agree to any and every proposal that gives Haman the power to enact his enmity in the first place. The fickleness of Ahasuerus means that danger may come again at any time.

Moreover, in the parallels between *Esther* and *Samuel*, there is a substantial shift in power held by the characters in *Esther* compared to *Samuel*. Both Saul and David are placed in parallel to queens, Vashti and Esther, whose power is adjunct to a foreign king. They are not rulers in their own right, and they lack traditional forms of power because of the social hierarchical position of their sex. Moreover, as Crawford has observed, Esther is also an orphan and part of a Jewish minority, diminishing her power further (Crawford 1989, 167).

The shift in gender and hierarchy is also reflected in the shift in means to defeat the enemy. In contrast to David's military attack against the Amalekites in battle, Esther uses patience, beauty, food and wine, and entreaty to Ahasuerus to bring about the rescue of her people. To an extent she also employs deceit when she does not reveal that she is Jewish to Ahasuerus (Est. 2:20). Adelman (2015, 198–230) has argued that there is a pattern of associating deception with the feminine throughout the Hebrew Bible, and through examining the Joseph and Esther stories side by side she suggests Esther's discretion is also gendered. Esther's hidden ethnicity is contrasted with Mordecai's overt ethnicity, known at the city gate.[15] She avoids confrontation by delaying her request to the king for help until the second feast. Her words to the king in 5:4, 5:8, and 7:3 emphasize her subordination to him, culminating in her request in 8:5-6 where she uses four conditional clauses. Whether Esther is a cipher for the Jewish diaspora acting collectively or an example of Jewish individual action and response to danger in the diaspora (Beal 1999, 54;

---

15. See also Koller (2014, 77–8); and Klein (1995, 149–75) argues that Esther acts behind the "mask of 'feminine shame'" to bring about salvation to the Jewish people.

Humphreys 1973, 211–23; Koller 2014), Esther's "feminine" identity and behavior are in contrast to the "masculine" military salvation from enemies brought about through Kings Saul and David.

Therefore, the "feminization"[16] of Saul and David, when paralleled in *Esther*, points to the characterization of Esther's action as passive and responsive. Although Mordecai is also paralleled with Saul, we observe that he is, in turn, paralleled with Vashti. Admittedly, both Vashti and Mordecai resist in a confrontational manner, refusing the orders of Ahasuerus,[17] but both acts of resistance lead to danger, rather than redemption. Only Esther's "feminine" strategy is successful. Furthermore, as the power of Mordecai and Esther increases in the story, so too the story focus shifts to Mordecai from Esther in Esther 9, in a sense "masculinizing" the central figure in the story. The foregrounding of the male character also coincides with the use of physical violence against the enemies, reminiscent of the military violence of Saul and David (Sweeney 2000, 272–3).

Having identified the shift in hierarchy from Saul and David, to Vashti and Esther, respectively, at least until the revenge and foregrounding of Mordecai in ch. 9, the Saulide ancestry of Esther and Mordecai also falls into this pattern. Not only is the role of David paralleled with a queen, it is paralleled with a Benjaminite queen. It is a "demotion" in two senses. And yet the demotion is necessary: the Davidic King Jeconiah's presence in exile is juxtaposed with Mordecai's ancestry in 2:5-6; but Jeconiah has not brought deliverance. A different tactic, and protagonist, is now portrayed, one that represents the shift in hierarchy from Israelite monarchy to diaspora in the Persian empire. Moreover, the theme of reversals is central to the story of *Esther*,[18] and therefore an intertextual relationship that overturns gender and ancestry imitates the overall message in the book's literary artistry.[19]

These reversals and shifts in hierarchy are antitheses between text and intertext. Therefore, using W. Kynes' (2011, 291) definition of parody as "antithetical allusion," the royal court in *Esther* parodies the royal court in *Samuel*. Although it is possible that *Esther* satirizes the Israelite royal court, Saul's rejection, and David's replacement, by feminizing these characters and reversing Esther's ancestry,[20] it is more plausible that *Samuel* is used as a weapon, not object, of satire. Kynes argues

16. That is, according to the social constructions of gender in the Hebrew Bible.

17. Note that Vashti's resistance involves her staying in female space of the women's feast rather than entering the male space of Ahasuerus' feast (Klein 1995, 155).

18. For an overview of reversals in *Esther*, see Fox (2001, 158–63), including his table.

19. See Grossman (2009, 394–414), who argues that changing and reversals in analogies are used to "convey a sense of capriciousness and instability such that the reader feels unequipped to assess fully the situations that he [sic] reads about and the characters whom he [sic] encounters" (414).

20. The feminization of characters in *Samuel* and reversal from Davidic to Saulide protagonist potentially disrespects both kings of Israel in the *Samuel* intertext. Chapman (2004) has examined the feminization of warriors in the Hebrew Bible and other ancient Near Eastern texts, suggesting it discredits the warrior. Among other features, the feminization is often portrayed through association with sexual exposure or prostitution,

that ridicule and subversion are not essential aspects of parody and the parody can respect or even reaffirm the earlier text, satirizing instead the contemporary context.[21]

The parody of the *Samuel* intertext satirizes the Persian court and highlights the diminishment of the Jewish position from the glory days of Judah and Israel's monarchy and self-determination. There is a new situation in the diaspora, and it is a parody of what the Judahite king's court once was. The use of *Samuel* as intertext is not due to hopes of either Benjaminite or non-Davidic savior; rather, it is because the book of *Samuel* deals with issues of political and divine sovereignty, the reversals wrought through divine sovereignty, and the institution of kings in concert with the divine sovereignty. It is an appropriate intertext because of its similarity in themes and its "ideal" as a point of contrast.

Moreover, contrary to many studies, *Esther* does not introduce a focus on human responsibility and action to bring about salvation: in the *Samuel* intertext, the military action of King David is also the means and the initiative for overcoming the Amalekite enemy. The change in human action is in the type of human action: the shift from king to queen is also a shift from military might to patience and deception. Only with success and the return of power to the Jews is human action again more typically "masculine" in the figure of Mordecai and the military-like slaughter of the opponents of the Jews.

God–Ahasuerus

Vashti and Saul are both rejected from royal rule in favor of a neighbor, and Esther and David replace Vashti and Saul, respectively, through a selection process of trial and error. The shifting rule of Persian queens parodies the shifting rule of Israel's first kings. However, there is a third parallel between the stories, another locus for parody: just as God rejects Saul and chooses David, governing the elevation of the lowly and humbling of the powerful, Ahasuerus governs the overturning of sovereignty in *Esther*.

---

related but not identical to the demand for Vashti's appearance at the men's banquet and Esther being brought into the king's harem.

21. Kynes (2011, 287). Certainly the "burlesque" or farcical features in *Esther* are all directed at elements in the story that do not have a direct intertextual relationship with *Samuel*. For example, one humorous element in the *Esther* story is, according to Berlin, that "Vashti's nonappearance at a party, becomes a crisis of state, with all the bureaucratic trappings that can be mustered" (Berlin 2001, xix). While it might be argued that Saul's misdemeanor in 1 Samuel 15 is as trivial as Vashti's misdemeanor, nowhere in the *Samuel* text is it suggested that all of the people, or all of the kingdom, would become disobedient as a result. Indeed, Saul is rebuked for listening to the people, rather than for the people listening to him (1 Sam. 15:15, 24). Thus, the humor, and any suggestion of ridicule, is directed at the components of the Persian court that find no parallel in the *Samuel* story.

Both the stories of *Samuel* and *Esther* are dominated by a theme of reversals. In the text of *Samuel*, God is the primary actor who overturns Saul's kingship in favor of David. In 1 Sam. 15:10, the "word of the LORD" comes to Samuel saying that he regrets making Saul king. When Samuel speaks to Saul he says explicitly, "[the LORD] has also rejected you from being king" (v. 23), and again that "the LORD has torn the kingdom of Israel from you this very day" (v. 26) in the verse echoed in Vashti's rejection. In 1 Samuel 16, God repeatedly "said to Samuel" and states explicitly, "I have rejected [Saul] from being king over Israel ... I will send you to Jesse the Bethlehemite for I have seen among his sons a king for myself" (1 Sam. 16:1).

Similarly, all of the reversals in *Esther* are directed by Ahasuerus. The king personally rejects Vashti and sends letters to the provinces (1:21-22), albeit on advice from Memucan. Although the king consults the law, the advice from Memucan includes issuing a royal order to be written into the law. Ahasuerus sets the royal crown on Esther's head (2:17). Ahasuerus gives his signet ring to Haman (3:11), but the destruction of the Jews is sent in the name of the king and the "couriers went quickly by order of the king." Ahasuerus directs the reversal of honoring Mordecai (6:10), and Ahasuerus directs letters reversing the command for the destruction of the Jews (8:9-10). Ahasuerus intervenes, albeit through intercession from Memucan, Esther, or Haman, to bring about each of these major reversals.

Linked to his role in directing reversals, the characterization and position of King Ahasuerus remain relatively stable throughout the book. As Levenson (1997, 8) points out, the book of *Esther* begins and ends with the greatness of Ahasuerus. He is devastated by an action as small as Vashti's refusal to come to his banquet; and yet this humiliation does not threaten his position as king, only ridicules him in the eyes of *Esther*'s audience.[22] In a story of reversals, Ahasuerus is neither humbled nor exalted, and he has no character development. Instead, he is the one who brings about reversals and remains static.

Moreover, Koller (2014, 99-100) has suggested, through connections to texts other than *Samuel*, that Ahasuerus is portrayed in a divine manner. In the elaborate descriptions of Ahasuerus' palace and furnishings, and repeated reference to the "citadel" (בירה), the tabernacle in Exodus and the temple, also called a citadel (בירה) in 1 Chron. 29:1, 19, is evoked. In Ps. 145:3, God's "greatness" (ולגדלתו) is praised, and in Ps. 145:11-12, "the glory of [his] kingship" (כבוד מלכותך); in Est. 1:4, Ahasuerus' "greatness" (גדולתו) is displayed and "the glory of his kingship" (כבוד מלכותו). The presentation of Ahasuerus' kingship and palace draws on imagery associated with God's kingship and the tabernacle or temple.

Divine sovereignty, at least according to the portrayal of divine sovereignty in *Samuel*, is now invested in Ahasuerus. In *Samuel*, the divine prerogative, and

---

22. Cf., Firth (2010a) argues that Ahasuerus too is brought low through ridicule. However, this ridicule is also consistent across the story, as part of the parody, as we will see shortly.

characteristic intervention, is to bring about reversal. Divinely wrought reversals are highlighted in Hannah's song (1 Sam. 2:4-8), for example, "The LORD makes poor and makes rich; he brings low, he also exalts" (v. 7). These actions of reversal are now the domain of Ahasuerus, rejecting Vashti, selecting Esther, endangering and then rescuing the Jews.

The parallels between Ahasuerus in *Esther* and God in *Samuel* establish the intertextual connection; but the antithetical differences between Ahasuerus and God demonstrate that Ahasuerus' power is satirized through parody of God in *Samuel*, just as the Benjaminite Queen Esther from the family of Saul parodies the Judahite King David. The demotion from divine to human follows the same pattern of power shift discussed earlier between Saul, David, and Esther.

Esther's means of delivering the Jews from an Amalekite enemy is markedly different from David's military tactics, but Ahasuerus' exercise of power and limitations are even more negatively contrasted to God's actions in *Samuel*. As Berg has demonstrated, all of the reversals, or shifts of power, in *Esther* take place at parties and are associated with drinking (Berg 1979, 31-5). This is ominous for Ahasuerus if a connection to Nabal in 1 Samuel 25, who is struck down dead while drunk, is taken into account (Firth 2010a), and it suggests a profound lack of knowledge informing his decisions.

The lack of knowledge is developed through other differences between *Samuel* and *Esther*. In *Samuel*, God's selection of David is connected explicitly with God's "seeing" in a way that humans cannot see, for example, in 1 Sam. 16:7: "the LORD does not see as mortals see; they look on the outwards appearance, but the LORD looks on the heart." By contrast, Ahasuerus is not even aware of what is happening when he leaves the room (Est. 7:7); he does not know that his own wife, Esther, is Jewish; he forgets what Mordecai has done to foil a plot and does not know what has been done to reward him (Est. 6:3). Similarly, as observed earlier, all of Ahasuerus' directions are prompted by intercession or advice by Memucan, Haman, or Esther, in contrast to God's refusal to capitulate to the prophet Samuel's reservations in 1 Samuel 8 regarding the anointing of a king. Ahasuerus' limitations are highlighted by the hyperbole in Memucan's advice concerning Vashti's disobedience to the king's command: he fears all women in the empire will rebel against their husbands. There is no parallel in God's response to Saul's disobedience. Returning to Hannah's song, God's reversals are conducted by Ahasuerus, but whereas "the LORD is a God of knowledge and by him deeds are weighed" (1 Sam. 2:3), Ahasuerus brings about the reversals without judgment or knowledge. Ahasuerus is not God, and so his function in the role of God is a subject for satire.

In summary, the role of God in *Samuel* is parodied in *Esther* through parallels to the role of King Ahasuerus. Ahasuerus embodies the sovereignty held by God in *Samuel*, but his abilities in exercising this sovereignty are satirized. The contrast to God's sovereignty in *Samuel* is a parodic weapon against Ahasuerus and the diaspora dependence on his sovereignty.

Koller (2014, 99) argues that Ahasuerus and the Jews have *replaced* God in the *Esther* story. Yet, the people have always been represented as doing God's "job," including David's first defeat of the Amalekites in the book of *Samuel*. Moreover, we have argued that Ahasuerus parodies rather than replaces God. The deficiencies in Ahasuerus may point to God's hidden action (Grossman 2011, 70)[23] or they may point to the "chance" of divine sovereignty; dependence on Ahasuerus is no more or less than dependence on lots. Compared to the Divine who sees people's hearts in *Samuel*, in *Esther* the outcome is brought about by a king who cannot see into the next room. The fact that the result is the same, the Jews are saved and gain victory over their enemies, may suggest that God has providentially brought about this result; or that chance has brought about the result, chance governed by Ahasuerus' fickle sovereignty. God also brings about reversals, even in a way that seems capricious; but this capriciousness is coupled with a claim to God's knowledge and ability to "see" in a way that Ahasuerus is not.

Conclusion

This essay has argued that parallels between Esther, Mordecai, and the Benjaminite line of Kish should be read as a parodic shift in power from the glory days of the Israelite royal court to diaspora political life. By identifying the structure of character parallels within as well as between texts, the extent of the parody comes into focus: Vashti is paralleled to the rejected Saul; Esther is paralleled to the replacement David, who will overcome the Amalekites; and crucially, Ahasuerus holds the divine sovereignty to reject and to select. The literary absence of God also brings this shift of power into focus: no longer is God governing the reversals of the kings and, via kings, the people; now the Persian king governs the reversals of his queens and, via queens, the Jewish people. This new situation does not endorse King Ahasuerus; instead, like Esther's profile, queen instead of king, Saulide instead of Davidic, divine sovereignty is invested in a drunk, pliable king, in place of the God of Israel.

The situation for the diaspora is not transformed; King Ahasuerus remains king at the end of the book of *Esther*, but safety is achieved. A new type of action is needed in light of the shift in power: action characterized by responsive opportunism and even deception, in contrast from the direct military exploits of King David, unsanctioned by a foreign king.

---

23. There is no reason not to allow that God's providence acts behind the scenes. Grossman hints at this same connection when discussing the midrash connecting Moses, Saul, David, and Mordecai: "Who chooses Mordecai and Esther, though? Who appointed them to the task of savior? There is no prophetic declaration nor any anointment ceremony. Moreover, the naked truth is that they are actually chosen by none other than Ahasuerus!" Grossman sees the possibility of providence behind this: "A man sees only what is visible, but God sees into the heart—even the heart of Ahasuerus—and influences it" (Grossman 2011, 70).

Part III

ESTHER IN DIALOGUE WITH THE LATTER PROPHETS

Chapter 6

AT THE TABLE: BANQUETS IN ESTHER AND ISAIAH IN INTERTEXTUAL CONVERSATION

Andrew T. Abernethy

What does Esther have to do with Isaiah? Esther emphasizes the particularism of the Jewish people and does not anticipate (at least explicitly) a change in the exilic, diasporic way of life for God's chosen people. Isaiah, on the other hand, prophesies about a grandiose restoration of Jerusalem where the faithful from all nations—not simply Israelites—will stream to Zion to experience God's blessing. What is more, one will search in vain for significant linguistic affiliations between Esther and Isaiah so as to suggest that texts in one book are meant to allude to or echo the other. So, one can rightly ask, what is the basis for an essay that reads Esther in dialogue with Isaiah? After a brief methodological reflection, I will illustrate the interpretive benefits of bringing Esther and Isaiah into dialogue via the meal scenes of Esther and the eschatological banquet in Isaiah 25.

Intertextuality

When it comes to defining "intertextuality," one can distinguish between author-centered and reader-centered approaches (Miller 2011). This essay adopts a reader-centered approach.

Author-Centered Intertextuality and Esther

Author-centered intertextuality has two varieties. The first can be described as "inner-biblical exegesis" or "inner-biblical allusion" (Miller 2010, 305).[1] The premise is that an author of a text (phenotext) writes in such a way as to guide an audience to interpret the text via recourse to an already existing text

---

1. Miller believes that author-centered intertextuality should be termed "inner-biblical exegesis" or "inner-biblical allusion," but a second variety of author-centered intertextuality, described below as tradition-affiliation, would not fit within either label.

(genotext) (van Wolde 1997, 5). For instance, there is strong reason to believe that the opening verse of Isaiah, "Hear O heavens; give ear O earth" (1:2; שמעו שמים והאזיני ארץ), alludes to Deut. 32:1, "Give ear O heavens ... and hear O earth" (האזינו השמים...ותשמע הארץ).[2] Although this is not an exact quotation, the lexical overlap (שמים, ארץ, אזן, שמע) and similarity in syntactic function of the lexemes (volitives; vocative nouns) provide a strong basis for believing the author of Isa. 1:2 (phenotext) wrote so as to expect a reader to call to mind Deut. 32:1 (genotext). This association guides readers of Isaiah 1 to read in view of heaven and earth's role in witnessing God's word in Deuteronomy 32. When one reads Esther, the sorts of lexical and content- and form-related elements that meet criteria for identifying an intentional allusion to Isaiah are lacking (Edenburg 2010).

Another variety of author-centered intertextuality focuses on what one might describe as tradition-affiliation. By tradition-affiliation,[3] I mean an expectation by an author that a reader will know to read his or her writing in association with an already existing set of traditional texts (whether read or learned aurally). From this vantage point, the author of Esther writes to provide an alternative to or complement to known literature. Jon Levenson (1976) is a prime example of this. He argues that prior to Esther, Second Isaiah and Third Isaiah were the prominent perspectives on exilic and postexilic life. God's faithfulness to and deliverance of exiles, according to Second Isaiah, will be evident when God restores Zion and returns exiles to Jerusalem as a second exodus. Third Isaiah encourages the despairing returnees to press on in their "labors on behalf of Zion" as they await Zion's glory (Levenson 1976, 445). A Zion-centeredness dominates the postexilic perspective, and the implication is that "Diaspora existence is seen as a curse" from which they need deliverance (Levenson 1976, 446). Within this backdrop, Levenson claims that "rejecting this solution, Esther presents a very different narrative" (Levenson 1976, 447). Esther reconfigures the motif of deliverance that is common in Second Isaiah to depict a deliverance of the Diaspora people from dangerous anti-Semites. Notably in Esther, the exiled Jews are not delivered to return to Jerusalem but rather for a continued existence in the Diaspora (Levenson 1976, 448–50). Esther, then, is "an alternative to the lack of political realism in Second Isaiah and his successors" (Levenson 1976, 449). Although there is a level of possibility to Levenson's approach, there are no concrete lexical affiliations between specific passages in either book to support his claims. Indeed, although Levenson suggests that Esther adapts Second Isaiah's use of the second exodus motif, no linguistic affinities verify this. So, without access to Esther's author, it is impossible to know with confidence that Esther was intentionally written to be read in contrast to Isaiah.

---

2. All translations are my own unless otherwise noted.
3. On the place of traditions within intertextuality, see Stead (2012, 361).

Reader-Centered Intertextuality and Purpose

Without any concrete evidence that the author of Esther is referring a reader back to texts in Isaiah, this essay utilizes a reader-centered intertextuality. Reader-centered intertextuality identifies the reader as the one responsible for bringing texts into conversation with one another. The dialogue between the discrete texts accomplishes two purposes: (1) illumination of each individual text by better recognizing its fit (similarities and/or differences) within a larger social and literary fabric[4] and (2) emergence of a new horizon of vision through the associative reading, a vision that could not emerge unless the two texts were coordinated together.[5] Although virtually any text can be read in dialogue with any other, the benefits of reader-centered intertextuality become most apparent when the sets of texts have something in common (van Wolde 1997, 6–7). In this essay, the common use of the meal motif between Esther and Isaiah will focus our attention, and a recognition that these two books are part of the same religious canon provides a further basis for reading these texts in dialogue.[6]

Feasts in Esther and Isaiah

One could say that an entire 'world' ... is present in and signified by food. (Barthes 2008, 32)

---

4. Reader-centered intertextuality is not as avant-garde as some suppose. Even Schleiermacher (1998, 5–29) notes how essential it is to understand a grammatical utterance as a choice by an author from a larger language system and therefore the utterance must be understood in light of the language system as a whole (i.e., texts have meaning by being understood in light of other texts in the grammatical world of the author). A non-extreme use of Kristeva and Bakhtin recognizes the dialogical coordination between a "self" (the one who creates literary expression) and the wider grammatical fabric of society.

5. For more on how texts operate uniquely (in contrast to speech) to open a new horizon of vision before its readers, see Ricoeur (1976, 25–37 and 1981, 94).

6. Melton and Thomas (2021) also identify the canon as warranting intertextual readings, noting that Midrashic interpretation has long read texts across the canon in association with one another. For an overview of Midrashic interpretation, see Kugel (1986, 77–103). According to Kugel (1990, 360, 363), this practice "reflect[s] the overall 'canonizing' concern of rabbinic exegesis" and "demonstrat[es], nay celebrat[es], ... the unity and interrelatedness of the canon." As one example between Esther and Isaiah, Rabbi Samuel bar Nachmani introduces Esther by appealing to each part of Isa. 55:13: "Instead of thorn bushes [Haman], a Cyprus [Mordechai] will spring up; instead of the nettle tree [Vashti], the myrtle [Esther] will spring up. And the name of the Lord will become a sign [lesson of the book of Esther]; for times, forever; irretractable [days of Purim]." See Midr. Est. 9 Meg. 10A, B *Traktat Megilla*, vol. 1 of Börner-Klein and Hollender (2000, 161–2).

Table 6.1 Feasts in Esther

Feasts	Setting	Host	Guests	Other Details
1. Est. 1:3-4	Susa Third year of king Palace	King Ahasuerus	All rulers/servants Army Nobles Rulers of provinces	Displays riches 180 days
2. Est. 1:5-8	Susa At end of Feast 1 Palace courtyard	King Ahasuerus	All people of Susa (great or small)	Seven days Lavish Abundant wine No compulsion Vashti's fate turns
3. Est. 1:9	Susa At time of Feast 2 Royal House	Queen Vashti	Women	
4. Est. 2:18	Susa Esther named Queen	King Ahasuerus	All rulers/servants	Provinces receive gifts and tax relief
5. Est. 5:4-8	Susa After fasting three days	Queen Esther	King Ahasuerus Haman	During משתה יין
6. Est. 6:14–7:9	Susa Next day	Queen Esther	King Ahasuerus Haman	During משתה יין Haman's fate turns
7. Est. 8:17	Every province and every city After decree to reverse Jews' fate (third month, twenty-third day)	–	Jews in all provinces	Joy
8. Est. 9:18	Susa twelfth month, thirteenth–fifteenth day	–	Jews in Susa	Joy Sets precedent for Jews in villages
9. Est. 9:22	Every province Every year Twelfth month, fourteenth–fifteenth day	–	Jews in all provinces	Joy Decree of Mordechai

The focus now is to bring the nine feasts in Esther into dialogue with the eschatological feast in Isa. 25:6-10, in view of the two purposes of intertextuality noted above. There are nine feasts that hold the book of Esther together.[7] Table 6.1 offers a bird's-eye view.

The feast motif propels the book's narrative. The book opens with three feasts: two by King Ahasuerus (1:3-4, 5-8) and one by Queen Vashti (1:9). After the Queen refuses to submit to the voyeurism requested by the king at his second feast, she is deposed and her replacement is sought. Once Esther is named queen in place of Vashti, the first action we read of is the king having a feast in Esther's

---

7. It is unlikely that the comment "Now the king and Haman sat down to drink [לשתות], but the city, Susa, was in turmoil" (3:15) is a reference to a feast, as all other occasions use the noun משתה to designate a feast event. For an overview on feasts and fasting in Esther, see Berg (1979, 31–47).

name (2:18), presumably a celebration that a queen has been found who will model acquiescence to the male sovereign. Ironically, Esther gets the upper hand in their relationship in the rest of the narrative through feasts. She hosts two feasts that ingratiate the king—with the help of inebriation[8]—to save her people (5:5-8; 6:14–7:9). With the king's power now at her disposal, Esther ensures that a written decree is given to reverse the previous decree to kill the Jews; this results in a great feast among the Jews (8:17). When the day originally set for the extermination of the Jews comes to pass with the Jews having vanquished their enemies, a great feast is held (9:18), which sets the stage for it becoming an annual feast in honor of this event (9:22).

As for Isa. 25:6-10, it is the only eschatological feast in the HB.[9] It reads:

> [6] And the LORD of Hosts will make for all of the peoples on this mountain
>   a feast of rich foods, a feast of fine wines,
>   marrowed rich foods, filtered fine wines.
> [7] And he will swallow on this mountain
>   the face of the veil, the veil over all the peoples,
>   the covering that is spread out over all the nations;
> [8] he will swallow Death forever.
>   And the Lord YHWH will blot out tears from every face,
>   and the reproach of his people he will remove from over all the earth,
>   for YHWH has spoken.
> [9] And one will say in that day,
>   "Behold, this is our God; we have waited for him that he might save us!
>   This, YHWH, we have waited for him: Let us be glad, and let us rejoice in his salvation.
> [10]   For that hand of YHWH has rested on this mountain,
>   and Moab was tramped down under him
>   like trampling down straw in the waters of a dung heap."

This text unfolds in two segments: the feast (25:6-8) and celebration (25:9-10). These two texts cohere around the expression "on this mountain" (בהר ה־ה; vv. 6, 10) that points back to the announcement of the LORD of Hosts' eschatological

---

8. Spoelstra (2014) attempts to explain Esther's entire משתה as a drinking feast because it is described as משתה יין. He argues that since the king was not drunk enough when he asked for her request at the first feast, Esther invites the king to a second drinking feast. The problem with this is that משתה יין most likely refers to the second part of the feast (the *symposion*) that takes place after the meal (*deipnon*). On the *symposion*, see Miles (2015, 133); Ruiz-Ortiz (2017, 165–7).

9. For interpretations of this passage within the book of Isaiah as a whole with help from cultural anthropology, see Abernethy (2014 and 2018).

Table 6.2 Feasting in Isaiah 25

Feast	Setting	Host	Guests	Other Details
Isa. 25:6-10	Mount Zion Eschatological future	King Lord of Hosts	All peoples	Menu: Rich foods/wines Mythic menu: Death (Mot) Tears blotted out Reproach removed Celebratory song

rule on Mount Zion (בהר ציון) in 24:23. While ch. 24 conceptualizes divine rule in terms of judgment, the text before us expresses the positive side of divine rule in terms of a feast and celebration. If one were to chart this feast as we did Esther's feasts, we find the following in Table 6.2.

The flow across this passage is apparent. What begins as a feast that YHWH throws for "all peoples," where he offers the richest of fare (25:6), becomes an occasion for a display of power by the Host, as he ingests the great enemy, Death (25:7-8a), and eradicates all occasion for sorrow and shame (25:8). This scene of feasting gives way to a chorus of praise for God's salvation for his victory over their enemies (25:9-10).

Mutual Illumination

There are five prominent insights into the particularities of each text that arise from reading these texts in dialogue. These insights derive from recognizing similarities and differences between the passages, so I have ordered these five so as to move toward increasing dissimilarity.

The Grammar of Kingship Feasts In all three texts, feasts hosted by King Ahasuerus and in Isa. 25:6, we find the king is the subject, the verb is עשה, the object is משתה, and there is an adjunct prepositional phrase that begins with ל+כל.

All nine references to feasting in Esther use the term משתה to designate a feast. The narrator refers to the queens making a משתה through the verb עשה, but they lack the adjunct לכל. In Vashti's case, her feast is simply for נשים ("women" [1:9]). In Esther's two feasts, her audience is narrowed down to the king (לו; "for him" [5:4]) and the king and Haman (להם; "for them" [5:8]). Within Esther then, the coordination of עשה, משתה, and לכל appears to be the language of a feast hosted by a king as one finds in Table 6.3. In Isa. 25:6-8, YHWH is certainly viewed through a royal lens. In 24:23, one reads ... כי־מלך יהוה צבאות בהר ציון ("for YHWH of Hosts reigns on Mount Zion"); so when 25:6 sets the feast בהר הזה ("on this mountain"), it is natural to interpret this feast as being hosted by King YHWH on Zion (MacDonald 2008, 160, 191-4). The combination of עשה, משתה, and לכל in 25:6 as in Est. 1:3, 5, and 2:18 highlights the practice of kings in providing a feast for a great number of people. As one looks across the entire HB/OT, six out of the seven occasions where עשה, משתה, and לכל coordinate refer to a king hosting a

Table 6.3 Comparison of Feasts in Esther and Isaiah 25

Est. 1:3 In the third year of his ruling, **he made a feast for all** of his rulers ...	בִּשְׁנַת שָׁלוֹשׁ לְמָלְכוֹ **עָשָׂה מִשְׁתֶּה לְכָל־שָׂרָיו**....
Est. 1:5 ... the King **made for all** the people found in Susa, the acropolis, from great unto small a **feast**	**עָשָׂה** הַמֶּלֶךְ **לְכָל־הָעָם** הַנִּמְצְאִים בְּשׁוּשַׁן הַבִּירָה לְמִגָּדוֹל וְעַד־קָטֹן **מִשְׁתֶּה**....
Est. 2:18 and the king **made** a great **feast for all** of his rulers.	**וַיַּעַשׂ** הַמֶּלֶךְ **מִשְׁתֶּה גָדוֹל לְכָל־שָׂרָיו**....
Isa. 25:6 And the LORD of Hosts will **make for all** of the peoples on this mountain a **feast** ...	**וְעָשָׂה** יְהוָה צְבָאוֹת **לְכָל־הָעַמִּים** בָּהָר הַזֶּה **מִשְׁתֶּה**....

feast (Gen. 40:20 [Pharaoh]; 1 Kgs 3:15 [Solomon]; Est. 1:3, 5; 2:18; Isa. 25:6). This insight is not insignificant for Isa. 25:6, as some through the years have been prone to interpret this text as a covenant meal (e.g., Hagelia 2003).

These texts, then, illuminate the grammar of the royal feast in their respective texts.

Abundance and Greatness at Kingship Feasts Another similarity between these texts is that royal feasts are occasions for the king to display his abundance and greatness.[10] In King Ahasuerus' first feast, the narrator speaks of the king "showing the riches of the glory of his kingdom and the preciousness of the beauty of his greatness" (1:4).[11] No doubt, the length of this feast—180 days!—contributes to the impression of both the king's greatness and his generosity. The king's second feast, for men of Susa, is shorter (7 days), but his luxurious furnishings grace the temple garden: "There were white cotton curtains and blue hangings tied with cords of fine linen and purple to silver rings and marble pillars. There were couches of gold and silver on a mosaic pavement of porphyry, marble, mother-of-pearl, and colored stones" (1:6 NRSV). As drinks were served in goblets of gold (1:7), the king's generosity—not to mention his licentiousness—is highlighted: there are to be no limits on the amount of wine one can consume (1:8). Along with displaying his wealth and generosity at the feasts, King Ahasuerus seeks to promote his greatness further by displaying the beauty of his queen, Vashti. Ironically, however, amidst the king's display of wealth and grandiose, Vashti's refusal exposes the limits of the king and results in his shame (1:12).

The feast in Isa. 25:6-8 also depicts a king's greatness at the feast. Initially, this is seen in how the menu is described. Twice the food is described as 'rich" (שְׁמָנִים). The term for wine is not among the more common terms, such as יַיִן or תִּירוֹשׁ (cf., 24:7, 9); instead, שְׁמָרִים occurs, which refers to the most potent and excellent wine that settles at the bottom of a cup (Ps. 75:9).

---

10. Briant (2002, 286–97) offers a useful overview of extravagance at royal banquets in the Persian Empire.

11. The awkwardness of the Hebrew is retained in this translation for emphasis.

Although the luxuriant quality of the menu highlights King YHWH's greatness and generosity, it is his actions at the feast that receive the most attention. These actions in comparison to those of King Ahasuerus reveal a significant contrast between these kings and the nature of their kingdoms. For King Ahasuerus, his attempt to gain glory for himself comes *at the expense of another*, Vashti. In the case of King YHWH, he reveals his glory by acting *for the benefit of* the others at the feast. The reason he swallows Death is because it has loomed over the people (25:7-8a). What is more, the king blots out tears from every face and removes the reproach from his people (25:8). Another contrast is seen in King Ahasuerus's inability to succeed in his attempted display of his power; Vashti refuses. In the case of King YHWH, he vanquishes a cosmic power, Death,[12] without a hint of challenge or battle.

By bringing Esther's feasts into dialogue with Isaiah 25, it becomes apparent that royal feasts are often occasions for kings to depict their greatness and the nature of their kingdom. The differences between these texts expose dynamics in each of these texts respectively. In the case of the book of Esther, the contrast with King YHWH reveals how a feast meant to display Ahasuerus' greatness turns into an occasion for exposing the self-centeredness of King Ahasuerus and the comical limits of his feigned power. In the case of Isaiah, the contrast with King Ahasuerus displays the benevolence and incomparable power of King YHWH.

Rejoicing in Conjunction with the Feast In Esther, rejoicing is a feature that accompanies the feasts of the Jews in view of their deliverance. When Mordechai receives a position of honor, "the city of Susa shrilled and rejoiced (שׂמח)" (8:15). This rejoicing (שׂמח; vv. 16-17) extends to all the Jews in the provinces after the king's decree to protect the Jews reaches them, and they hold a feast as a result (8:16-17). Again, rejoicing (שׂמחה) and feasting overtake the Jews after their enemies are vanquished on the date previously designated by Haman for their slaughter (9:18-19). To commemorate this event, Mordechai commands Jews in every province to make the fourteenth and fifteenth days of the twelfth month days משׁתה ושׂמחה (9:23). This motif in Esther strategically reverses the occasion of lament and fasting by the queen and Jews earlier in the book (4:3, 16; 9:31).[13]

As one turns to Isa. 25:6-10, mindful of the association between feasting and rejoicing from Esther, vv. 9-10 fit the conceptual pattern of rejoicing in proximity to feasting. The audience extols God for his saving works, calling on one another: "Let us be glad, and let us rejoice [נשׂמחה] in his salvation!" (25:9).

---

12. For a mythic background on death as Mot, see Cho and Fu (2013, 120-1). Another option is to interpret death as a symbol of Israel's enemies, namely Egypt (cf., Hays 2011, 322-3).

13. See Berg (1979, 37-9). The interconnectedness of fasting and feasting in chs 4 and 9 is a major argument for seeing Purim as organically coordinated with the book (cf., Ruiz-Ortiz 2017, 35).

By being alert to the intersection between rejoicing and feasting in these books, a significant distinction emerges. Although rejoicing accompanies the feast of King YHWH in Isa. 25:9, it is noteworthy that rejoicing in the book of Esther is exclusive to the feasts of the Jews in the wake of deliverance through Esther and Mordechai (8:16, 17; 9:17, 18, 19, 22). In other words, there is no mention of rejoicing at the feasts hosted by King Ahasuerus, Vashti, or Esther. It is reserved in Esther for a response to deliverance that stems from Esther's initiative (and God's use of it) not the frivolity of a Persian king;[14] perhaps, in a book that does not mention God explicitly, the motif of rejoicing Esther underscores a reader's hunch that God is at work to deliver his people.

Centralization and Decentralization In Esther, the feasts move from being centralized in Susa to being decentralized across the Persian Empire. King Ahasuerus, Queen Vashti, and Queen Esther host the first six feasts in the book within Susa, on palace grounds. It is fitting for royalty to host a feast at the capital of the kingdom, and one finds the same in Isa. 25:6 with King YHWH's feast being on Mount Zion.

One finds in Esther, however, that the feasts of most interest in the book are decentralized and democratized. Feast 7 is בכל־מדינה ומדינה ובכל־עיר ועיר ("in every province after province, and in every city after city" [3:17]). The use of בכל, along with מדינה and עיר, highlights how widespread the rejoicing that turns into a feast is among the Jews. In Feast 8, decentralization continues as Jews in the provinces (fourteenth day) and Susa (fifteenth day) hold feasts to celebrate their protection from their enemies (9:17-18), which created a pattern for Jews of the villages to celebrate this festival as well (9:19). Finally, Mordechai makes a decree for כל־היהודים אשר בכל־מדינות המלך אחשורוש הקרובים והרחוקים ("all Jews who are in the provinces of King Ahasuerus, those near and far" [9:20]) to hold this festival. The import of this decentralization of the Jewish feast cannot be understated. The Jews, now absent from Zion and their homeland, can hold this feast across the empire wherever they find themselves. If a feast is a window into a world, a social reality, the decentralized nature of this feast reveals a world for the Jews where geographical centralization is not an essential element in their identity as the people of God.

Inclusion and Particularism A dialogical reading between the feasts in Esther and the feast in Isa. 25:6-10 directs us to attend to the topic of inclusion and particularism. We can begin by comparing the participants in King Ahasuerus' three feasts (Feasts 1, 2, and 4 in the chart above) and those at King YHWH's feast in Isa. 25:6. King Ahasuerus' feasts display a limited inclusivism. Feast 1 is for those with important governmental roles from across the Persian Empire: "for all the

---

14. The lack of explicit mention of God in Esther could be due to a shift in the postexilic era toward speaking less directly about God and the use of female protagonists. For more, see Melton (2021).

rulers, servants, the army of the Medes and Persians, governors, and rulers of the provinces" (Est. 1:3). Feast 4 is also for "all of his rulers and servants" (2:18), which suggests a similar audience to the one in Est. 1:3. The inclusivity here is apparent, in that these rulers represent the regions across the empire, yet the exclusivity is seen in that only the governmental elite participate in this 180-day feast. Feast 2 is "for all the people found in Susa, the acropolis, from great unto small" (Est. 1:5). Inclusivity is apparent in that "all the people" (כל־העם) from Susa, regardless of status, participate in this feast, yet limiting the participants to those in the capital city exposes its boundaries.

A striking contrast emerges through reading Isa. 25:6 and the feasts of the king (Feasts 1, 2, and 4) from Esther in dialogue. Yes, it is admirable that King Ahasuerus would include כל־העם of Susa (Est. 1:5), but Isa. 25:6 specifies that King YHWH's feast is לכל־העמים. Furthermore, King YHWH's display of power at the feast, when he swallows death, is on behalf of כל־העמים and כל־הגוים (25:7). Notably, there is no indication that Isa. 25:6 limits participation to only representative leaders from the nations, as King Ahasuerus does in his first feast. Instead, if Isa. 25:1-5 informs our sense of who will participate, the poor (דל) and oppressed (אביון) will partake as well (25:4). Thus, by comparing the feasts of King Ahasuerus and King YHWH, the limited extent of the former's social vision of inclusion and the far-reaching extent of the latter's inclusivism becomes more apparent.

Particularism is also apparent in both books. As for Esther, she hosts her meals with a very *particular* purpose: to preserve the lives of the Jews. In line with this vision, the resulting celebratory feasts are all ליהודים ("for the Jews" [8:16-17; 9:16-19, 20-22]). Some interpret this particularism in the book of Esther as *anti-Gentile*, but the celebration pertains to victory over *enemies* of the Jews, not simply over Gentiles (Levenson 1976, 443–4).

To a lesser extent, one finds a level of particularism imbedded within the universalism of Isa. 25:6-8. Although עם is plural throughout vv. 6-7, the shift to the singular in v. 8 suggests an enduring particularism: "and the reproach of his people he will remove from over all the earth" (והרפת עמו יסיר מעל כל־הארץ).[15] As YHWH swallows Death for the benefit of all peoples, he will also remove any reproach and shame associated with his people, Israel, from all nations.

In summary, in order to understand a particular text, it is vital to read intertextually. The result is an ability to read each text more clearly due to a growing understanding of how each text fits into the fabric of the linguistic tapestry, the linguistic world, of which it is a part. I have identified five types of insights that a dialogical reading leads readers to be aware of in each text: the grammar of kingship feasts, abundance and greatness at kingship feasts, rejoicing in conjunction with the feast, centralization and decentralization, and inclusion and particularism.

---

15. On particularism in this feast, see Polaski (2001, 192).

Dialogical Imagination

As this essay concludes, we ponder how the coordination of these texts from Esther and Isaiah promotes a dialogical vision. As noted above, at its best, the emerging vision should not smooth over the particularities of each text. I offer three perspectives on how a coordinated, canonical vision might emerge from reading the feasts in Esther in dialogue with the feast in Isaiah 25.

The first perspective pertains to *time*. A dialogical vision needs near and far temporal lenses of reference. On the one hand, Esther affirms the value and delight of being able to celebrate a festival dispersed throughout the known empire. This celebration would take place perpetually throughout the near future. Even if all is not as it should be, there is still a place for festal celebration in the present time. On the other hand, Isaiah 25 depicts an eschatological vision of feasting where YHWH's rule is established, Death is abolished, and tears and reproach are absent. The near and the far are to be held together without dismissing one or another; both have their place in canonical vision.

The second perspective pertains to *place and participants*. A dialogical vision from feasts in Esther and Isaiah holds in tension decentralization and centralization, particularism and inclusivism. In Esther, there is a movement from centralized feasts in Susa to decentralized feasting among Jews throughout the empire. In Isa. 25:6-8, the feast is centralized in Zion, King YHWH's capital, and includes those from all nations. Rather than construing these tensions as attempts to correct or reject opposing views, a dialogical reading—where each voice is respected—holds the two together. Canonical vision retains a place for upholding the particularism of God's displaced people amidst feasting while also anticipating a future when universalism will have priority amidst the centralization of divine rule in Zion.

The third perspective pertains to *the host* of the feasts. The book of Esther's canonical vision offers several angles into the hosts of feasts. Pagan kings may feign power through their feasts, yet such feasts may turn out to be an unexpected means toward ensuring the well-being of God's people. God's people, like Esther, may find themselves hosting pagan feasts as means to a greater end, as Esther does in hosting the king and Haman. Furthermore, amidst scattering, minority communities can host their own feasts to celebrate their preservation. These angles on meal hosting in Esther guard against being blinded by the supposed invincibility of kings aired by royal celebrations, commission God's people in positions of power to utilize secular practices like feasts as means for divine ends, and empower the marginal to celebrate amidst their lowly status in an earthly kingdom. In the case of Isaiah 25, the host is God himself whose generosity is abundant and whose power operates benevolently to overcome the greatest threat to humanity. A coordinated vision retains all of these vantage points on the host.

Thus, I have offered three perspectives on how a dialogical reading of feasts in Esther and the feast in Isaiah 25 results in a coordinated, canonical vision: perspectives on time, people and place, and the host.

Conclusion

What does Esther have to do with Isaiah? Although at first glance one might say "very little," these two books serve as dialogue partners within the canon so as to enable readers to see each text more clearly and to invite readers to ponder how these books contribute to a coordinated, canonical vision. We are forced to adjust our glasses to be able to see near and far, Jew and Gentile, Zion and Diaspora, and a world where banal kings, unlikely queens, a marginal populace, and ultimately the Divine King vie for prestige, power, survival, identity, and victory through the symbolic potency of feasts.

Chapter 7

THE FRUIT OF MOURNING: ESTHER ENRICHED BY THE LATTER PROPHETS

Heath A. Thomas

Introduction

This essay explores linguistic and thematic correspondence between Esther and the Latter Prophets (particularly Isaiah and the Twelve) in terms of Israel's mourning in the prophets and the mourning of the people of God in Esther. I shall note links between action in Esther 4 and the call to mourning, fasting, and weeping Joel, Jonah, and Isaiah. The actions of Mordecai, Esther, and the Jews in the book of Esther display petitionary mourning, anticipating divine action to end the mourning process. Intertextuality between Esther and the Latter Prophets creates expectation of divine response to mourning but leaves open the ways in which God might end the mourning rite. Mourning in Esther evinces features of postexilic penitential acts in line with other texts from the postexilic era, though in a different register than the penitential prayers of Ezra 9, Nehemiah 9, and Daniel 9.

Investigating intertextuality has become commonplace in biblical studies. Often, intertextuality is defined in terms of authorial influence and reception, while more recent studies assess intertextuality in terms of readerly interests that generate associations between texts without a necessary historical precedent (see Grohmann and Kim 2019, 1-14). Without foreclosing upon one or the other possibility, this chapter raises a slightly different question: In what ways does Esther's presence in the tripartite Hebrew Bible create the possibility of the Latter Prophets enriching the reading of Esther? One could argue Esther as quite late, and therefore the book's composer intentionally utilizes earlier texts to open horizons of understanding for the reader in relation to the meaning and purpose of the book.[1] Berlin and

---

1. Scholarly consensus places the book within the Persian or Hellenistic periods between 400 and 200 BCE. For discussion, see Berlin (2001, xli). Berlin dates the book between 400 and 300 BCE, after the reign of Xerxes and before Hellenization after Alexander the Great. By contrast, Macchi (2018, 38-9) dates the book to *after* the Hellenization of Alexander the Great.

others have approached intertextuality in Esther from this vantage point. Previous research, for instance, marks connections between Joel and Esther in terms of historical dependence Esther owes to Joel; Joel's prophetic material was available to Esther's writer, and Esther's writer used it (Jobes 1999, 135–7).

However, the argument advanced here does not attempt to date Esther with respect to Latter Prophets that share similar language, or vice versa. Rather than an historical investigation, the kind of intertextuality engaged in this essay reads the Latter Prophets as cotexts of Esther to see how Esther might be enriched hermeneutically without making a claim to necessary historical dependence. What Seitz says of Joel's relation to the Minor Prophets applies here, albeit in a modified form. When discerning the associations between Joel and the Minor Prophets, Seitz (2016, 9) states there "is no really good way to speak of this dimension *in strictly diachronic terms*, because we must allow for the strong possibility of mutual enrichment, of reciprocal association, both now imbedded in what we must attend to as the character of the presentation of the Twelve in its present form."[2]

Seitz's notion of "mutual enrichment" gestures toward the reading advanced in this essay. Intertextuality here assesses what kind of readerly horizons emerge when Esther is read in concert with the Latter Prophets, the kinds of hermeneutical vistas open for the reader of the text when one establishes intertextual connections. Intertextuality—broadly understood as allusion or echo of another text through repetition of terms, phrases, scenes, or action—becomes a way to identify and explore how the Latter Prophets enrich the reading of Esther, particularly in the ways both corpora present mourning.

Mourning in the Latter Prophets

If this essay draws lines of "mutual enrichment" between the Latter Prophets and Esther in terms of mourning, then it is necessary to explore briefly mourning in the Hebrew Bible. Mourning is not an emotional state but rather it is a ritual process. Mourning in the Hebrew Bible derives first and foremost from bereavement, and mourning the dead is a basic ritual act.

Saul Olyan (2003, 26) taxonomizes the ritual process of mourning into four major types: mourning the dead, petitionary mourning, non-petitionary mourning that marks disaster, and non-petitionary mourning rites associated with skin disease. Mourning the dead marks bereavement, while petitionary mourning adds lament and petition. Non-petitionary mourning does not cry out to God but

---

2. I do not want to suggest that Esther's association with the Latter Prophets is *equivalent to* Joel's association in the Minor Prophets. Joel's intertextual association with the Twelve is well-established and well-trod. But in both cases (Joel and the Minor Prophets as well as Esther and the Latter Prophets), literary and canonical association provides sufficient warrant to read one text in the light of others.

still exhibits characteristics of mourning the dead. Finally, mourning associated with skin disease is a unique category somewhat different from the others but still rooted in a ritual process.

For petitionary mourning, language of lament often accompanies the terms "to mourn" (אבל), or "to wail"/"mourn"/"lament" (ספד), or "a lament" (קינה).³ Still, laments do not need this language, because lamenting is a form of speech that may not exhibit such *termini technici*. Elsewhere I have defined lament as "a kind of prayer that voices a complaint to God about distress, and it is uttered to persuade God to act on the sufferer's behalf" (Thomas 2018, 67). Laments may utilize the technical language, but they employ a multitude of terms, questions, phrases, and complaints to petition the deity to change the sufferer's situation. The goal in lament is to experience a change of situation, oftentimes it is petitionary prayer that God will act on behalf of, rather than against, the sufferer (Thomas 2018, 67–76).

As they express grief and pain through a prayer, it is no wonder that laments often emerge in contexts of mourning, especially petitionary mourning in the prophets. "The Prophetic Books are filled with language, imagery and forms related to the expression of lament and mourning. This is a reflection of the dominant negative tone of the prophets as they address a community threatened with or experiencing the discipline and judgment of Yahweh" (Boda 2012, 473).

Whether connected with lament or not, biblical mourning represents a *process*, and thus expects a movement from the ritual state of mourning to a different ritual state: joy, often identified with "dancing" (Anderson 1991, 82–97; Olyan 2003, 1–61, esp. p. 4 n. 7).⁴ Mourning is a ritual movement, a liminal process, in which the mourner undergoes symbolic change: from normal "life," to symbolic "death," to anticipated renewed "life." So mourning is not designed to persist interminably in the biblical corpus.⁵

---

3. Still, this language appears regularly in laments in the Latter Prophets. For examples of language "to mourn" (אבל) in prophetic texts, see: Isa. 3:26; 19:8; 24:4, 7; 33:9; 57:18; 60:20; 61:2-3; 66:10; Jer. 4:28; 6:26; 12:4; 14:2 16:7; 23:10; 31:13; Ezek. 7:12, 27; Hos. 4:3; 10:5; Joel 1:9-10; Amos 5:16; 8:8, 10; 9:5; Mic. 1:8. For examples of language "to wail"/"mourn"/"lament" (ספד) in prophetic texts see, for instance: Isa. 32:12; Zech. 7:5; 12:10, 12; Ezek. 24:16, 23; Amos 5:16; Mic. 1:8; Jer. 4:8; 6:16; 16:4-6; 22:18; 25:33; 34:5; 49:3; Joel 1:13. For examples of "a lament" (קינה) see, for instance: Jer. 7:29; 9:9, 19; Ezek. 2:10; 19:1, 14; 26:17; 27:2, cf., v. 32; 26:17; 27:2, 32; 28:12; 32:2, 16; Amos 5:1; 8:10.

4. Cf., Ps. 30:11; Isa. 66:10; Jer. 31:13.

5. But see Gen. 37:35, where Jacob refuses to cease mourning due to the loss of the perceived death of Joseph, his favorite son. His behavior, however, is not to be emulated, as Olyan (2003, 36) rightly avers. See also Olyan's discussion of a similar motif in the Gilgamesh epic (2003, 36). The interminable mourning in the book of Lamentations exacerbates the dire sadness of the book all the more. See Pham (1999).

As a ritual, mourning symbolically *inverts* the normal order of living and associates the mourner with the world of the dead (Anderson 1991, 82; Feldman 1977, 13–30, 91–108; Kruger 2005).[6] Mourners may be identified as nonpersons (symbolically) who avoid food through fasting, avoid sex, shave the head, lament, put ashes or dust on the head, and tear their clothes or wear sackcloth (Anderson 1991, 49).[7] These actions are designed to express grief, identify with the world of death, but they also anticipate change.

The *agent* that moves the mourner from desacralized life to renewed life varies. Mourning can break open into new life through the role of *comforters*. Pham (1999) highlights the role of the comforter (מנחם) within the mourning rite. Anderson (1991, 84) states that the comforter provides consolation that "can imply either the symbolic action of *assuming the state of mourning* alongside the mourner, or it can have the nuance of *bringing about the cessation of mourning*" (italics his).[8] So, for instance, when Isa. 40:1 declares, "Comfort, comfort, says your God," what is displayed is an *end* to the mourning on display in Isaiah 1–39 and a renewed vitality for the people of God.[9] Some comforting agent has provided the cessation of mourning and enabled renewed vitality with God, described as an end to her warfare, pardon for iniquity, and just recompense for her sins (Isa. 40:2).[10]

Sometimes the agent of change is the *prophet*, transforming mourning into renewed vitality. In Isa. 40:1, for example, the plural imperative of "comfort" may

---

6. See Olyan's comments that association with the dead, in practice, means a separation from the cult and "quotidian" life (2003, 59, 39–60). Nonetheless, it is an inversion of the normal order and signifies the *problem or threat* that death poses to the normal order of life. Note especially the law for purification for corpse-contamination in Numbers 19. One should note that the leper, too, symbolically associates with the dead (or an incomplete human being) who engages in a ritual process that anticipates new and restored life (healing of leprosy, or "cleanness"). "As for the leper, he, too, suffers a kind of death" (Feldman 1977, 37, see also pp. 38–41).

7. For biblical examples: Deut. 26:14; 2 Sam. 3:31; 14:2; Est. 4:3; Qoh. 7:2, 4; Jer. 47:5; Ezek. 27:31; Joel 2:12; Amos 8:10; Mic. 1:8, 16.

8. According to Pham (1999, 28), the comforter "tries to comfort or to mitigate the mourner's grief in two main ways: first, by identifying with the mourner through participating in the mourning rites; and, secondly, by speaking to the mourner, giving him or her advice on how to get over his or her pain."

9. This is true regardless of the identity of the subject of the plural Piel imperative (נַחֲמוּ, "comfort") spoken of in v. 1. For discussion, see Goldingay and Payne (2006, 63–6).

10. The lack of a comforter can mean that mourning persists interminably. For example, persistent mourning comprises the reality of the book of Lamentations. A central figure in the book, the daughter of Zion, emerges as a mourner with "no comfort" from her friends, lovers, or God in Lam. 1:2b, 7c, 9b, 16b, 17a, 21a. See Thomas (2013, 96–129). Persistent mourning emerges in the daughter of Zion's words: "On account of these things I weep, my eye constantly streaming with water. For far from me is a comforter [מנחם], one who restores my life" (Lam. 1:16a) (Thomas 2013, 131).

be a group of prophets who speak words of comfort signifying the mourning of God's people is over.[11] The text reads, "Comfort, O comfort my people, says your God. Speak tenderly to Jerusalem, and cry to her that she has served her term, that her penalty is paid, that she has received from the LORD's hand double for all her sins" (Isa. 40:1-2, NRSV).

In other texts, the cry of lament becomes the vehicle to cry for a change of ritual state, and *divine response* enables the traverse from mourning. Olyan signifies this combination of mourning and lament as "petitionary mourning." Petitionary mourning presents a "combination of shared characteristics with mourning the dead and distinct features of its own," so petitionary mourning is "a discrete ritual activity distinguishable from mourning the dead, and, at the same time, as a type of mourning broadly conceived" (Olyan 2003, 64). For petitionary mourning, these actions may be accompanied with prayer to God to enact change. In cases of petitionary mourning in the prophets, such debasement couples with petitions to the deity to reverse judgment and forgive sin, or they may attempt to forestall divine judgment through humility and penitence. As such, mourners place themselves in positions that expect ritual movement from symbolic "death" to renewed "life," or as prophetic texts indicate: from mourning to joy, gladness for sorrow (Jer. 31:13), gladness instead of mourning and a garment of praise instead of a faint spirit (Isa. 61:3).

Petitionary mourning exhibits the same phenomenal acts one associates with mourning the dead: tearing one's clothes, throwing ash or dust on the head, wailing, weeping, wearing sackcloth, and fasting. One finds instances of petitionary mourning in texts like Ezra 9:3, 5; 10:6; Neh. 1:4; 1 Sam. 30:4; 2 Sam. 13:19; Joel 1–2. For our purposes, I want to focus upon Joel 1–2, because scholars associate it with Esther 4.

In Joel 1–2 a locust plague afflicts the people of God (whether this is a metaphorical or literal locust plague is irrelevant for our argument) (see Thomas and Bartholomew forthcoming). The prophet calls the priests, elders, and the inhabitants of the land to mourn and fast with typical language of mourning in Joel 1:13-14. In these verses, the language of mourning stands out. Wearing sackcloth (בַּשַׂקִּים, v. 13), lamenting (וְסִפְדוּ, v. 13), and fasting (צוֹם, v 14) emerge as a call to transform normal life into the inverse world of mourning. What distinguishes the experience from normal mourning over the dead is the cry to God: "put on sackcloth and lament (וְסִפְדוּ)" and "cry out to the LORD (וְזַעֲקוּ אֶל־יְהוָה)." The people's petitionary mourning apparently encourages God to "relent" from the disaster that is coming (Joel 2:14). The call for the fast (צוֹם) in 1:14 redoubles with a command for fasting, weeping, and lamenting (וּבְצוֹם וּבְבְכִי וּבְמִסְפֵּד) in Joel 2:12.

Joel 2:17 specifies that the temple comprises the location where the mourning ought to take place. This is likely because the temple marks the location where God hears and responds to the people.[12]

---

11. For discussion, see Goldingay and Payne (2006, 63–6).

12. "The holy temple of Yahweh is the judgment seat where God authoritatively renders his holy judgment. In the Minor Prophets, the prophet Jonah longs for *this* place in his time of trouble; his petition goes up 'into your holy temple' (Jon 2:4, 7). Jonah's prayer goes

Again, the mourning actions appear alongside the petition of the people, where the people ask YHWH to spare the people so they are not put to shame (Joel 2:17). And apparently God grants the people's request: they are saved from destruction. Joel 2:18-27 comprises a restoration oracle in which God removes the enemy threat, grants his people provision and protection, and there will be the clear knowledge of God. As the final two verses reveal, God proclaims over Israel that their honor will be restored and their fast will be reversed: they will eat and be satisfied and not be put to shame (Joel 2:26-27).

In this act of divine power, the state of mourning inverts to a renewed state of vitality before God. Where there was threat, there is now peace. Where there was the threat of lack, now there will be plenty. Where there was the threat of God's negative action toward the people, now God is in the midst of Israel and they shall never again be put to shame. As Olyan (2003, 67) states, "Petitionary mourning ends with the change in the community's circumstances."

Mourning in Esther

Narrative action in Esther 4 stands out in light of our discussion on mourning, above. Upon hearing of Haman's plot to kill the Jewish people, the text indicates Mordecai responds with absolute abandon: "Mordecai tore his clothes and put on sackcloth and ashes, and went through the city, wailing a loud and bitter cry" (Est. 4:1). By tearing his clothes and girding himself with sackcloth and ashes, Mordecai removes himself from the normal realm of the living and associates with the dead, in mourning. He mourns the calamity that has befallen the Jews. When the Jews understand their reality, "great mourning" emerged among them, "with a fast, and weeping, and lamentation; many lay in sackcloth and ashes" (Est. 4:3). The people join Mordecai in mourning. Mordecai approaches Esther about the plot to provide relief from the threat, and at this point his famous statement emerges, "Who knows? Perhaps you have come to royal dignity for such a time as this" (Est. 4:14). In her commitment to the plot to engage the king about the Jews' plight, Esther requests that Mordecai "hold a fast" (וְצוּמוּ) (Est. 4:16) on her behalf, which will persist for three days; Esther would fast (אָצוּם) along with her retinue as well. After this time of fasting, Esther would go to gain audience of the king. Upon her visit, Ahasuerus reverses course against the Jews, and Haman receives his just

before Yahweh in the temple to receive the divine verdict. In Mic. 1:2, it is from the holy temple that Yahweh is a witness against all the peoples and all the earth. As a witness against the lawlessness of his world, God then renders judgment from the temple against his people and land (Mic. 1:3-7). It is the *temple* where Yahweh's faithful ones look because it is there that he will give his divine decree. This is the place where God vindicates the righteous and punishes the wicked" (Thomas 2018, 134).

desserts. Mordecai and Esther move to positions of prestige and power, and the Jewish people are saved.

In assessing the chapter, some recognize elements of mourning in Esther 4, without marking its significance. Ringgren (1962, 390), for instance, remarks Mordecai and the Jews' response in Esther 4 represents typical mourning rites ("üblichen Trauergebräuche"), but he treats it lightly. So, too does Loader (1992, 246), who says that Mordecai's actions represent visible, undisguised grief ("Mordechais erste Reaktion ist unverhohlene, sichtbare Trauer"), without expounding its import.

Similarly, Day interprets mourning in Esther 4 as clarifying the emotions of Mordecai and the Jews. She says that mourning acts of wailing, wearing sackcloth, and ashes reflect Mordecai's "mood"; Mordecai "makes apparent to all his emotional state through sight and sound" (Day 2005, 78–9). For Day (2005, 79), the phenomenal acts displayed in Esther 4 are "typical expressions of grief and despair." Unfortunately, Day's characterization does not appropriately engage the ritual significance of mourning, indicated above, and its import on the text.

Jean-Daniel Macchi explores the ritual mourning of Esther 4 more fully, but he remains unclear about its significance. He notes Mordecai's actions in Est. 4:1-2 initiate mourning and reveal his leadership—after his example the rest of the Jews mourn as well (Est. 4:3). Macchi notes that the outward acts of mourning here are accompanied with cries to God for help in other texts (cf., Jon. 3:5-8); the cry for help is not apparent in Esther 4. Macchi (2018, 169) states, "Consequently, there is some ambiguity in our text: are these gestures simply an expression of angst, or are they a call for help? The reader is invited to understand that even if the attitude of the Jews does not exclude the hope for divine assistance, it certainly manifests a profound sense of uncertainty about the future."

Contrasting Day or Macchi, Olyan (2003, 25) links the text specifically with ritual mourning in the fashion of Joel 2 (explored above). He states, "Under the rubric of petitionary mourning I include many narratives that describe mourning behaviour that anticipates disaster or punishment, as these state or imply a petitionary purpose"; he includes in this category Neh. 1:5-11; Joel 2:17; Dan. 9:4-19; 2 Kgs 19:15-19; 2 Chron. 20:6-12; 2 Sam. 12:16-20; and Est. 4:16. For Olyan, mourning in Esther 4 exhibits petitionary mourning, as we described above.

Hazony is not interested in a taxonomy of mourning rites as much as the hermeneutical significance of mourning in Esther 4. Mourning prepares of the reader to expect divine response in Esther 4. Hazony relates the mourning rites initiated by Mordecai and the Jews (Est. 4:1-2) and then Esther and her entourage (Est. 4:12-16) with the petition for God to save them:

> Despite the absence of God's name, the reader is expected immediately to recognize that the Jews of the empire, including Esther and Mordechai, have joined together in rituals of grief and contrition whose purpose is to petition God to aver the evil that has befallen them and save their lives. (Hazony 2016, 196)

Table 7.1 Intertextual Connections between Esther and Joel

Esther	Intertextual Connection	Explanation of Intertext
Est. 4:3	Joel 2:12	אֵבֶל גָּדוֹל לַיְּהוּדִים וְצוֹם וּבְכִי וּמִסְפֵּד שָׂק וָאֵפֶר יֻצַּע לָרַבִּים "there was great mourning among the Jews, and <u>fasting</u>, and <u>weeping</u>, and <u>lamentation</u>; many lay in sackcloth and ashes" // שֻׁבוּ עָדַי בְּכָל־לְבַבְכֶם וּבְצוֹם וּבִבְכִי וּבְמִסְפֵּד׃ "return unto Me with all your heart, and with <u>fasting</u>, and with <u>weeping</u> and with <u>lamentation</u>."
Est. 4:14	Joel 2:14	"who knows?" (וּמִי יוֹדֵעַ) // "who knows?" (מִי יוֹדֵעַ)

For Hazony, Mordecai's mourning in Est. 4:3 is petitionary, and it echoes the mourning of Joel 2:12. Because of this, Joel's mourning and repentance echo in Esther, leading the reader to expect God to act on the Jews' behalf, just as he did in Joel. Others identify connections between Joel and Esther as well (Beal 1999, 66; Berg 1979, 52 n. 33). We shall turn to links between Est. 4:14 and Jon. 3:9 below but presently note the shared language and terminology that emerge between Joel 2 and Esther 4, as Hazony identifies it (Table 7.1):

As the table reveals, resonant language between the texts of "fasting, weeping, and lamentation" (צום+בכי+מספד) deserves explanation. That the same terms recur in the same order between texts is conspicuous, as this is the only time this triad appears in that order.[13] Hazony rightly sees the actions of Mordecai and the Jews resonant with the divine call of Joel 2:12, so that their actions represent the turn to God in hopes that he would deliver. The intertextual interchange between texts draws out the hope of divine response in the light of authentic petition.

Further, the interrogative "who knows?" from the prophet (in Joel) and from Mordecai (in Esther) marks a turning point in the action of both texts: after this interrogative, the reader witnesses a reversal of fortunes of those under threat. After this question in Esther, the narrative shifts to a reversal of fortunes: Haman is shamed and Mordecai, Esther, and the Jews are saved and honored (Esther 5–10). After this same interrogative in Joel, God responds to his people and reverses their fortunes (Joel 2:18-27). So Hazony (2016, 198) states, "The fact that the text in Esther refers to these other texts in this way leaves no doubt that the Esther narrative, too, portrays the Jews as crying out to God and pleading for their salvation, even though this is not said explicitly."

Like Hazony, Jobes (1999, 135) believes Esther 4 echoes Joel 2, but she emphasizes the notion of repentance more strongly than Hazony. Esther's use of metalepsis "thus places the readers of Esther 4 within a field of 'whispered or

---

13. Similar lexemes recur in 2 Sam. 1:12, but not in the same order: "And they mourned and wept and fasted until evening (וַיִּסְפְּדוּ וַיִּבְכּוּ וַיָּצֻמוּ עַד־הָעָרֶב) over Saul and Jonathan, his son, and for the people of the LORD, and for the house of Israel, because they fell by the sword."

Table 7.2 Intertextual Connections between Esther and Jonah

Esther	Intertextual Connection	Explanation of Intertext
Est. 4:3	Jon. 3:5-9	אֵבֶל גָּדוֹל לַיְּהוּדִים וְצוֹם וּבְכִי וּמִסְפֵּד שַׂק וָאֵפֶר יֻצַּע לָרַבִּים "there was great mourning among the Jews, with <u>fasting</u>, and weeping, and lamentation; many lay in <u>sackcloth</u> and ashes" // "and they proclaimed a fast" (וַיִּקְרְאוּ־צוֹם) + "and they wore sackcloth" (וַיִּלְבְּשׁוּ שַׂקִּים)
Est. 4:14	Jon. 3:9	"who knows?" (וּמִי יוֹדֵעַ) // "who knows?" (וּמִי יוֹדֵעַ)

unstated correspondences' between events of this chapter and the words of the prophet in Joel 2."[14] The association connects the Jews' mourning in Esther 4 to Israel's repentance in Joel 2. "The author of Esther portrays the Jews' response of 'fasting, weeping, and wailing' in the face of this calamity as the repentance called for by Joel" (Jobes 1999, 136). In this way, Joel and Esther interact to demonstrate the possibility of divine deliverance through human repentance. "For the first time in this story, Esther identifies herself with God's people and responds to the prophetic call to repentance [through Joel 2:15–16a] by joining with the Jews of Susa in this fast" (Jobes 1999, 137). Metalepsis invites the readers of Esther 4 to interpret the mourning as a way to gain divine intervention.

Previous readings assessing intertextuality between Joel and Esther rightly emphasize the significance of mourning in Esther 4. However, attention must be given to the ways Esther 4 resonates with other texts in the Latter Prophets beyond Joel 2, nuancing the presentation beyond repentance. Jon. 3:5-9; Isa. 37:1; and Isa. 58:5 intersect with Esther 4, as we shall see below. Hazony (2016, 198–9) draws attention to Jon. 3:9, but note other correspondences between Est. 4:3 and Jon. 3:5-9, as well (Table 7.2).

The language of fasting and wearing sackcloth echoes the mourning of the Ninevites in Jonah, as one notes above. Further, the interrogative by the Ninevite king ("who knows whether God will relent and forgive?") is matched with Mordecai's statement to Esther "who knows?" whether she has come to the kingdom for a time like this. Shared language between texts invites reading them alongside one another. If Jonah presents the possibility of God relenting from judgment against the Ninevites because of their mourning, then Esther may present the possibility of divine deliverance of the Jews because of their mourning.

If this correlation remains possible, then Esther's narrative nuances the nature of deliverance. The king of Nineveh asks the question whether God will relent and forgive, but Mordecai presses the same question to Esther as she enjoys privileged position in the royal court. Although the "kingdom" that she has come

---

14. Metalepsis is a figure of speech in which reference is made to one text through an allusion or citation to another text. For further study, see Brown (2016, 29–41).

into mentioned in Est. 4:14 is, on the surface, the kingdom of Persia under the authority of King Ahasuerus, the interplay between Jonah and Esther draws the possibility of a secondary reading. As Hazony (2016, 199) says, "By coming into worldly royalty, Esther placed herself in position to act in the service of another king entirely. The secondary meaning of Mordechai's question ['who knows?'], emergent on the first, is this: Who knows whether it was for such a time as this that you have come into the service of the true king, God?"

Admittedly, this intertext is less convincing than Joel, whose language resonates more clearly with Esther. The constellation of terminology is more specific between Joel 2 and Esther 4. Correspondence between Jonah 3 and Esther 4 likely is a result of stock imagery and mourning language rather than direct borrowing. However, common imagery and language—stock or otherwise—is enough to note common concepts. Mourning, fasting, and sackcloth engender divine response. What is said of Joel could be said of Jonah: petitionary mourning leads to God's salvific intervention.

Beyond Jonah, one notes resonance that runs through Isaiah and Esther 4. See the correspondence in Table 7.3. To my knowledge, scholars have not recognized correspondences between Isaiah 37 and Esther 4. When read alongside Isa. 37:1, Mordecai's actions resemble Hezekiah's. Mordecai tears his clothes like Hezekiah (וַיִּקְרַע אֶת־בְּגָדָיו), indicating dejection and humility in mourning (cf., Josh. 7:6; 1 Kgs 21:27; 2 Kgs 22:11//2 Chron. 34:19). Moreover, both Hezekiah and Mordecai don sackcloth (שָׂק). Their responses derive from duress over a calamitous decree: Mordecai with the decree of Jewish persecution at the hands of a Persian king; Hezekiah with the decree of Judahite destruction at the hands of an Assyrian king.

These intertextual clues gain prominence when assessing plot development between the stories. Esther's plot mirrors other books, like Daniel 1–6 and the Joseph story (Berlin 2001, xxxiv–xli). Similar plot development also emerges

Table 7.3 Intertextual Connections between Esther and Isaiah

Esther	Intertextual Connection	Explanation of Intertext
Est. 4:1	Isa. 37:1//2 Kgs 19:1	וַיִּקְרַע מָרְדֳּכַי אֶת־בְּגָדָיו וַיִּלְבַּשׁ שָׂק וָאֵפֶר וַיֵּצֵא בְּתוֹךְ הָעִיר וַיִּזְעַק זְעָקָה גְדֹלָה וּמָרָה "Mordecai <u>tore his clothes and put on sackcloth</u> and <u>ashes</u>, and went through the city, wailing a loud and bitter cry." // וַיִּקְרַע אֶת־בְּגָדָיו וַיִּתְכַּס בַּשָּׂק וַיָּבֹא בֵּית יְהוָה: "When King Hezekiah heard it, <u>he tore his clothes</u>, covered himself with <u>sackcloth</u>, and went into the House of the Lord."
Est. 4:1	Isa. 58:5	שָׂק וָאֵפֶר "<u>sackcloth and ashes</u>" // וְשַׂק וָאֵפֶר "and <u>sackcloth and ashes</u>"

between Isaiah 37 and Esther 4. In Est. 4:4-17, Esther and Mordecai interact through intermediaries (Hathach, Esther's maidservants, and her eunuchs). In Isa. 37:2-35, Isaiah/God and Hezekiah interact through intermediaries (Eliakim, Shebna, and priests). The climactic moment in Isaiah 37 is Hezekiah's prayer (Isa. 37:14-20) and God's response (Isa. 37:21-35) while the climactic moment in Esther 4 lies in Mordecai's request (Est. 4:13-14) and Esther's response (Est. 4:15-16). In both instances, mourning anticipates response, and in both texts, mourning precedes intervention and deliverance: one from the hand of God and the other from the hand of Esther. Similar storytelling and plot development in Esther 4 to Isaiah 37 carry the correlation.

Differences between the texts, however, appear as narratives progress. Mordecai goes to the outer court of the palace (Est. 4:1) in his ritual state of mourning, while Hezekiah mourns in the "House of the Lord" or the temple (Isa. 37:1). Spatial differences hint at expected response. Hezekiah goes to the temple presumably because it marks the place where God hears and responds to the cries of his people (Thomas 2018, 134). But in Est. 4:1, Mordecai goes to the palace of Ahasuerus.

The differences between the royal houses are striking, as place nuances the nature and expectation of deliverance. If God delivered through the prophecy of Isaiah when Hezekiah went to the temple, then how will God deliver his people in Persia? The narrative reveals Esther as the instrument of deliverance. Mordecai requests an audience with her for help. When read alongside Isaiah 37, Esther 4 opens a horizon of readerly expectation for divine deliverance, but spatial differentiation between the two narratives nuances divine action. If God "shows up" in Esther 4, it will be through the action of Esther rather than the miraculous intervention of God to subdue the threat, as witnessed in Isa. 37:36-37. The book of Esther subtly exposes the *possibility* of divine response without saying it explicitly. One should note that this kind of allusive subtlety emerges elsewhere in Esther's narrative technique. As Grossman (2011, 245) says, "The reader who fails to sense the hidden level of the story will miss its main messages and morals."[15]

Esther also echoes Isaiah 58, as the figure, above, reveals. It shares the collocation "sackcloth and ashes" with Est. 4:1//Isa. 58:5, as Moore (1971, 47) pointed out long ago. This great Isaianic text on the efficacy of true mourning and repentance becomes a cotext from which one interprets the actions of Mordecai and the Jews in Est. 4:1. If Mordecai's actions are interpreted in the light of Isa. 58:5, then they may be understood as true repentance and commitment to the Lord: he lies in sackcloth and ashes at the decree of the Lord, while he is acting on behalf of his people. "The prophets recognized the value of rent garments and the ritual weight of sitting in sackcloth but only when accompanied by an inwardly directed process or—as Isaiah emphasizes—ethical repentance" (Grossman 2011, 114).

Grossman takes this intertextual clue to distinguish Mordecai's actions and inner motivations in Est. 4:1 and Esther's actions and motivations on display

---

15. Grossman argues that the book revels in concealment and revelation. Subtlety and subtext comprise the nature of Esther's narrative style.

throughout the remainder of the chapter. Mordecai sits outside the court of Ahasuerus, mourning on behalf of his people and seeking the favor of God. But in the inner court of Ahasuerus, Esther does not understand, nor can she see, the significance of Mordecai's clothing. In fact, she is shocked and appalled at his external visage, because she does not share his inner disposition of pain and anguish at the fate of the Jews. Her response is to get Mordecai some different clothes to wear, presumably because she does not share the same heart as Mordecai (Est. 4:4-5). Esther's lack of understanding on the reason for Mordecai's sackcloth reveals her lack of spiritual vision and fidelity to her people. However, this will change in the ritual world as Esther turns to mourning by the end of ch. 4. Esther's commitment to mourn *alongside* the Jews indicates her commitment to the ethical demand of true repentance and dependence upon the Lord. Or as Grossman (2011, 119) states,

> In this chapter, Esther underwent a transformation. It began with the narrator's subtle criticism of Esther for her assimilation to the norms of the palace. By the end, Hadassah, Queen Esther's hidden Jewish identity, had come to the fore, expressing self-sacrifice for the sake of her people. Esther's proclaiming a fast for her people testified to not only a change of garment but a change of heart.

Intertextuality between Isa. 58:5 and Est. 4:1 opens a reading that correlates the mourning of Mordecai, the Jews, and finally Esther to the appropriate ethical repentance and mourning that God expects in Isaiah 58.

Conclusion

When Esther is read alongside the Latter Prophets, mourning emerges as significant for both the moral and theological vision of the book. Although not stated overtly, Esther's allusive echo of Joel 2 suggests Mordecai and the Jews' mourning as *petitionary*. The oblique way the book of Esther points to petitionary mourning marks a good example of the subtlety of the book's storytelling. Intertextuality opens a horizon for the reader to interpret the mourning as petitionary without explicitly stating it.[16]

Esther's oblique echo of Jon. 3:9 accomplishes something similar as the Joel intertext, but takes it further in the way that it presents the echo in the narrative.

---

16. In this regard, it is possible that the Greek versions of Esther, sensing the allusive nature of Mordecai and the Jews' action, fills in the petition itself in the additions of Esther; in both the Old Greek and Alpha-text of Esther, the petitions of Mordecai and Esther to God emerge at the point of their mourning, which resonates with penitential prayer. This is true whether it is the Old Greek of Esther or the Greek Alpha-text of Esther. For further study, see Kahana (2005). For the characteristics of penitential prayer, see the seminal three-volume work: Boda, Falk, and Werline (2006–8).

By using the same mourning acts and terminology of the Ninevite king, the text enables the reader to see the mourning as petitionary, here to avert a great disaster. For the Ninevites, it is the impending judgment of God, but for the Jews, it is the impending doom because of the Persian decree. Interestingly, the placement of Mordecai's question to Esther in the narrative of Esther 4 enables one to see that it is *Esther* who may be the means of deliverance for her people; her turn toward mourning in the conclusion of the chapter enables the reader to see, with Hazony, that Esther's moment may indicate her service in the kingdom of God rather than the kingdom of Ahasuerus.

Isaiah (in ch. 37 and 58:5) enriches Esther's meaning by correlating Mordecai's actions and Hezekiah's. Isaiah 37 anticipates divine response to the Assyrian threat, leading the reader to consider whether similar response would occur in Esther 4. However, the plot development in Esther contrasts against Isaiah 37, differentiating both the immediate source of deliverance and juxtaposes God's palace in Isaiah against Ahasuerus' palace in Esther. If God shows up in Esther, it will be in close connection with the actions of Esther. That Esther undergoes a moral transformation emerges from intertextuality between Esther 4 and Isaiah 58. Mordecai's true moral repentance and humility becomes a model for divine response; Esther must embody that same repentance. By the end of Esther 4, she has achieved the moral vision of Isaiah 58, engages in petitionary mourning, and is positioned to deliver her people.

If this intertextual reading between Esther and the Latter Prophets is felicitous, then it needs to be measured against other great penitential texts of the Persian period and beyond: the penitential prayers of Daniel 9, Ezra 9, and Nehemiah 9. These texts explicitly recount Israel's story, admit sin, and petition God to deliver. Esther does not make the bold declarations of these penitential prayers. Although these prayers "pray the tradition" of God's people, the penitence on display in Esther is achieved through mourning and intertextual interchange between Esther and the Latter Prophets, rather than explicit prayers of confession and a plea for forgiveness.

Part IV

ESTHER IN DIALOGUE WITH THE WRITINGS

Chapter 8

IN A WORLD WITHOUT GOD: READING ESTHER ALONGSIDE PSALMS

David G. Firth and Brittany N. Melton

Reading Esther alongside the Psalter may seem an odd thing to do. Granted, both are part of the canon, but they are remarkably different works. Esther, in its MT form (which will be the focus of this chapter), is famously the book of the Bible that definitely does not mention God.[1] Indeed, it seems at points to go out of its way to avoid mentioning God. For example, in Est. 4:15-16, Esther directs Mordecai to arrange a fast, something she also does with her attendants. Elsewhere in the Hebrew Bible, however, fasting is associated with prayer.[2] But here, precisely at the point where it seems that mention of God (or at least a religious act which invokes God) is pertinent, the text is silent. A fast is called, but the question of what the fast should achieve is not made explicit. There are several points in the text where readers may well infer God's involvement, such as the seeming divine passive of הפך at Est. 9:1 amidst an unexpected reversal, but there is still no point at which God's involvement is directly stated. Alongside the absence of reference to God, Esther also avoids mention of the land and the temple, both places of great importance in Israelite religion. Why these things are avoided is beyond the scope of this chapter, but avoidance of them is a key part of how the book is composed.[3]

By contrast, the Psalter is saturated with references to the deity. Every psalm either mentions or addresses God. In the midst of complaint and times when God might seem absent, the psalmists remember God (e.g., Psalm 77), and this provides a shape for their future, typically displaying a "movement from divine absence to divine presence" across individual laments (Burnett 2010, 137).[4] The question "how long" (occurring 4× in Psalm 13) occurs often enough to let us

---

1. Though this may also be true of Song of Songs (see Melton 2018, 58–83; Sun 2021).
2. A feature present in AT (5:11) at this point.
3. This holds true for MT Esther regardless of whether one sees the Greek versions making God more explicit (see, e.g., De Troyer 2003) or the MT editing God out of an alternative Hebrew *Vorlage* (Clines 1984).
4. For "The Divine Metaphor of Absence and Presence as a Binding Element in the Composition of the Book of Psalms," see Doyle (2010).

know that not all psalmists were content with how God was acting or present in their lives. But as a text, the Psalter is focused on God and his relationship to creation as a whole, Israel as a nation, and the various individuals whose voices are heard. Where Esther avoids the use of religious language, the Psalter looks for ways to speak of God. Given the concentration of God-speech in the Psalter, both points where psalmists speak of God and points where God is reported as speaking,[5] it is perhaps unsurprising that the temple is also an important dimension of the Psalter's theology. Even in places where the temple is not expressly mentioned, there are numerous points where the text assumes some reference to the cult.[6] For example, Ps. 116:13 speaks of lifting "the cup of salvation," an act that assumes some sort of temple ritual, even if the details are currently obscure (see, e.g., Seybold 1996, 455–6).[7] Likewise, although the land of Israel is perhaps less prominent than speech about God or ritual activity, the Psalter still has numerous references to the land (e.g., Pss. 78:54-55; 105:11). These three themes (God, temple, and land) come together in Psalm 79, where the theme of the exile leads to these three elements being central in prayer. Esther, by contrast, allows the exile (which has now become the diaspora) to stand and avoids all overtly religious language.

Despite these obvious differences, there is value in reading Esther and Psalms together. In this treatment, there is no assumption that one text is prior to the other. As a later book in the Hebrew Bible, it is often the case that Esther presumes knowledge of earlier texts,[8] but we cannot make that assumption here. It is not unreasonable to assume that many psalms do precede Esther, but the final form of the Psalter is likely to have emerged in a broadly similar period to Esther, making decisions about dating priority rather tenuous.[9] As such, the approach taken here is to treat these as distinctive works, but without assuming one has influenced the other. That is, each can be read on its own terms without reference to the other, yet recognizing there is also value in reading them together.

As a heuristic example, this chapter reads Psalms 9–14 and Esther alongside each other. There are several reasons why this is beneficial. At a superficial level,

---

5. On the function of passages where God speaks in Psalms, see Jacobson (2004, 82–130).

6. See Creach (2005), who argues that the present form of the Psalter does not require that the Psalms emerge from the cult, merely that they use language derived from it. But in either case, the temple looms large in the background.

7. Biblical quotations throughout follow the ESV translation.

8. For the view that Esther presumes knowledge of Samuel, see Firth (2010a).

9. Note, e.g., that 11Q5 (=11QPsa[a]) may well be a Psalter that arranges the book very differently from the MT Psalter, and it is probably to be dated to the first half of the first century AD. If so (and much is debated), then it offers a very different theological response to the Davidic monarchy (see Wilson 2005, 242–4), but the important point for our purposes is that it could indicate that discussion about the final form of the Psalter was still active in the latter part of the first century AD. Even if it is not a Psalter but a text that supports liturgy in some way, we cannot move the final compilation to much before the latter part of the second century AD if the heading of Psalm 30 references Hanukkah.

we can note that each makes use of the idiom of speaking in one's heart—for example, Psalm 14 famously opens by declaring אמר נבל בלבו אין אלהים. In response to Ahasuerus's question about what was to be done for the man the king desired to honor, we read that Haman's response is prefaced by ויאמר המן בלבו (Est. 6:6). So, there is a clear verbal similarity to be noted here. We should not place too much weight on this, since the idiom of speaking in one's heart clearly means "to think," and it occurs frequently outside these texts (e.g., Isa. 47:10). But on closer inspection, we can note that the similarities between these two texts go beyond the occurrence of an idiom, since in both cases the cited thoughts will be shown to be fundamentally flawed, suggesting that they have more in common, even at the level of language, than simple repetition of an idiom. We can even push this further by noting that the world that Psalm 14 imagines (and rejects) is one in which God is believed to be absent, or at least sufficiently distant that God need not be considered in making ethical choices. In imagining this world, Psalm 14 comes much closer to the world as it is represented in the book of Esther. As will become clear, Psalm 14 forms part of a small collection that runs from Psalm 9 that explores the idea of a world without God in a series of poems that take up the issue of theodicy.

Psalms 9–14 and a World without God

A great deal of current research on Psalms explores the possibility of collections within the Psalter (see, e.g., the foundational work of Wilson 1985, 139–98). Although this has come to varying conclusions about the ways in which these collections work and whether or not there is a storyline that can be traced through the Psalter, we take a narrower focus in this chapter and note that there are important features that indicate Psalms 9–14 are presented as a small collection. Within the Psalter, Psalms 1–2 are now widely read as an introduction to the Psalter, even if the exact function of that introduction is disputed.[10] Following this, there is now broad agreement that Psalms 3–14 form an initial collection (see Hartenstein 2010). Irrespective of whether or not Hartenstein's proposal that Psalms 9–10 are a later insertion to this collection, his basic observation about the structure of this collection, with Psalms 3–7 and 9–14 pivoting around Psalm 8, is probably correct. Psalms 3–7 are all complaint psalms, while Psalm 8's meditation on creation is clearly different in tone, though it also has numerous linguistic connections to the small group that preceded it (see Vesco 2006, 136–7). Whereas Psalms 3–7 are all individual complaints[11] and Psalm 8 the only praise poem addressed entirely to

---

10. Note the suggestion of B. Janowski (2010, 281, drawing on Athanasius) that these psalms are like a door into a temple formed by words.

11. The "I" who speaks has been identified as the king by some commentators, but there is nothing explicitly royal in these psalms, though of course the title of Psalm 3 suggests the psalm be read in light of David's experience during Absalom's revolt. But irrespective of the implied speaker, these are all poems in which an individual speaks.

Yahweh, Psalms 9–14 are distinct in that they show a mixture of forms, all of which can be shown to address the issue of theodicy, especially the question of why the righteous suffer. Although no final answer is given, they work together to enable the question to be addressed through a combination of expressly didactic material and prayer.

In considering the profile of Psalms 9–14, we should note that they also have a range of features in common, which supports the idea that they are a collection. We should begin by noting that although MT separates Psalms 9–10 into two psalms, it makes clear that they are a single poem (hence LXX keeps them as a single psalm). This is clear from language that is common to both and a shared theme for the complaint. But more importantly, although it is no longer complete (and may never have been exactly), the origins of the poem as a single acrostic can still be seen, with the break occurring only at כ (Ps. 9:19 [18]),[12] so that 10:1 then provides the ל lines. Further, Psalm 10 has no title, the only psalm in Psalms 3–14 without one;[13] and this seems to be a means by which the Masoretes allowed readers to see that they had divided the one poem into two psalms.[14] Once the unity of Psalms 9–10 as a single poem is acknowledged, then it can be observed that the boundaries of Psalms 9–14 are formed by 9–10 and 14. Taken as a single poem, one divided around the need for humans to understand their limitations (9:21 [20]), it can also be noted that this means that the boundaries of the collection are marked by those who say *in their heart that there is no God* (10:4; 14:1). In both cases, the balance of the poem will demonstrate that the thoughts which are cited are to be rejected. Indeed, a recurring motif of each poem in this collection is that they use the motif of citing the speech of opponents to show that such thinking is fundamentally flawed (see Jacobson 2004, 30). Psalm 10:1-11 cites the thoughts of the wicked three times to do this, while this pattern is repeated in Pss. 11:1b-3, 12:5 [4], and 13:5 [4], so that by the time we reach the statement of the fool in 14:1 we already know that this is flawed thinking, though the use of wisdom motifs there makes this point particularly clear.

As we trace the language that is rejected through these psalms, we can see how the issue of theodicy is explored, and most particularly through the motif of practical atheism. That is, having created a boundary through Psalms 9–10 and 14 in which the world is envisioned without God, these psalms explore the effect of imagining such a world even as they reject this perspective. Space prohibits a detailed treatment of each psalm, so more general observations will be given, though they should be sufficient to show the similarities to the world that is portrayed in Esther.

---

12. English versification has been cited in brackets throughout where it differs from the Hebrew.

13. Indeed, in Book 1 of Psalms, apart from Psalms 1–2, Psalm 33 is the only other psalm that lacks a title.

14. Ho (2019, 36-7) includes this Masoretic move in his category of "tacit techniques" for linking psalms.

Psalms 9–10 develop their emphasis on human limitations in comparison to God while acknowledging that not everyone consistently experiences God as the good and just figure that is proclaimed in worship. That is why there is a shift at Ps. 9:14 [13] where, having outlined reasons to be thankful to God as the one who is just, the poet then asks for grace, with YHWH called upon to see the psalmist's affliction (cf., Lam. 2:20; 5:1). In doing this, the poem begins the process of holding together the reality that life is not always experienced as beneficially as some might suggest, while still desiring that YHWH should act. This is why YHWH is summoned to arise in 9:20 [19], in preparation for showing humans their limits. All of this prepares for Ps. 10:1-11, which offers a series of complaints to YHWH about the wicked. In this section, there are three points at which the words of others are cited, each of which is intended to show the limitation of human beings, even as they also reveal that many act in a way that does not recognize this. So, in Ps. 10:4 the thought that "There is no God" is first introduced. Whereas Psalm 14 will assign these words to the fool (נבל), here they are the words of the wicked (רשע). Within the Psalter, Psalm 1 has already made clear that the counsel of the wicked is something to be avoided, so readers have good reason to reject this statement. But within Psalm 10, the immediate context also makes clear that these are people who are troublesome, not least because such people seem to prosper and Yahweh's judgments seem to have no impact on them (v. 5), observations that might trouble a simplistic reading of Psalm 1. Nevertheless, having characterized the thought that "there is no God" as an expression of wickedness, the psalm makes clear that this is not a view to be tolerated, even as it also accepts that there will be those whose experience does seem to enable them to flourish in a life of wickedness. For this reason, a second thought (again with אמר בלבו) is introduced in Ps. 10:6. Here, there is a development of the thoughts of such people, who reason that if YHWH's judgments have not so far affected them, then they will remain secure (contra Ps. 15:5). Accordingly, such people seek out opportunities to prey on the weak, leading to the thought (again with אמר בלבו) that God has forgotten them and will not act against the wicked (Ps. 10:11). Clearly, these people are not denying the existence of God in an absolute sense, which would be an anachronistic projection onto an ANE worldview. This practical atheism assumes that the powerful can act against the weak with impunity and that YHWH will not act, which runs counter "to wisdom's view of the world, [in which] the hidden God of creation is present even in the most secret corners of human social life and holds human beings accountable for their deeds" (Burnett 2010, 99, citing Ps. 10:4, 11). This is precisely the reason why Ps. 10:12 immediately prays that YHWH arise and remember the afflicted, leading to the closing hope that humans would again learn their limits (10:18). Psalm 8:6 [5] had stressed that humans were a little less than God, and these psalms then explore the problems of those who do not continue to recognize that important distinction.

Psalm 11 then explores life in a world where the structural violence described in 10:1-11 is experienced by a particular psalmist. This psalm also has important links to Psalms 9–10 (see Vesco 2006, 157), and these are more important than a proposed temple ritual for asylum (see Seybold 1996, 60). In this case, the quoted speech is not from enemies but from misguided counselors who look at a situation where the wicked (הרשעים) seemingly act with impunity against the righteous.[15] Although Psalm 11 can be read on its own terms (and bringing psalms into small collections does not remove that layer of interpretation), the situation of the wicked acting like this is precisely the world imagined in Ps. 10:1-11, where the wicked posit a world in which God does not act. But this advice is not accepted, and the poem pivots on the observation that YHWH is in his temple, enthroned in the heavens, before offering assurance that YHWH does see the actions of the wicked (Ps. 11:4).[16] This establishes a context in which the psalmist can then desire that YHWH would act presently[17] while continuing to trust that YHWH's love for the righteous will eventually see God act on their behalf. Nevertheless, although the psalm rejects the idea that YHWH is inactive, it does not require that this be the immediate experience of all, meaning that the righteous may well experience injustice and violence at present.

Psalm 11 outlines a society in which wickedness (as in the rejection of YHWH's reign) is prominent, and this theme continues in Psalm 12. In this instance, the damage done to society is specifically through the speech of the ungodly, an important theme given the emphasis on the speech within this collection (as well as Proverbs). The problem of untrustworthy speech is raised in vv. 2-3 [1-2] before asking that YHWH cut off the lips of the boastful. It is notable that when their speech is cited once more in v. 5 [4], they claim they can prevail through their own words, closing with a rhetorical question that assumes they have no master. Yet again a claim of practical atheism is found, and it occurs at the turning point of the middle poem (treating Psalms 9–10 as a single unit) within this collection. Therefore, the motif of practical atheism is raised in the opening and closing psalms of the collection and is also the turning point of the middle poem. It is against such speech that the poem then cites YHWH as speaking, the first time YHWH is said to have spoken in this collection, with a promise that he will act for the poor. That is, the weak who have suffered through the wicked are the ones for whom YHWH will act, challenging the shape of a society that acts as if God is not active. This is why the value of YHWH's words are particularly stressed in v. 7 [6], preparing for the closing two verses to declare that YHWH would guard the community[18] even though they live in a world where the wicked (רשעים) are active.

Psalm 13 is often read as the classic expression of the individual complaint, but it is also important to note the effect of its placement in this literary setting (see Prinsloo 2013, 797; Vesco 2006, 165). When read straight from the end of Psalm 12,

---

15. This assumes that citation runs through to v. 3. See Jacobson (2004, 32).

16. On the structure of the poem, see Prinsloo (2013, 778–9).

17. This seems to be the force of the jussives here, though GKC §109k indicates they could still function as imperfects.

18. Retaining MT's תשמרם rather than the common emendation (seen in some manuscripts) to תשמרנו.

with its assurance that YHWH will keep the poor, the fourfold "how long" with which this psalm opens has particular resonance. We know that YHWH keeps the righteous, but when will this be experienced?[19] Moreover, Ps. 11:7 had promised the righteous that they would see YHWH's face, but presently the poet's experience is that it is hidden (13:2 [1]).[20] Whereas the previous psalms in the collection thus explore this issue primarily from the perspective of the community, here it is the experience of the individual that is primary. But we note that the question "how long" assumes that there is no current experience of YHWH acting, setting this psalm also among those that wrestle with the practical atheism expressed in hypothetical citation of the enemy in v. 5 [4]. Here, in Psalm 13, the poet protests about YHWH to YHWH because of his perceived absence (or concealment, *verberging*), something that was regarded as an appropriate response to this issue (see Coetzee 1998).

At this point, Psalm 14[21] formally returns readers to the issue of practical atheism, though in doing so it brings this collection to a close. Whereas Psalms 9-10 had left the issue of practical atheism until the second half of the poem, here it is brought to the beginning, though the reader knows immediately that the citation with which the poem begins is to be rejected. In part, this is because each citation within the collection has been rejected (even if only implicitly in Psalm 10), but more obviously because the rejection of God is said to be the words of a fool. As Psalms 11-12 envisioned the problems of practical atheism expressed in the damage done to a community, so here the attitude of the fool is expressed through those who act in ways that undermine societal well-being. In response to this problem, Psalm 14 pivots on v. 4 (see Botha 1995, 19-20), which advises the audience through a rhetorical question to note that such an attitude ignores the fundamental reality of YHWH's interaction with the world and God's people in particular. Since YHWH is a refuge for the poor, it seems likely that the psalm identifies them as YHWH's people, indicating that the ones who deny God are those who might in fact seem to be prospering. But the poem insists that this is not how it will always be, even as it closes with a wish that YHWH's salvation might be seen so that God's people can rejoice.[22] As long as they experience the seeming triumph of those who ignore God, such rejoicing is void, but when salvation comes, rejoicing will follow.

---

19. Cf., 13:2 [1] with Lam. 5:20 for a prolonged experience of waiting for restoration compounded by the recurrence of "how?" (Lam. 1:1; 2:1; 4:1).

20. See further *The Hidden God: The Hiding of the Face of God in the Old Testament* (Balentine 1983).

21. The poem is nearly identical to Psalm 53. However, the different locations in which we find these poems lead to differing issues of interpretation. See Botha (2015).

22. Cf., Lam. 3:55-66, which displays confidence that God will take up the supplicant's cause by acting against all those who "plot against [him]" (vv. 60-61). The plot of Haman against Mordecai readily comes to mind as a parallel scenario.

Esther and a World without God

That Esther can be read as a text in which God is absent is perhaps self-evident. This might be more accurately expressed by saying that Esther omits mention of God at the literary level, but the presence of numerous allusions to other parts of the Hebrew Bible through the book encourages readers to wonder if God is present in some way.[23] As Melton (2018, 68) frames the matter, it seems the book affirms God's involvement but is unwilling for any of the characters to confirm this. If so, then this represents a close parallel to the experience outlined in Psalms 9–14.

Obviously, there is no point at which anyone expressly declares "there is no God" in Esther. Thus, Esther's sense of divine absence is explored differently from the Psalms, but this is largely because the Psalter is full of references to God, and so a sense of divine absence can only be created through explicit statement. For example, in Esther God never speaks, so divine silence can be reasonably inferred, but in Psalms 10 (v. 11) and 14 (v. 4) a "break in communication between God and man [sic]" is described explicitly in terms of a lack of attention (Balentine 1983, 57). Whereas Esther develops a sense of divine absence through a literary model that avoids mentioning God, the Psalter explores it by temporarily setting up a model that is counter to its dominant strategy of celebrating God's presence. Although the means contrast significantly by which this world without God is evoked, there are remarkable parallels that should be noted.

First, we should note that Esther reports on a world in which the powerful seem to act with impunity against the weak. Even the book's introduction, with its reports of Ahasuerus's feasts (Est. 1:1-9), makes clear that there is a significant differential between the needs of the poor and a king who can spend such extraordinary sums on feasting. This contrast is especially clear in Est. 2:1-18 when a replacement for Vashti is sought. Here, the king has no compunction in creating a system in which his own sexual gratification is placed before the needs of the rest of society, and in so doing spends lavishly in creating a twelve-month system for the women taken into the custody of Hegai simply so that they might please him on the one night they spend together before they are then passed to another area of the harem. Mordecai's concern for Esther, an orphan within his family (Est. 2:7), is presented as a notable contrast. As a Jewish exile, he acts with concern for the weak as opposed to a king who considers only his own needs. At this point in the story, Ahasuerus seems to embody the attitude of the wicked expressed in Ps. 10:5, as someone who seems to prosper while acting without reference to God. This situation is exacerbated when Haman arranges for the issuing of an edict for the destruction of the Jews (Esther 3). Much like the wicked described in Ps. 10:1-11, Haman plans to attack the weak with no assumption that God would act against him.

---

23. Melton (2018) demonstrates that it participates in a dialogue on this theme within the *Megilloth*. See Melton (2018, 35–8) for an overview of proposals for divine presence in Esther.

Second, Haman's edict places the Jews into the sort of social context presumed by Psalms 11–12, in which society as a whole appears to have no foundations. He is one who has clearly lied to the king even as he flatters him (cf. Ps. 12:4 [3]) and "loves violence" (Ps. 11:5), illustrated by the inordinate size of the gallows he constructs and his desire to obliterate all the Jews in Persia on account of his hatred of one man (Est. 5:14; 3:6).[24] This is a world from which one may well wish to flee because the wicked believe they can act with impunity (cf., Ps. 11:2). Indeed, when Haman is finally unmasked by Esther to the king, she describes him first as a "foe" (צר) and an "enemy" (אויב) before specifically calling him "this wicked Haman" (Est. 7:6).[25] Although language of enemies is widespread throughout the Hebrew Bible, it is particularly common in the Psalter. For our purposes, it is noteworthy that the combination of "foe" and "enemy" also occurs in Ps. 13:5 [4] when citing the potential speech of those acting against the psalmist (though with the addition of 1cs pronominal suffixes: איבי...צרי). Within Esther, Haman had accepted the invitation to the feast with the king and queen while expecting to triumph over Mordecai, but this wish had been subverted in the events of Esther 6. Just as his anticipated triumph had been lost, so Psalm 13 also anticipates the point when the enemy will fail, though exactly how God would do this is not mentioned. Haman's wife Zeresh and his "wise men" arguably anticipate his downfall along this same reasoning (Est. 6:13). By contrast, Haman experiences his downfall as an unanticipated reality, as he seems to think he answers to no one but the king he is manipulating (cf., Ps. 12:5 [4]). In referring to Haman as רע (Est. 7:6), Esther uses a term for the wicked that is less common than רשע in Psalms 9–14, though Ps. 10:15 does ask YHWH to act against them, breaking their power. It is also interesting that the "wicked" who will be shown their limits from Psalm 9 include "nations that forget God" (v. 18 [17]).[26] Read alongside this background, we can see that Haman's fall can be understood as an example of YHWH destroying the power of the wicked even in a foreign nation. And indeed, just as Ps. 14:7 had anticipated rejoicing in a change of circumstances, so also the Jews rejoice in their deliverance (Est. 8:17; 9:17, 19); their sorrow is followed by gladness and "relief from their enemies" (Est. 9:16, 22) who no longer exalt over them (see Ps. 13:3 [2]; cf., 14:7).

In treating Psalms 9–14 there was one absence on which we did not comment, and that is that although these poems ask in various ways for YHWH to break the power of the wicked, they never specify the means by which this is to be done. God is asked to rise and judge the wicked, but no mechanism for this is given. A reader who only reads the Psalter may expect this to be only through direct divine intervention, especially if YHWH does indeed watch over the way of the

---

24. Ps. 10:7-9 also presents an apt description of Haman, and Ps. 14:4 could serve as a comment on his grotesque ability to envision the destruction of God's people amidst indulgent feasting—"evildoers who eat up my people as they eat bread."

25. Consider also Esther exposing Haman's wickedness in 7:6 alongside Ps. 10:15, which asks God to call wickedness to account.

26. See also Ps. 9:20: "Let the nations know that they are but men!"

righteous (Ps. 1:6). But this is not required, and even Psalm 1 does not specify that the wicked are destroyed this way. Wickedness may be destroyed because it is inherently unable to sustain a society in the way that righteousness does, but Esther proposes another option, which is that God acts through his people when they commit themselves to him. In contrast to Duvall and Hays (2019, 90), who assert "the complete absence of any reference to God in the book of Esther is a reminder that they are still in exile, separated from the blessings and protection that the relational presence of God would bring," it would seem this is exactly the type of divine presence that perhaps is evidenced in the book (i.e., *protection* of God through impeccably timed reversals and the courage of his people to stand up to the wicked).[27] Here again, it should be reiterated that the means by which justice will come is not spelled out in Psalms 9–14; it is simply to be anticipated that wickedness against the righteous will not go unanswered forever. Has God "hear[d] the desire of the afflicted" in Persia and "do[ne] justice to the fatherless [Esther] and the oppressed [Mordecai], so that man [Haman] who is of the earth may strike terror no more" (Ps. 10:18) through courage of the afflicted ones? These psalms not only shed light on the theological context in which we might read Esther, but Esther also sheds light on how we read these psalms.

Conclusion

Although Esther and Psalms might not be texts that we would immediately associate with one another, reading them alongside one another sheds light on the important theological issues of theodicy and seeming divine absence. Both Psalms 9–14 and Esther wrestle with the issue of divine absence, something that is more explicitly associated with the question of theodicy in Psalms. But once the connections between the texts are recognized, it turns out that even Esther, a book that seems to avoid mentioning God, can also be a significant resource for engaging with the issue of theodicy. Divine absence is a theme in Esther that is easily recognized, even if readers must wrestle with the question of whether this is a literary strategy or a theological position. When we see how closely Psalms 9–14 and Esther intertextually map onto one another, we have more reason for thinking this is a theological choice. Conversely, if this is a theological choice, then the relationship with Psalms 9–14 also means that Esther is, perhaps unexpectedly, an important resource for reflecting on the questions of theodicy.

---

27. See further Melton (2018, 149–63).

Chapter 9

READING ESTHER WITH PROVERBS: COMPLEXIFYING CHARACTER, THEME, AND IDEOLOGY

Suzanna R. Millar

Introduction

In the 1950s and 1960s, a flurry of studies claimed to have discovered "wisdom influence" in biblical narratives, often comparing them to the book of Proverbs. The "wisdom" label was excitedly applied to, for example, the Joseph saga (von Rad 1953), Succession Narrative (Whybray 1968), and the book of Esther (Talmon 1963). Talmon proposed to read Esther as a "historicized wisdom-tale" (1963, 426), which displayed the sayings from Proverbs applied to life. Talmon's suggestion has been influential (e.g., Loader 1978; van Uchelen 1974; Wilson 1990). He found similarities to Proverbs in, for example, the book's lack of Jewish religiosity, history, and institutions; depiction of the "wise courtier"; paradigmatic character types; and exemplification of just consequences. However, Talmon's proposal has also been seriously questioned: Crenshaw (1969, 141) asserts that "it is difficult to conceive of a book more alien to wisdom literature than Esther," and Fox (1991b, 143) asserts that "Esther is not affiliated with Wisdom by even the broadest definition." Furthermore, recent scholars have seriously questioned the very idea of "wisdom influence" (Kynes 2015; Sneed 2011), and even of "wisdom literature" (Kynes 2019).

This chapter will thus not use Proverbs to determine "wisdom influence" in Esther. My intertextual method is synchronic rather than diachronic. I propose to read Esther and Proverbs as mutually enlightening, observing what happens when they interact. I suggest that when they do, the complexity of each is revealed, in their representations of characters, themes, and ideologies.

Character

Talmon (1963, 440) likened Esther to Proverbs for depicting static character types. In both, he said, characters lack depth and development, merely representing virtues and vices. Scholars have subsequently found this to be a gross distortion of the complexity in Esther (e.g., Fox 1991b, 143). Esther herself is changeable and psychologically real, refusing to conform to simple paradigms of wisdom. Such simple paradigms are, most assume, found in Proverbs. Indeed, it offers a cast of antithetical personae: Lady Wisdom and Lady Folly, wise man and fool, righteous and wicked, father and son. However, this superficial polarization masks complexities (Millar 2020, 89–110), which Esther can help reveal.

Theme

Talmon (1963, 427) based his approach on thematic connections, "general trends and ideas" evident in both texts. He demonstrated this by applying individual proverbs to situations in Esther. And indeed, this follows the conventions of the proverb genre: proverb meaning resides not in the text alone but in its application to circumstances (Kirshenblatt-Gimblett 1973).

However, this search for "proverb correlates" has been widely criticized as methodologically unsound (e.g., Fox 1991b, 143). First, applying one proverb alone ignores potential alternatives. Proverbs is not single-voiced but is strewn with competing opinions and even contradictions (e.g., Prov. 17:27-28; 26:4-5; Hatton 2008), showing awareness that situations can have diverse interpretations. By applying a single proverb, the speaker claims to offer *the* interpretation. Talmon thus pronounces his verdict, but we might sound the contradictory voices. Second, some proverbs that Talmon invokes do not straightforwardly support his case. Indeed, proverbs—with their concise form, ambiguous syntax, and open-ended imagery—often have numerous possible interpretations, making them multi-applicable (Millar 2020). Talmon might highlight one interpretation, and we discover another that does not so readily apply. Talmon then, in the manner of a proverb-speaker, reduces the thematic complexity in both texts. Fresh intertextual analysis may shed new light.

Ideology

Ideological analyses are increasingly popular in biblical studies. Esther provides particularly fertile terrain for, for example, postcolonial and feminist critics (e.g., Beal 1997). The power dynamics of empire, age, ethnicity, gender, and status interact fractiously and propel the story forward. These dynamics are less evident in Proverbs. While some suggest that the book's origin was in the wranglings of the court (Talmon 1963), its current form subsumes politics with a moralizing tenor. Viewing it in light of Esther can help expose the powers at play.

These three concerns—character, theme, and ideology—will weave through my analysis below. To limit the study, I will focus mainly on Esther herself in the MT, in her relationship with authority (§1), seduction (§2), and justice (§3). I will bring Esther's story into interaction with Proverbs, exploring the complexities revealed in both.

Authority

Parental Authority

Both books begin by focalizing youths: Proverbs' anonymous young man (נַעַר; Prov. 1:4) stands alongside Esther the young woman (נַעֲרָה; Est. 2:7). Proverbs celebrates youth with the sincerity of moralized rhetoric: Wisdom herself is a child brought up (אָמוֹן),[1] playing in delight (Prov. 8:30). By contrast, a shadow is cast over Esther's youth: both parents dead, she is brought up (אמן) by her cousin Mordecai (Est. 2:7).

For both, though, youth is characterized by obedience. Filial relationships act as mechanisms for social control of an unpredictable generation. Proverbs moralizes this intergenerational power balance. In its prologue, the father's voice mingles with Lady Wisdom's, and throughout, obedience is connected with becoming wise (e.g., Prov. 4:1-5; 7:1-5; 10:8; 13:1; 15:5). At the start of her story, Esther embodies the paradigmatic submissive youth. She twice allows herself to be "taken" (לקח), first into Mordecai's guardianship (Est. 2:7), then into the king's harem (2:8). In both settings, she exhibits perfect obedience (2:10, 15, 20).

On the surface, then, Proverbs' נַעַר and Esther the נַעֲרָה are commendable for their filial submission. But there are cracks beneath this façade. For all its insistence that the generational hierarchy maps onto the moral hierarchy, Proverbs remains aware that not all instructors are wise, not all advice should be followed (e.g., Prov. 12:26b; 16:29). The נַעַר is close to the "simpleton" (פֶּתִי), who may be swayed to a foolish course (1:32; 7:6-23; 14 15).

Mordecai's advice to Esther—to conceal her ethnicity (Est. 2:10, 20)—is morally ambiguous. Possibly, it constitutes wise restraint in speech. Thus Talmon (1963, 447) notes that Mordecai "[knows] that secretiveness goes with the wise courtier's metier (Prov. xii 23) and that talkativeness spells disaster (ib. xiii 2 [sic, xiii 3 intended?])." Talmon here invokes two proverbs and claims them as the proper interpretation of Mordecai's character: he is a prudent man who conceals knowledge (12:23), not one who opens his lips and comes to ruin (13:3). But no situation is monolithic, and a proverb can capture only one aspect of it. We might apply to Mordecai and Esther not only laudatory proverbs advocating restraint (e.g., 10:19; 11:12; 17:27) but also more damning proverbs condemning deception (e.g., 6:17-19; 12:17-19). We thus expose Proverbs' ambivalence about a central theme in Esther: concealment.[2] Is Esther the understanding one who remains silent (Prov. 11:12) or the liar who gives ear to the destructive tongue (17:4)?

Esther, then, vacillates between the types of youth offered by Proverbs: wise son and naïve simpleton. But she further ambiguates this dynamic, instigating a role reversal that sees her as "parent" and Mordecai as "child." In ch. 4, Mordecai initially wishes to "command" (צוה) Est. (4:8), but instead she "commands" (צוה) him, and

---

1. The meaning of this term is disputed. Common interpretations are "one brought up" (KJV), "master workman" (ESV), and "constant(ly)" (NIV) (Fox 1996).

2. Beal (1997) describes Esther as *The Book of Hiding*.

he obeys in everything (4:15-17). Her removal to the palace and marriage to the king have functioned akin to a rite of passage to adulthood,[3] and her character has developed, acquiring authority and voice. By the end of the book, Esther and Mordecai have joint command over the festivities of all Jews (9:29-32).

Refracting this back onto Proverbs illuminates a potential progression there too. Proverbs may present, not static, unchanging characters but "the process of maturation from receptive child to responsible adult, from dependent to patriarch" (Brown 2002, 153). William Brown traces how, as the book progresses, its complexity increases in form and content, and its social purview widens. Though it begins with a naïve child (chs 1-9), it ends with a king and matriarch (ch. 31). The interpellated reader develops, Esther-like, from obedient and submissive to wielding patriarchal authority (Brown 2002, 181).

Royal Authority

In the scene preceding Esther's assumption of authority, the ambiguity of obedience is exposed. Should Esther obey her guardian and plead before the king (4:8)? Or should she obey the king and refrain from appearing before him (4:11)? Esther obeys neither, rather assuming control herself. But the question emerges of clashing loyalties: family or state, parent or monarch? This frictional relationship is evident in both texts. In Esther, Ahasuerus' palace functions as both domestic and political space. Esther's interactions with her husband and king occur in the bedroom, throne-room, and banquet hall, hybrid spaces for personal and procedural wranglings. The final chapter of Proverbs subsumes the political within the domestic (Brown 2002, 181), as King Lemuel is chided by his mother (Prov. 31:1-9), and the mistress of the household is extolled in terms fitting for a queen (31:10-31; Brown 2002, 181).

Wherever their prime loyalties lie, both books note the dire consequences of rebelling against royal power. When Mordecai refuses to bow to Haman, the highest court official (Est. 3:2), the extermination of all Jews is declared (3:8-11); and Esther fears that disobeying the king will cost her life (4:11, 16).[4] Similarly, certain proverbs describe a fearsome king: "The king's anger is a messenger of death; a wise man will appease it" (Prov. 16:14); "The king's terror is a growling like a lion; whoever enrages him forfeits his life (/sins against himself[5])" (20:2).

Talmon (1963, 441-3) applies these proverbs to Ahasuerus, arguing that they show him as a traditional wisdom type, the irascible "witless king." This character type is "conceited, irritable and unpredictable," acting with anger and haste. And indeed, the proverbs might be taken negatively, as Talmon assumes. The "messengers" of 16:14 (be they human, divine, or metaphorical) may deliver

---

3. McGeough (2008, 51) discusses (though does not affirm) this suggestion.

4. We might also compare the fate of Vashti. The king's terrifying nature is heightened in LXX Esther (e.g., 5:6-7, 13).

5. Heb: חוֹטֵא נַפְשׁוֹ. See discussion in Millar (2020, 186–7).

death undeserved. The "lion" of 20:2 is a common biblical metaphor for terrifying enemies (e.g., Isa. 5:29; Jer. 50:17; Joel 1:6; Ps. 7:3[2]), naturally ferocious and indiscriminately violent. Elsewhere in Proverbs the lion depicts a "wicked ruler" (28:15).

Yet leonine and deathly grandeur may be appropriate qualities for a king; 16:14 occurs in a proverb cluster that glorifies the king (16:10-15), using for him language reserved elsewhere for God (Kim 2011). The king, like God, brings both life (16:15) and death (16:14), and has leonine ferocity (20:2). Elsewhere in the ANE, the lion is a rote characterization in royal self-glorifications.[6] These proverbs may thus see the king as "the earthly embodiment of divine *mysterium tremendum*" (Brown 2002, 180). Talmon's application ignores these possible alternatives.

Furthermore, these proverbs might be applied, not to King Ahasuerus but to Esther in her interactions with him. Esther fears that she will enrage him and forfeit her life (Prov. 20:2; Est. 4:11, 16), and attempts to assuage him with wise words (Prov. 16:14). Proverbs here maps moral language onto the political sphere. The "wise" (חכם) man appeases the king, while the one who enrages him "sins" (חטא).[7] In the ethical context of Proverbs, these terms are moralistic. Applying them to Esther, however, removes this moralism. With the knowing wink of inverted commas, Talmon (1963, 433) thus describes "the 'wise' courtier" who succeeds through the "ruthless application of ... ruses."

Seduction

Silent Seduction

Esther plays out in the context of empire. Persia is the prevailing power, centered on the citadel at Susa, where Esther and Mordecai live as representatives of a minority Jewish culture. Their ethnicity is immediately evident in their introduction: אִישׁ יְהוּדִי הָיָה "a Jewish man there was ..." (Est. 2:5). And the danger of their ethnicity is apparent: Mordecai commands Esther not to make it known (2:10, 20), and he possibly claims it as the reason for his own disobedience (3:4). Jewish laws become the pretext for Haman's attempted ethnic cleansing (3:8-9).

The dynamics of interacting ethnicities raise the question of who, in this story, are the "foreigners." From the perspective of the implied narrator, the Jews are the in-group; other peoples are foreign. It is with the Jews that the story's sympathies lie. Yet, within the political dynamics of the story-world, Persians are the in-group; the Jews are foreign. They are ethnic Others, a diaspora people under Persian power.

Esther is thus afforded both insider and outsider status; she is both quintessential Israelite and foreign woman. This has interesting resonances with Proverbs.

---

6. E.g., Adadnarari II: "I am king, I am lord, I am powerful ... I am a virile lion ... I am raging" (Strawn 2005, 58).

7. The root חטא is almost always morally imbued. Even if the phrase חוֹטֵא נַפְשׁוֹ is translated "forfeits his life," the moral connotations may ring out.

Proverbs is, ostensibly, unconcerned with ethnicity. And yet, unease about foreignness manifests itself at pivotal moments, in warnings about the "Foreign Woman" (נָכְרִיָּה; 2:16; 6:24; 7:5; 23:27). Like Esther, she lives within a prevailing order, threatening to disrupt it. Some contend that נָכְרִי ("foreign") should not be taken literally here, as describing ethnicity, but rather metaphorically, as describing a dangerous outsider (Tan 2008, 3–13). But even if so, this metaphor depends on an ideological assumption about ethnic foreignness: it is dangerous and unwanted. In Proverbs, ethnicity and morality coalesce: the Foreign Woman is outside ethnic norms, so must be outside ethical norms too. Thus, it is little surprise that she is associated with the "strange woman" (אִשָּׁה זָרָה; 2:16; 7:5), "evil woman" (אֵשֶׁת רָע; 6:24), and "prostitute" (זוֹנָה; 23:27).

The Foreign Woman is particularly dangerous because of her exotic allure (note her Egyptian linens and exotic spices; 7:16-17). Throughout the history of empires, foreign females have been depicted with beauty and "luxuriant and seemingly unbounded sexuality" (Said 2003, 187). Thus, the king's harem is made up of women, probably multiethnic, from all the provinces: the most beautiful in the land (2:3). Indeed, Esther is introduced via her physical appearance: she "had a beautiful form and attractive appearance" (2:7). Physical beauty is ambiguous, sometimes associated with moral rectitude or divine favor (1 Sam. 16:12), sometimes with immorality and seduction (Ezek. 16:15). Esther's beauty might position her like Lady Wisdom, whose allure goes beyond that of precious jewels (Prov. 3:15), or like the Foreign Woman, whose beauty must not be desired (6:25). Capturing the ambiguous quality of feminine wiles, Proverbs concludes that grace is deception and beauty vanity (שֶׁקֶר הַחֵן וְהֶבֶל הַיֹּפִי; 31:30). Thus, when Esther acquires "grace" (חֵן) from the king (Est. 2:15, 17), this may not be straightforwardly positive. Indeed, the woman of grace (אֵשֶׁת חֵן) who attains honor may have a moral status akin to violent men (Prov. 11:16).

In the king's harem, Esther undergoes a year-long beauty regime: "six months with oil of myrrh and six months with spices and ointments" (Est. 2:12). Cosmetics function as communicative devices, culturally encoded social signifiers. Specifically, they may communicate sexual intention (Quick 2019). Esther's use of myrrh and spices may whiff of the Foreign Woman's, for the latter takes "myrrh, aloes, and cinnamon" (Prov. 7:17) to fragrance her conjugal bed. It is the scent of seduction (cf., Song 1:13; 5:5, 13; Ps. 45:8). Proverbs' moralism retches at the odor, but Esther casts no moral aspersions.

An overnight sexual tryst is indicated in both texts. In Esther, each young virgin comes to the king by evening and leaves the following morning (Est. 2:14). Esther dutifully follows this protocol (2:15-17). Similarly, the Foreign Woman goes out by twilight (Prov. 7:9) and invites her lover to be with her until morning (7:18).

The difference lies in the manner of and judgment given to the women's behavior. The Foreign Woman is brazen, assertive, and verbose. Esther is passive and silent. In effect, Esther simultaneously plays both roles from the vignette of Proverbs 7: Foreign Woman and naïve youth. Furthermore, Esther's behavior is not judged negatively but follows a pattern of acceptable female sexuality (e.g., Genesis 38, Ruth 3). In a value system structured by the politics of the Persian court, Esther plays her assigned role, submissive within a gendered hierarchy. By contrast, Proverbs' Foreign Woman subverts patriarchal norms by playing the dominant partner and transgressing marital expectations. Sexuality, though, does not completely separate the Foreign Woman from her positive counterparts. Both she and Lady Wisdom are embraced (חבק; Prov. 5:20; 4:8); both she and the good wife offer saturation (רוה) in love (7:18; 5:19; Aletti 1977). Proverbs' paradigms of wisdom and folly are not as polarized as is sometimes asserted, and Esther conforms wholly to neither.

Smooth-Spoken Seduction

If Esther seems passive and silent in Esther 2, this soon changes as she becomes increasingly active and outspoken. Esther crafts a plan to save her people, preparing two sequential banquets, to which she invites Ahasuerus and Haman. The opulence and intoxication of each "wine party" (מִשְׁתֵּה הַיַּיִן; 5:7; 7:2) provide opportune circumstances to ply the king. Esther's strategy is appropriate in a book whose comico-serious plot is structured by the revelry of feasting (Berlin 2001, xxiv). Perhaps in a cynical comment on political absurdity, the wine-soaked banquet hall is the setting for major political decisions.

Proverbs is uneasy about such inebriation (20:1; 23:20-21, 29-35). Tongue in cheek, we might warn Ahasuerus with the words of Lemuel's mother (Prov. 31:3-5):

> [3] Do not give your strength to women,
> *[not even to beautiful Queen Esther]*
> your ways to those who destroy kings.
> [4] It is not for kings, O *[Ahasuerus]*,
>   it is not for kings to drink wine,
>   or for rulers to take strong drink,
> *[not even at Esther's wine party]*
> [5] lest they drink and forget what has been decreed
> *[like Haman's decree]*
> and change the judgment[8] over all the afflicted.
> *[like the judgment over the Jews]*

If Ahasuerus was so warned, he does not heed the advice. He succumbs to Esther's ploy and changes the judgment.

Speaking at these banquets, Esther tries her skills of courtly rhetoric. Her language is stylized and verbose, speaking of the king in the third person, with polite jussives rather than abrupt imperatives. She proliferates declarations of deference: "If I have found favor in the king's sight," "if it please the king" (5:8; 7:3).

---

8. The phrase translated "change the judgment" is usually taken negatively, as "pervert the rights" or similar, which makes sense within the context of Proverbs. However, the Hebrew—וִישַׁנֶּה דִּין—is more neutral.

She is self-deprecating and plays into Ahasuerus' ego (7:4), before her dramatic accusation (7:6).

Talmon (1963, 437) pronounces the verdict on Esther's rhetoric: she "quite decidedly masters courtiers' speech." Like the gracious speaker of Prov. 22:11 and the soft-tongued of 25:15, smooth-spoken Esther persuades the king (Talmon 1963, 436). Yet Proverbs is ambivalent about speech, such that Esther conforms to no straightforward paradigm. If these proverbs might demonstrate Esther's wisdom, others might display her folly. Indeed, both Lady Wisdom and Lady Folly are adept in verbal arts. Lady Folly speaks with "smooth words" (Prov. 2:16; 5:3; 6:24; 7:5, 21), with lips that "drip honey" (5:3). Her prime tool of seduction is her tongue.

Lady Folly's speech is particularly dangerous and effective because it resembles Lady Wisdom's (Aletti 1977; Camp 2000, 80–3). Both women, Esther-like, stage feasts. And both call out identically, as though to Ahasuerus and Haman, "Whoever is simple, let him turn in here!" (Prov. 9:4, 16). The naïve simpleton is their target, who is precariously ill-equipped to distinguish between their calls. But the true contrast is stark: Wisdom's Feast is characterized by clarity and life (9:6); Folly's by secretiveness and death (9:17-18). Esther's feast, paradoxically, embodies both poles. Like Lady Folly, Esther moves in secrecy and seduction. She lures the men to the banquet without revealing her intentions and offers "deceptive food" (23:3). Her invitation will result in death for one unsuspecting guest (Est. 7:7-10; Prov. 9:18). But, like Lady Wisdom's, her call is noble, ultimately intended to reveal the truth (in her case, of Haman's plot), and directed to the fundamental aim of life for her people (Est. 7:3-4; Prov. 9:6).

Justice

Human and Divine Initiative

God is never mentioned in MT Esther. This has provoked extensive ink-spilling about divine activity "behind the scenes," allegedly drawing Esther close to the wisdom books (e.g., Talmon 1963, 427–30). I cannot fully address this issue but will focus on Esther's own response to possible divine activity. In her famous exchange with Mordecai, she is told that if she does not act, "relief and deliverance will rise for the Jews from another place" (4:14). Mordecai is sure that the Jews will be delivered (נצל) but less clear about how. The "other place" is sometimes taken as a veiled reference to the deity (Berlin 2001, 44); sometimes as a comment on Jewish resilience (Fox 1991b, 244). Similarly, several proverbs are certain of deliverance (נצל), without specifying any divine or human agent (e.g., Prov. 10:2; 11:4, 6; 12:6). Strikingly though, deliverance in Proverbs is morally circumscribed: it comes through righteousness (צְדָקָה; Prov. 10:2; 11:4, 6) to the upright (יְשָׁרִים; Prov. 11:6; 12:6). In Proverbs, the criterion for deliverance is ethics; in Esther it is ethnic.

Mordecai is suggestive but uncertain about Esther's role: "Who knows whether you have not come to the kingdom for such a time as this" (4:14). Mordecai raises the tentative possibility of providence, his "who knows" voicing the perpetual "perhaps" of divine inscrutability. Though the divine hand is more evident in Proverbs, similar sentiments are found there too: "From Yahweh are a man's steps; as for a person, how can he understand his way?" (Prov. 20:24).

If Mordecai is implying a divinely ordained task, then Esther might accept or resist it. Here we enter the fraught interplay of divine and human initiative frequently sounded in Proverbs. Proverbs never resolves this, and several proverbs exasperate it (Millar 2020, 212–18). In effect, Esther's moment of decision dances on the possible interpretations of Prov. 16:9. Her response—accepting or rejecting providence—will determine which interpretation pertains.

"The heart of a man devises his way; Yahweh establishes his step" (Prov. 16:9). The first half of this proverb concerns human initiative; the second half divine initiative. Ambiguities stem from the unclear relationship between the halves and the referent of the suffix on צַעֲדוֹ, "his step." If Esther accepts providence, the proverb might be understood by synonymous parallelism: A human (like Esther or Mordecai) has responsibility to devise plans and initiate action, *and then* Yahweh will uphold "his" (the human's) plans. If, however, Esther rejects providence, then antithetical parallelism might pertain: Esther can devise whatever plans she will, *but* Yahweh will establish "his" (own) steps nonetheless, saving the Jews by another means.

Esther accepts, but with no easy confidence of success. She immediately calls a fast (4:16). Though she does not explicitly command prayer,[9] this communal posture of submission strongly suggests supplication of a higher force. God is not guaranteed to endorse the initiative; he must be called upon to act. The fast should, in effect, synchronize human and divine footfall: "his" (Yahweh's) step brought in sync with "his" (the human's).

Poetic Justice

On the surface at least, Esther's plot is driven by human initiative. But it is punctured by several notable "coincidences," perhaps suggestive of an unseen directing force. Ahasuerus "just happens" to use the account of Mordecai to cure his insomnia (6:1-2), and as he is planning how to honor him, Haman "just happens" to enter the court (6:4). Later, Ahasuerus "just happens" to see Haman throw himself on Esther (7:8).

There is an inevitability about this coincidence-strewn and peripeteian plot: justice will be done, fortunes reversed, wrongs righted. And the punishment will fit the crime. Thus, after Haman happens upon the court, he is forced to honor Mordecai in the very way he wanted to be honored himself (6:11). After he happens to be seen falling upon Esther, he is executed on the very gallows he had built for Mordecai (7:10). This poetic justice makes amply applicable the proverb-speaker's

---

9. Compare LXX Esther, in which both Esther and Mordecai pray at length.

words: "Whoever builds a pit will fall into it; whoever rolls a stone, to him it will return" (26:27). Whoever builds a gallows, we might add.

This proverb could be applied here piously, as an expression of divinely ordained world order. Yet Esther's tone teeters on the impiety of carnivalesque (Berlin 2001, xxi–xxii), and the proverb may quip about the ironic twist of fate that frequently structures "gallows humour" (O'Neill 1983, 153). What's more, the events leading to Haman's death contain moral ambiguities. In Esther 7, Haman falls on Esther's couch to plead for his life. Seeing this, Ahasuerus mistakenly thinks that Haman is assaulting Esther (7:8). Action proceeds quickly: Haman's face may be covered (7:8),[10] the verdict is pronounced (7:9), Haman is executed (7:10). Thus, the immediate reason for his execution—his assault of the queen—is a false accusation. Esther (alone?) knows the true situation yet refuses to correct the mistake. If the book's overall structure tends toward Proverbial justice, the immediate circumstances do not. And Esther herself comes close to that most feared "false witness" (Prov. 6:19; 12:17; 14:5; 19:5; 21:28; 24:28).

Violence

In other ways too, the "justice" of the book raises ethical quandaries. Most notably, Esther and Mordecai meet violence with violence. They issue a degree giving Jews permission "to destroy, to kill, and to annihilate" (לְהַשְׁמִיד וְלַהֲרֹג וּלְאַבֵּד) anyone who threatens them, women and children included (Est. 8:11; cf., 3:13). In the citadel, Esther pleads that the bloodbath continue for an additional day (9:13). Ultimately, they kill 75,000 enemies (9:16). Many have been troubled by this apparent brutality and vindictiveness (Harvey 2014, 39–43, 49–55).

Indeed, by the standards of Proverbs, it seems at first condemnable, contravening prohibitions of violence (e.g., Prov. 3:31; 16:29; 21:7; 24:1-2) and vengeance (20:22; 24:29). Yet Esther and Mordecai's actions may extrapolate Proverbial logic. Proverbs has twin emphases on human agency and the downfall of the wicked. It is not a far step to make the former responsible for the latter. Other ambiguities about violence emerge too. Ostensibly, Lady Wisdom offers peace (Prov. 3:17), while Lady Folly is as destructive as a sword (5:4), fire (6:27), or snare (7:23). And yet, a disturbingly violent outburst punctures Lady Wisdom's first speech. She laughs and mocks at the calamity of her enemies, reveling in their distress, and refusing to listen to their cries (1:26-28). The violence expected of Folly interjects itself into Wisdom, as it does into Esther.

What's more, such behavior may be rewarded: "a woman of grace takes hold of honor; violent people take hold of wealth" (Prov. 11:16). Above, I briefly commented on the juxtaposition of characters in this proverb, suggesting that the negative connotations of "violent people" may color the "woman of grace" in an unpleasant hue. But the reverse may also be the case: the face-value positivity of "grace" refracts onto the "violent people," dressing them with moral worth. The

---

10. The meaning of this verse is somewhat unclear (Fox 1991b, 283–4).

close interplay of ambiguous characters, jostling together in cryptic parallelism, makes multiple interpretations possible, highlighting the complexity in Proverbs' portraits of character.

Conclusion

In his argument for "wisdom influence," Talmon characterized both Esther and Proverbs as straightforward works, lacking in depth and complexity. Our intertextual analysis, however, has revealed just the opposite. Reading Esther in light of Proverbs suggests that the *character* Esther is not simply a paradigm of wisdom but much more complex. She interacts with and adopts the guise of several Proverbial players: obedient child, naïve youth, and wise instructor; Foreign Woman and Lady Wisdom; agent of justice and false witness. Embodied in the same individual, these characters are not straightforwardly antithetical. And indeed, in Proverbs itself, we find points of correspondence between the apparent opposites, complexifying its alleged simplicity.

The *themes* in Esther cannot be straightforwardly captured in individual proverbs. Any attempt to do so throws up the thematic ambiguity of Esther and the multiplicity of Proverbial perspectives. Thus, Proverbs condones silence but condemns deception. Esther is rife with concealment, which hovers between the two. Proverbs advocates eloquence but forbids seductive speech. Esther exemplifies eloquent seduction. At times too, we have found proverbs applied to Esther as though they straightforwardly summarize a theme (e.g., Prov. 11:6; 16:9, 14; 20:2), yet our analyses have unearthed ambiguities.

Attention to the *ideologies* of both texts has revealed that both worlds are undergirded by power dynamics: instructor/child; insider/foreigner; king/courtier; male/female. These dynamics are evident in Esther, as essential engines driving the plot. They are not given explicit value judgments, but the turn of events demonstrates where loyalties lie. In Proverbs, these dynamics are moralized: a deft ideological move maps social hierarchy onto moral hierarchy. However, Proverbs' complex view of character problematizes this: the instructor is not always wise; the king not always righteous.

Taken individually, both Esther and Proverbs might at first seem clear and straightforward. But this intertextual analysis has complexified the picture. The friction between the texts has not sanded away their rough edges but rather removed their façades, exposing the complex structures beneath.

Part V

ESTHER IN DIALOGUE BEYOND THE HEBREW BIBLE

Chapter 10

TRAUMA, PURITY, AND DANGER IN THE LXX PRAYERS OF ESTHER AND JUDITH

Helen Efthimiadis-Keith (Keith-van Wyk)[1]

Introduction

LXX Esther (henceforth, *Esther*) and Judith's prayers (Add. Est. C:14-30, Jdt. 9:2-14)[2] have often been favorably compared as to their narrative situation, structure, type, and sociohistorical context. It is correctly noted, for example, that they are centrally situated and catalytic for the reversals of fortune that occur thereafter. Similarly, they are aimed at eliciting God's deliverance of the Jews and empowerment of the female intercessors. They may further be dated to roughly the same period, namely the late Hellenistic/early Roman period, prior to the destruction of the Second Temple (Van Der Walt 2008). It has been noted, incorrectly in the case of Judith (Efthimiadis-Keith 2014, 872–6), that both prayers subscribe to Deuteronomic ideology and contain elements common to petitionary prayers of the Second Temple period (Balentine 2006, 4–5). Their emotionality has been noted severally (Ego 2015; Gera 2014, 311, 322). What has not been noted is that they turn on the concept of purity—of the intercessor in *Esther* and of the nation in *Judith*. Neither have they been analyzed from a trauma perspective.

In this chapter, I will focus on purity and danger in these prayers, analyzing them comparatively through the lens of trauma. I begin with a brief description of each prayer, its textual context, and its structure.

---

1. Associate Professor in Biblical Hebrew and Hebrew Bible/Old Testament, University of Kwazulu Natal.

2. "*Esther*"/"*Judith*" refer to the LXX books, whereas "Esther"/"Judith" refer to the characters. The essay is based on the B-text, using the NETS numbering and versification. All English translations stem from the NETS, while Greek quotations are taken from Rahlfs' Septuagint. Additions to Esther will henceforth be referred to by their representative letter, e.g., B.

Textual Context and Structure of the Prayers

As indicated, the prayers' textual context is similar. In *Esther*, the Jews stand to be annihilated because of Aman's hatred for Mardochaios (henceforth, Mordecai), who refuses to bow before him (Est. 3:1-6).[3] Aman is Artaxerxes' vizier (3:1-2) and Holofernes is Nebuchadnezzar's chief general (Jdt. 2:4). These men are given *carte blanche* in dealing with the "hostile," "disobedient" Judeans (Est. 3:2-3, 8-12, B:4-5; Jdt. 2:5-12, 4:1–5:2). As such, Aman aims to annihilate them in one day (Est. 3:7), and Holofernes aims to destroy the Jews by capturing the Bethulians' water spring (Jdt. 7:7, 12-22, 29). The terrified Jews engage in vigorous prayer and mourning rituals (Est. 3:15, 4:1, 3-4, C; Jdt. 4:2, 9-15, 6:18-19, 21). Mordecai instructs Esther, through her eunuch, to intercede on the Jews' behalf with Artaxerxes, her husband (Est. 4:7-8). She is hesitant, fearful, as no-one could approach him unbidden on pain of death. To make things worse, he had not called her for thirty days. She could die (4:10-11). After Mordecai's thinly veiled threat (4:13-14), Esther calls for a three-day fast (4:15) and goes through an extensive self-degrading mourning ritual (C:7-13) before praying. After her prayer, she dresses in royal finery (D:1-2, 5) and approaches Artaxerxes in terror, fainting twice (D:3, 7, 12-15). However, she executes a clever plan to out Aman by inviting only him and Artaxerxes to two successive banquets (5:4, 8). At the second, she implores the king for her and her people's lives (7:1-6). Aman is hung and the Jews are saved through a second edict (negotiated by Esther) granting them the right to defend themselves (8:5-12, E). The Jews rejoice and rout their enemies (8:15–9:11, 9:12-15). Mordecai becomes vizier (8:2, 15) and Esther (with Mordecai) institutes the Purim feast in celebration and remembrance of the day that God gave the Jews the victory (9:29-31, see also 7:22-23, 9:17-19).

With *Judith*, Judith hears of the ultimatum that the Bethulians have given God (Jdt. 8:1, 9): should He not save them in five days, they would surrender to Holofernes (7:23-31). Contrary to Esther, Judith shows no fear. She upbraids the elders for trying to force God's hand and promises that God will deliver them by her hand before the five days are up (8:10-36). She too engages in (less severe) self-deprecating rituals before her prayer. Having prayed, she dons her finery (10:1-4) and descends to the enemy camp with her maid (9:5-11). Claiming that the Jews had defiled themselves by eating forbidden food, she promises the lust-struck Holofernes that she would lead him right into Jerusalem in victory once she hears that the people had sinned by also eating items reserved for the priests (11:12-19). After a private banquet,[4] at which Holofernes aimed to seduce her, Judith decapitates the drunken man and returns to Bethuliah with his head in her food basket (12:10–13:11). The Jews are elated, praising God and Judith.

---

3. For an analysis of Mordecai's refusal to bow, see Ego (2010).

4. Regrettably, spatial constraints prevent me from dealing with the similarities and differences between the banquet scenes throughout these books. For a discussion of some of these and their relation to other biblical banquets, see Gera (2014, 132, 370, 383-4).

As with *Esther*, where gentiles are converted for fear of the Judeans (Est. 8:17), Achior, an Ammonite general, converts after verifying the decapitated head as that of Holofernes (Jdt. 15:10). "Fear and trembling" falls on the Assyrians when they realize that Holofernes is dead, and they flee (15:1-3). The Jews rout them and Judith leads a triumphant march to the temple where she dedicates her war spoils to God (13:12–16:20) *Judith* then notes that nobody terrified the Jews again in Judith's time or for many days after her death (16:25). Similarly, in *Esther*, all the Jews' enemies perished, with none resisting the Jews out of fear: "For the rulers ... esteemed the Judeans, for the fear of Mardochaios weighed upon them" (9:2-3).

As is evident, *Esther* and *Judith* share many similarities in plot and content. The women's petitionary prayers also have much in common. Beginning with "a typical address and a number of epithets for God" (McDowell 2006, 39), they contain common petitionary themes, like the Jews' election, the difference between God and idols, a description of the enemy's fearsomeness, and a declaration of the intercessor's innocence, devotion, or piety (McDowell 2006, 39). Most importantly, both are concerned with maintaining the temple's purity (C:20), although Judith's concern is far more elaborate.

Following Westermann (1931, 202, 204),[5] the structure of these prayers may be represented as in Table 10.1.

Table 10.1 Structure of Esther's and Judith's Prayers

Structural Element	Esther's prayer Add C		Structural element	Judith's prayer
1. Address	C:14b	↔	1. Address	9:2a
2. Personal petition - I-complaint - trust motifs	C:14c-15		3. Retrospect	9:2b-4a
3. Confession of trust / retrospect	C:16		6. Petition to hear her	9:4b
4. Confession of sin - declaration of God's righteousness	C:17-18		3. Confession of trust	9:5-6
5. Enemy complaint	C:19-21	↔	5. Enemy complaint	9:7
6. Petitions	C:22-25b		6. Petitions	9:8-10
7. Declaration of innocence	C:25c-29		3. Confession of trust	9:11
8. Collective petitions	C:30a-c		9. Personal petition	9:12-13
9. Personal petition	C:30d		8. Collective petition	9:14

---

5. Westermann's versification has been replaced by that of the NETS, and the connection between the various elements in each prayer has been added.

Purity, Danger, and Petition in the Prayers of Esther and Judith

The preceding table shows that the prayers share certain structural parallels, suggesting a possibly common literary origin (Van der Walt 2007, 318). Furthermore, they have a similar concern with purity, yet one that differentiates them the most.

Esther's Prayer

Esther's prayer "turns" on her declaration of innocence. Hailing God with "O my Lord, you alone are our king" (C:14b), she immediately requests God's help with the dangerous situation she is facing (C:14c-15). Her request is followed by a brief retrospect on Israel's election and God's fulfilment of His promises to the Jewish forefathers (C:16). The subsequent confession of sin (C:17-18) identifies Esther as the intercessor-representative of her Jewish contemporaries. Like her, they are alone, having no-one but God to help, and in grave danger (C:14c-d). The confession is brief, telescoping Israel's breach of divine covenant into its representative sin, idolatry (C:17-18a) (see Boda 2006, 30), and leads to a declaration of God's righteousness in punishing them (C:18b). Underpinning her confession is the Deuteronomic representation of Israelite history in which the God rightly punished the sinful Jews through the Babylonian exile (Morrow 2006, 103). This Deuteronomic ideology colors the rest of Esther's prayer.

Linking idolatry to their current situation, Esther states that their enemies have "put their hands in the hands of their idols" to annul God's statutes; destroy His inheritance, house, and altar; and make the gentiles glorify a fleshly king (as God) forever (C:19-21). Esther, therefore, asks God not to surrender His scepter to idols but to turn their enemies' plans against them (C:22-25b). She pleads that God give her a soothing word when she faces Artaxerxes, to turn his heart against Aman, and save His people by His own hand. Finally, she prays for God to help her in her aloneness as she has none but Him (C:25c-29)—what I will call the loneliness formula.

Her final collective petition (C:30a-b) is preceded by an elaborate declaration of her innocence vis-à-vis her thwarted-but-desired ritual purity. Her declaration, which also hinges on Deuteronomic theology, is divided into two sections based on God's omniscience and informed by her hatred of the impurity she has had to endure.

In the first section (C:25c-26), Esther states that she abhors "the glory of the lawless" that she has obtained by marrying a gentile king, and "the bed of the uncircumcised and of any foreigner."[6] Hereby, she characterizes gentiles as those who are lawless, foreigners, and uncircumcised. By reverse implication, the Jews are law-abiding, circumcised, and members of God's elect. They are ritually pure, intact in corporate body, whereas the gentile "outsiders" are not. The strong "us"

---

6. "The problematic nature of sexual intercourse with foreigners [is that] it breaks down the divinely instituted boundary between Israel and gentiles" (Thiessen 2018, 169).

versus "them" distinction befits a threatened, traumatized group trying to maintain its traditional identity in what may be termed a pluralistic, traumatizing society (see Douglas 1966, 123, 161).

The second section (C:25c-26) picks up on Esther's hatred of her royal glory. She abhors her crown, wearing it only in public appearances, even as she abhors a menstrual cloth! Given Jewish menstruation taboos (see Maccoby 1999, 30–46), this statement is very strong. With menstruation, the boundaries of the female body are breached from the inside, as it were, so that it is no longer intact and so defiled (see Douglas 1966, 122). Thus, a menstrual cloth symbolizes defilement. She finds her defilement all the more abhorrent for it is Artaxerxes' uncircumcised penis that breaches her body's integrity and defiles her (see note 4). As Esther represents the Jewish collective, the menstrual cloth also speaks to the internal and external breach of the collective body[7] by means of idolatry, forced exile, loss of the temple and ritual expiation system, dispersion among "unclean" foreigners, and the impending trauma.

Interestingly, the impending breach of the collective body is caused by an "insider," Mordecai, attempting to uphold personal (and so communal) purity by not "worshipping" an "outsider." Just as Esther cannot avoid the breach of her body resulting from menstruation and undesired sexual activity, so too can the impending collective rupturing not be avoided because of Mordecai's stand, as his prayer (C:2-10) is at pains to show.

That remaining intact is a matter of ritual purity is underscored by at least two factors:

(a) The use of βδελύσσομαι, which reflects abhorrence of ritual defilement and occurs no less than three times in Esther's declaration:
   1. "[I] abhor the bed of the uncircumcised and of any foreigner."
   2. "I abhor the sign of my proud position."
   3. "I abhor it like a menstrual cloth."

Abhorring her crown is intimately linked to her abhorrence of sharing the gentile king's bed: had her body boundaries not been breached and defiled with their first encounter, her body would not have had to endure the abhorred sign of her station, and the continued breach of her body as queen.

(b) Having clarified her abhorrence, Esther offers three signs of her attempt to maintain ritual purity:
   1. "Your slave has not eaten at Haman's table,"
   2. "And I have not honored the king's banquet,"
   3. "Nor drunk the wine of libations."

---

7. Concerns about bodily defilement usually reflect a community's threatened boundaries (Douglas 1966, 123–6).

While it is hard to imagine how Esther managed to maintain these aspects of purity as queen, she nevertheless attempts to convince God of her predicament and unwelcomed ritual impurity so that He may answer her prayer: she is not an idolater, and she has maintained *kashrut*. She has not derived any pleasure in being queen since the day of her "change," and her only joy has been in Him. She deserves her appeal to be heard despite the impurity of having married a gentile king.

Clearly, Esther's petition hangs on her thwarted-but-desired ritual purity. Furthermore, it is driven by her fear and personal needs at crucial points:

1. She begins with a personal petition for God's help based on the loneliness formula and the danger she is facing (C:14c-15).
2. The last part of her first collective petition (C:23-25b) begins with her need for divine encouragement and ends with a cry for God's help, couched in the same loneliness formula.
3. Her last collective petition (C:30a-c) is followed by a petition for her own deliverance from fear (C:30d).

Thus, Esther's understandable fear frames her whole prayer and guides her Deuteronomically based declaration of innocence on which her petitions for herself and her people stand. This is not the case with Judith's prayer, as we will see below.

Judith's Prayer

Judith's prayer (Jdt. 9:2-14) is predicated entirely on an analogy between Dinah's rape (Genesis 34) and the Jews' current situation. Addressing God as "Lord God of my father Simeon" (Jdt. 9:2), Judith describes the rape in barely euphemistic words that may reflect the actual act (9:2) (Gera 2014, 306):

> [They] ravaged the virgin's vulva for defilement
> And stripped naked the thigh for shame
> And polluted the vulva for disgrace

Extolling Simeon's deceit (9:3, 13-14, see Gen. 34:13), Judith asks God to crush the Assyrians by *her* hand as *He* had crushed the Shechemites by Simeon's (Jdt. 9:7-10). Judith's ascription of Simeon's vengeance to God is most arresting, particularly as the Shechemites' humiliation included the pillage/rape[8] and "captivity" of their women (9:4, my emphasis):

> *you* handed over their wives for pillage and their daughters for captivity

---

8. Προνομή denotes "'a foraging, foray, raid' ... When cities are 'foraged' they are robbed of all their goods. Similarly, when women are 'foraged' they are robbed of their virtue or raped" (Efthimiadis-Keith 2004, 226).

Judith's rendition of events differs from Genesis 34 in which Jacob roundly condemns his sons' actions (v. 40).⁹ This difference is consonant with traumatic memory, in which past memories are altered to suit the survivor's present; *Judith's* author *needs* Judith's rendition/memory of events in order to spur her/his community to similarly rout their enemies (see Jdt. 9:7-14). The incongruity of a woman extolling God's (!) desecration of "other" women while condemning Dinah's (9:4) may also be understood through the lens of trauma, in combination with Douglas's (1966) work on purity: (im)purity is reserved for the "in-group," so that the same action (rape) that defiles a member of the "in-group" may not be viewed as a defilement when inflicted on members of the "out-group." Further, God *must* be seen as the avenger of the "in-group," repaying rape with rape, otherwise He cannot be relied upon to avenge His people now. The author's use of altered memory is, therefore, designed to embolden the "weak" Jews in her/his context to take up arms against their enemies for their intended "rape" of the Jerusalem temple (9:7, 11) (similarly Flesher 2007, 101–4).¹⁰

Verbal and sexual deception link the first and second parts of Judith's prayer (9:2-6, 7-24). Dinah's rape is characterized as an act of deceit that is avenged by Simeon and Levi's deceit (9:3). Judith asks God to grant her the power she has contemplated to rout the Assyrians. That this power refers to deceit is clarified by parallels in 9:3, 10, and 13 (Efthimiadis-Keith 2004, 223–4, my emphases).

> ... their bed which, *deceived,* felt ashamed at their *deceit* . . .
> and **you struck down slaves with lords and lords upon their thrones** (9:3)
>
> ... [P]lace in the hand of me, the widow, *the strength that I have contemplated.*
> *By the lips of my deceit* **strike down the slave with the ruler and the ruler with his attendant** ... grant my *word and deceit* for their wound and welt. (9:9-10, 13)

Judith emphasizes that Simeon's deception culminated in the Shechemites' destruction *upon their beds*: Jacob's sons used a phallic symbol, a sword, to kill them as they lay in post-circumcision pain (9:3). That Judith identifies with Simeon, and describes herself as a widow and a female, suggests that she too will use verbal *and* sexual deceit. Her use of sexual deceit is confirmed by the stated purpose of her post-prayer beautification (10:4): "she made herself up provocatively for the charming [literally: the deceit] of the eyes of men" (10:4), while her verbal deceit is demonstrated masterfully in her

---

9. Jacob's sons had deceived the Shechemites into thinking that they and Jacob's clan would become one after their circumcision (Gen. 34:13, 17, 22). Jacob's sons were therefore killing and defiling "in-group" members, which may account for Jacob's lament that they had made him hateful among the inhabitants of the land, opening him and his people up for annihilation (34:30).

10. The second part of Judith's prayer (Jdt. 9:7-14) links Dinah's rape with the impending "rape" of the temple by using words, concepts, and allusions drawn from the first part (9:2-6). For example, Judith uses the words βεβηλόω (to desecrate), μιαίνω (to pollute, defile), and μίασμα (defilement, pollution) to describe both rapes (9:2, 3) (Thiessen 2018, 170).

interactions with Holofernes (11:1-23). That her prayer coincides exactly with the evening incense offering (9:1) signifies that God has heard her prayer, granted her request, and does not find her intended use of verbal and sexual deceit abhorrent (Efthimiadis-Keith 2004, 228–9). Moreover, judging by 9:5-6, Judith regards her plan "as a righteous act of salvation that has been fore-ordained and 'prepared' by God just as Simeon's had" (Efthimiadis-Keith 2004, 227).[11]

I will now briefly compare the women's prayers to highlight fundamental differences that make them more dissimilar than alike.

Comparing Esther's and Judith's Prayers

The prayers share many similarities, the most obvious being that they are uttered by women secluded from their communities for the deliverance of their people. They are preceded by mourning rituals that prepare the women for intercession and followed by re-beautification processes that prepare them to deal with their male antagonists. The prayers are similarly concerned with God's temple, and informed by themes of deceit, sexuality, and ritual purity. They clearly describe their communities' predicaments and what they wish God to do. They request God to become known, to Jew and gentile alike, by thwarting the intentions of their enemies. Moreover, as we have seen, they have similar structural elements.[12] However, these similarities are superficial, hiding fundamental differences that echo the different theologies at play, impact on the women's agency (and so that of the intended audience), and reflect the audience's desired response.

As indicated, Esther's prayer is strongly influenced by the Deuteronomic interpretation of Israel's history. The absence of this element from Judith's prayer can be traced back to her repudiation of the Bethulians' belief in God's retributive justice.[13] As the Bethulians' desperation reaches fever pitch, ἐβόησαν—they cried out (Jdt. 6:18), becomes ἀνεβόησαν—they shouted out aloud (7:19, 23), and when their cisterns run dry, they approach their leaders with words of divine retribution strikingly similar to Esther's confession of sin (7:24-28):

God has sold us into their hands … (7:25)
our God and the Lord of our fathers,
who punishes us according to our transgressions
and … the transgressions of our fathers. (7:28)

---

11. Thiessen (2018, 176) rightly points out that the community's high praise of Judith means they have no problem with her methods either.

12. Reading intertextually allows for further parallels, e.g., one may see a likeness between Esther's personal predicament and Dinah's rape. Both women are taken against their will and subjected to undesired, defiling, sexual attention.

13. My comments on retributive justice in Judith's prayer are adapted from Efthimiadis-Keith (2004, 216–19) and Efthimiadis-Keith (2014, 872–5).

On the basis of this assumption, they wish to breach the corporate body and defile themselves as Holofernes' slaves and Nebuchadnezzar's devotees. As a result, Ozias, their leader, institutes a five-day ultimatum: if God does not deliver them within five days, then he will do as the people wish (7:26, 30-31). However, Judith upbraids the Bethulian leadership for "hold[ing] to account the purposes of the Lord" (8:16), that is, trying to force His hand. For her, the ultimatum shows that they are testing God, putting themselves above Him (8:12), and risk provoking Him to anger (8:14). Instead, God is a free agent who can choose if and when he will protect them (8:15). Her counsel that they "wait for his deliverance" and call upon Him so that he can hear them, "if it pleases him" (8:17), is grounded not only in God's freedom but also in the people's innocence or ritual purity: idolatry is not their sin, she says. Rather, it was a sin for which their forefathers "were handed over to the sword" (8:19). Therefore, the people may indeed hope that God will not disdain them (8:20). God is also not punishing them for the sins of their fathers. Rather, He is "testing" them, *because* they have drawn near to Him, as he had tested the patriarchs (8:24-27). Judith's "theology of testing" significantly challenges the Deuteronomism to which the Bethulians and Esther subscribe (7:28; 8:27). "It replaces punishment with 'trial' and sinfulness with righteousness as it locates the origin of this trial in the righteous action of those affected" (Efthimiadis-Keith 2004, 217),[14] creating a powerful model of agency (similarly Thiessen 2018, 184), unlike that of *Esther*.

Esther's and Judith's Prayers through the Lens of Trauma

From a trauma perspective, Judith's and Esther's divergent theological positions may indicate different levels of processing past and present trauma. Given their origin from the same sociohistorical milieu, the differences may also indicate two divergent opinions on dealing with impending communal trauma. Be that as it may, this sociohistorical milieu would have been fraught with intergenerational trauma as the traditions and stories of the past were transmitted from one generation to the next[15] and the actions of traumatized persons influenced the thinking and actions of those in present communities. Esther's Deuteronomic self-blame is just as much a response to trauma as Judith's active, empowered approach. Self-blame and untoward guilt are survival strategies that attempt to make sense of traumatic experiences. The traumatic shattering of core beliefs (Frechette and

---

14. I was intrigued by Flesher's (2007, 99-101) similar arguments, noting especially her insightful comment: "In typical Deuteronomic penitential thought, God is righteous and the people culpable. However, Judith has already declared the people innocent. The key to this dilemma—God is righteous and the people are innocent—is God's testing of the people" (100).

15. Esther's retrospect specifies such a passing down of traditions. The same may be said of Judith's retrospect, even though it is not overtly stated.

Boase 2016, 5) may lead to "toxic assumptions," which can cause a preponderance of negative emotions and mood and negatively affect the victim's sense of self, agency, safety, and relation to the world and God (Frechette and Boase 2016, 5). Trauma survivors may, therefore, "inappropriately blame themselves for their trauma, and yet [be unable to] take appropriate responsibility for their current actions and feelings" (Davis 2011, 106). This scenario clearly describes Esther's approach: collective and personal self-blame negatively impact her agency. She is fearful and cannot take responsibility for her own actions, thus she cannot act to change the situation herself but chooses to work through the king. Consequently, the intended audience may have experienced similar disempowerment and/or been encouraged to work behind the scenes as she does.

Ascribing one's suffering to God, as Esther does, is also a survival mechanism (Poser 2016, 36–7). It assumes that the God who was able and willing to inflict punishment justly through a traumatic event is the same God who is powerful enough to restore his repentant people out of love and mercy. It also allows survivors to maintain the concept of a just, holy, yet merciful God; and so allows "God" to survive (Poser 2016, 36–7). In other words, it prevents the dissolution of the survivor's religious identity, keeping her/him intact/pure in relation to God (God is not judged). And yet, this punitive view of God is maladaptive for the survivor, leading to increased dysfunctional mood (Lee, Roberts, and Gibbons 2013, 293; Matthews and Marwit 2006, 96), the perpetuation of feelings of hopelessness, delayed healing, and impaired agency through further fragmentation. We see this clearly in Esther's prayer: her Deuteronomic theology has immobilized her, as it may have immobilized her intended audience.

By contrast, not assigning untoward blame to oneself/one's community and seeing God as one who empowers people to intervene decisively in traumatic situations leads to enhanced healing, increased functionality, and so increased agency, as in *Judith's* case. Judith's non-Deuteronomic approach enables her to pray confidently. She is not a sinner that has to beg for a punitive God's involvement as Esther does. She, therefore, does not need to convince God of her innocence in order for Him to intervene, nor does she need to influence others to act on her behalf. Rather, *she* is the avenger of God's temple who is certain that God will act by *her* hand. Unlike Esther, she is the one acting, not the one being acted upon. Even so, Judith's theology of testing is significantly similar to Esther's approach in that it too allows for the survivor to maintain her/his religious identity and allows "God" to survive. However, it does so without immobilizing the would-be victim. The author would, therefore, be empowering *Judith's* intended audience to believe in God and themselves and take decisive actions to deal with the coming trauma—the desecration of the Second Temple—head-on.

Conclusion

As this essay has shown, the LXX prayers of Esther and Judith are emotionally laden responses to the traumatic events about to unfold in each story. They reflect certain theological themes that gained particular importance in the Second Temple period, such as the election of Israel, God's righteousness in punishing Israel, and the need for purity in God's elect. The essay focused on purity and danger in these prayers, analyzing them comparatively through the lens of trauma. It emerged that, even though the prayers have certain thematic and structural similarities, the theology underpinning them is fundamentally different, as is the sense of agency that these characters portray. While *Esther*, *Judith*, and the women's prayers in them have clear thematic, contextual, and structural similarities, the theological differences undergirding the women's prayers make them more dissimilar than alike. Deuteronomic theology informs Esther's prayer, impeding her sense of agency, so that she is reduced to a hesitant intercessor who has to prove her innocence/purity to God for Him to intervene through someone else. By contrast, Judith's beliefs in her own and her community's innocence/purity and God's positive role in the current situation makes of her a confident intercessor, one who fearlessly acts to bring about the deliverance of her people herself. As such, the prayers represent two options of dealing with the impending trauma: work behind the scenes to resolve it or take decisive action to avert it.

Chapter 11

ESTHER IN DIALOGUE WITH THE QUMRAN COMMUNITY

Seulgi L. Byun

Introduction

It is well known among scholars that the book of Esther is the only biblical book that has not been found in the collection of manuscripts at Qumran, a fact that may have significant implications for our understanding of the formation of the Jewish canon. In addition to the question of canon, the absence of the book of Esther at Qumran raises further questions: Did the conveners at Qumran even know of the book of Esther? If they did, how was it perceived and why is it not attested as a biblical book? And can we even talk about intertextuality in Esther and the Qumran texts at all?

Various explanations for the absence of Esther at Qumran have been suggested.[1] It is, of course, theoretically possible that the lack of any biblical texts of Esther at Qumran is simply coincidence and fragments may yet turn up,[2] but the more likely

---

1. There are many possible reasons why the Qumran conveners rejected the book of Esther as scripture. Some have pointed to the "secular" nature of the story. See, e.g., Pierce (1992, 77); Kalimi (2004, 101–6); Eisenman and Wise (1992, 100); and Dunne (2014). As is commonly known, there is not a single mention of God in Esther, and religious themes, such as prayer, worship, purity, the temple, and the law, are also curiously absent. Spiritual and ethical ideals foundational to the Hebrew Bible, such as righteousness, covenant loyalty, and holiness, are also missing. Furthermore, the story is full of pagan practices: the intermarriage of Esther to the Persian king; the pagan names of Esther and Mordecai that are derived from Babylonian gods (Ishtar and Marduk, respectively); the licentious nature of what can only be described as a sex competition that Esther enlists in; and the fact that Esther and Mordecai are part of the Jewish diaspora that chose *not* to return to Jerusalem but instead moved further eastward, a sign perhaps that they assimilated even further into Persian culture. Accordingly, some have argued that the purpose of the book of Esther was largely political with the survival of the Jewish people as the primary theme (Hazony 2016; Koller 2014).

2. E.g., Tov (1998, 289 n. 44) has argued that "the absence of the book should be ascribed to coincidence … (the destruction of the material) rather than to any other factor." However, Talmon (1995, 265) dismisses the idea that Esther will ever be found at Qumran; he points

explanation is that Esther had not achieved canonical status and was therefore not considered authoritative scripture.³ Whatever the reason, Talmon's (1995, 250) caution is instructive: "Nothing may be learned from [Esther's] absence regarding the question of whether or not the book was included in the 'canon of scriptures' ... nor about its status among the books which the יחד community had accepted."

Despite the absence of any Esther manuscripts at Qumran, it is still possible to demonstrate an awareness of the book of Esther if allusions, citations, or verbal parallels between the book of Esther and the texts at Qumran can be established. One must be careful not to conflate the absence of Esther at Qumran and the question of whether or not the conveners were aware of the book of Esther; they are two separate inquiries and must be considered independently. In this study, I will examine key texts in Esther and at Qumran that show literary dependence. I will begin by looking at the two manuscripts most commonly linked to the Esther story at Qumran: 1Q20, otherwise known as "The Genesis Apocryphon," and the fragments of 4Q550, or "Proto-Esther." The provenance of these manuscripts is debated, but there are some intriguing parallels to the Esther story that are worth considering. I will then examine several lexical parallels and allusions between Esther and the sectarian manuscripts at Qumran, texts that were written by the conveners and reflect their social, intellectual, and spiritual ideals.

Esther, Qumran Texts, and Literary Dependence

The Genesis Apocryphon

In 1961, J. Finkel argued that the author of the Genesis Apocryphon (1Q20), a badly damaged Aramaic document that retells some of the stories in Genesis, knew the book of Esther and alluded to it in the account of Sarah and Abraham at Pharaoh's court (1Q20 20:1-34). Finkel (1961, 179) identified several phrases, key words, and figures of speech that directly allude to the story of Esther, and he concluded that the "author was familiar with the Book of Esther" and furthermore he also sought to establish a literary connection between the two accounts by intentionally employing language from the book of Esther.

---

to fragments of Song of Songs and Lamentations, both of which are, like Esther, short books but well represented at Qumran. Another reason for Talmon's (1995, 266) skepticism is that "practically all of the manuscript finds at Qumran ... have been sorted and processed." Similarly, De Troyer (2000, 422) concluded, "To this point, I had been convinced that one would never find a book of Esther in Qumran ... I have strengthened my conviction that one will never find ... Esther in Qumran."

3. The rabbinical debates in the third and second centuries CE suggest that Esther was not considered canonical until the third century. See, e.g., the discussions of R. Judah in the name of Samuel in *b. Meg.* 7a. Cf., also *b. Sanh.* 100a.

Finkel's (1961, 169) first example is the description of Sarah as being more beautiful than "all maidens [בתולן] and brides" and "more lovely than all women [נשין]," which parallels Est. 2:17:

1Q20 20:6-7

וכל בתולן וכלאן די יעלן לגנון לא ישפרן מנהא ועל כול נשין שופר שפרה ועליא שפרהא לעלא מן כולהן

And all *maidens* and brides that enter under the wedding canopy are not fairer than she. And above all *women* is she lovely and higher in her beauty than that of them all.

Est. 2:17

ויאהב המלך את־אסתר מכל־הנשים ותשא־חן וחסד לפניו מכל־הבתולת

The king loved Esther more than all the other *women*, and she won his grace and favor more than all the *maidens*.

Finkel argued that the description of Sarah as being more beautiful than all the other maidens and brides, a gloss that is absent in the biblical account in Genesis 12, is a conscious allusion to Esther by the author of the Genesis Apocryphon to retell the story as if Sarah was in a beauty contest.

Another example of literary dependence is a phrase regarding an oath Pharaoh made to Abram in 1Q20 20:30: []לא וימא לי מלכא במומה די, "and the king swore to me with an oath that cannot [be changed/voided?]." Finkel (1961, 179) maintained that this language resembles the elevation of Mordecai in Est. 8:8: כי־כתב אשר־נכתב בשם־המלך ונחתום בטבעת המלך אין להשיב, "For an edict that has been written in the king's name and sealed with the king's signet may not be revoked."[4]

A third example, one that Finkel declared "a most definite proof," is the description of the parting gifts that Pharaoh gave Abraham, which is strikingly similar to the gifts that Ahasuerus gave Mordecai in Est. 8:15:

1Q20 20:31

ויהב לה מלכא [כסף וד]הב שגיא ולבוש די בוץ וארגואן

The king gave to her *[silver and go]ld* and much clothing of *fine linen and purple*.

Est. 8:15

ומרדכי יצא מלפני המלך בלבוש מלכות תכלת וחור ועטרת זהב גדולה ותכריך בוץ וארגמן

Mordecai left the king's presence in royal robes of blue and white, with a magnificent *crown of gold* and a mantle of *fine linen and purple wool*.

---

4. This example is less than convincing, as it relies on the reconstruction of a key word, and the similarities between the two texts are more conceptual with no direct lexical correlations. Given the context of the story, a plausible reconstruction of the lacuna might be "he did not touch her."

The use of the Aramaic expression בוץ וארגואן in 1Q20 is noteworthy in that it is the only occurrence of the collocation of the nouns בוץ and ארגואן in all non-biblical texts including Qumran and other Jewish and Rabbinic sources. Its occurrence in the MT is equally rare and is attested only twice, both times in Esther (1:6, and here in 8:15).[5] Talmon (1995, 256) agreed with Finkel that בוץ וארגואן is indeed a "direct quotation" of Est. 8:15, and he conceded that these three parallels clearly demonstrate that the author of the Genesis Apocryphon was "conversant with the tale of Esther and Mordecai."

In sum, there are three possible allusions to Esther in just one column of 1Q20, the story of Abram and Sarah at Pharaoh's court, and I concur with Finkel and Talmon that the author of 1Q20 knew the Esther story and alluded to it. But we must return to the question of the provenance and authorship of this manuscript. If someone at Qumran wrote it, one could definitively conclude that the conveners at Qumran knew of the book of Esther. In the years immediately following the discovery of 1Q20, it was the consensus view that 1Q20 was written by someone at Qumran. As Michaud (1957, 101–2) put it, "Les auteurs de l'oeuvre araméenne étaient vraisemblablement les moines de Qumran, c'est-à-dire les Esséniens" (see also Lignée 1963, 211–12; Reeves 1986, 415–19). However, in recent years, scholars have questioned the provenance of the Genesis Apocryphon.[6] One of the main arguments against a Qumran origin is that there is nothing in the text of 1Q20 that sheds light on the beliefs or customs of the Qumran conveners and only texts that reflect the unique ideology and intellectual world of the *Yahad* can be attributed to those at Qumran.[7] By way of contrast, almost all scholars attribute Jubilees to the Qumran conveners, as it insists on the solar calendar and sets fixed dates for key festivals, two core tenets of the Qumran community.

Thus, despite three possible allusions in the Genesis Apocryphon to the book of Esther—all of which are clustered closely together in a story where the plot is similar to that of Esther—Finkel's examples demonstrate that the *author* of the Genesis Apocryphon knew of the book of Esther, but they reveal little, if anything, of the Qumran conveners' knowledge of the book.

"Proto-Esther"

After Finkel's article, scholarly discussion on the relationship between Qumran and Esther lay dormant for about thirty years until J. T. Milik (1992, 321–99) published a lengthy and provocative article detailing six clusters of fragments from

---

5. In Est. 1:6, it is used to describe the elaborate cords that were draped on the pillars in Ahasuerus' garden.

6. See, e.g., Fitzmyer (1971, 23) for the strongest argument against a Qumran composition, a view that the majority of Qumran scholars hold today. See Machiela (2009, 7–8, 135–6) for a helpful summary of the discussion.

7. E.g., Talmon (1963, 252).

Cave 4 (4Q550ᵃ⁻ᶠ), which he labeled 4Qproto-Esther Aramaic.[8] Milik (1992, 321), argued that these manuscripts served as the "prototype," "model," "archetype," or "sources" for the various witnesses to the book of Esther, in particular the Latin version (*Vetus Latina*).[9]

There are three stories or plot lines that can be sketched out from these fragments. The first story involves two rival court officers vying for power in the court of Darius I. In the second story, a Persian king marries a foreign woman. The third story recounts how one court officer refuses to bow before the other officer. All three of these stories bear striking resemblances to the book of Esther, even if at a macro-narrative level. In addition to the plot lines, Milik identified onomastic evidence and similar phrases between these fragments and the book of Esther, and he concluded that 4Q550 is comprised of three successive layers that served as a prototype for the book of Esther and its ancient versions.[10]

Milik's translation of the 4Q550 fragments includes names that are found in the book of Esther, most of which are reconstructed. For example, in 4Q550 f2:3 the son of Patireza is reconstructed as Jair: [יא]יר בר לפתריזא איתי מלכא, "The king comes to Patireza son of Ja[ir]." This seems plausible, and if Milik is correct it mirrors Est. 2:5: ושמו מרדכי בן יאיר, "and his name was Mordecai, son of Jair." Milik suggested that Patireza and Mordecai should be equated, that is, Mordecai was the Hebrew name and Patireza the Persian name.[11]

Milik also claimed that he found Haman and his wife, Zeresh, in the 4Q550 fragments:

4Q550 f4:1-2

די תמר לשרתא א[נתתה ול... כנ]תה נד[י]ה [ ] פתריזא אב[ו]ך [ ]מן חמא די קם על עבידת [מלכותא] קדם מלכא

---

8. In addition to publishing the photos of the fragments, Milik provides a critical edition of the text, a history of interpretation of the fragments, and a commentary of the text.

9. "Je propose le sigle: 4Q pr(oto-)Esth(er) ar(améen) … s'agissant effectivement, à notre avis, de «proto-Esther», de «modèles», d'«archétypes», de «sources», des versions du livre d'*Esther* conservées en Hébreu, Grec, Latin (et jusqu'à un passage en Arménien)." It is not within the scope of this study to examine the relationship of 4Q550ᵃ⁻ᶠ with the LXX, AT (Alpha-Text), Proto-AT, and OL (*Vetus Latina*). For excellent discussions on the relationship between 4Q550 and the extant witnesses to the book of Esther, see Crawford (1996b, 307–25) and De Troyer (2000, 401–22).

10. Wechsler (2000, 130–72) has challenged Milik's theory that the six manuscripts that comprise 4Q550 are successive layers of the same story with Esther-like motifs. Instead, Wechsler argues that the fragments represent three independent, non-successive works that "fall into the 'Jew in the Foreign Court' genre" and supplement the stories not just in Esther but also in Ezra-Nehemiah.

11. Milik's suggestion to equate Mordecai to Patireza has some challenges. First, Mordecai is not a Hebrew name but a Babylonian theophoric name derived from Marduk. Also, Patireza's son is addressed elsewhere in 4Q550 (cf., 4Q550 f1 and f2:7).

Command Sharata [his wife, and her daughters that they be banished?]. Patireza your father, from Hama who arose concerning the service of ... before the king.[12]

If Milik is correct and שרתא is indeed a proper noun, it is very likely that this name corresponds to Zeresh, Haman's wife (Est. 5:10). As he points out in his commentary, Sharata has obvious connections to the Greek forms of this name: *Zôsara*, *Sôsara* (Alexandrinus), *Zôra*, and *Zara*. The name חמא needs no analysis, and Milik's reconstruction of א[נתתה is further evidence that this may be Haman from the book of Esther. At the very least, there is clear resemblance between this line and the characters in Esther.

Another reconstructed name that Milik discussed is a possible reference to Esther in fragment d:

4Q550 f5+5a:5

לגבר כותהׄ להתבה[מלי מל]כׄותך קאם באתר די אנתה קאם [   ] א[ֹנׄהאסׄ[תר]
Let a Kutean man be in charge of your kingdom holding power from the moment you yourself hold the power [As for m]e, Es[ther][13]

If the reconstruction אסתר had any legitimacy this would be incontrovertible evidence that 4Q550 is a prototype or a source for Esther, but, sadly, only the *aleph* is visible and the second letter is difficult to make out, as indicated by the open circle above the letter. This is a conjectural reading at best, and even Milik (1992, 364) concedes that "lecture et restitution incertaines."[14]

In addition to the possible onomastic connections, there are several parallels in the details of the story of the 4Q550 fragments to the book of Esther. One example is the reference to the "Books of His Father" in fragment a to the "Book of Records" in Est. 6:1: "On that night the king could not sleep, and he gave orders to bring the book of records, the annals, and they were read to the king."

4Q550a f1:3-5

בה בש<ע>תא ארכת רוחה די מלכא אׄעׄ[ירה אלהא   ס[פׄרי אב[וׄ]הי הׄתקריו קדמוהי ובין
ספריא אשתכח מנלה ח[דה חתי]מה חתמיןׄ שבעה בעזקתה די דריוש אבוהי ... השתכח כתיב כה
At that same hour the temper of the king was stretched [... the b]ooks of his father should be read to him and among the books was found a scroll [se]aled with seven seals of Darius his father ... it was found written within.

---

12. Reconstruction and translation by Milik (1992, 333–4).
13. Reconstruction and translation by Milik (1992, 337).
14. Milik mentions a few other names in 4Q550 that may relate to Esther in some way, but they are more dubious. For example, in 4Q550 f2:4, Milik reads בית ספרא "house of Saphra," the antecedent of which would appear to be Patireza. However, it is equally possible that this should be read "house of the scribe."

The similarities to Est. 6:1 are striking. The difference between the two texts is the inability of the king to sleep in the MT and the testing of the king's anger in 4Q550.¹⁵ However, one intriguing detail is the identity of the king. We are told that this king's father was Darius, which makes the present king Xerxes—the same king that is mentioned in MT Esther.¹⁶

Another section in 4Q550 with possible links to Esther is fragment d, the largest extant fragment. Milik's reconstruction of lines 3–4 is as follows:

4Q550 f5+5a:3-4

איתי נין עבד]יך גבר יהודי מן דבר בנימ[ין ... מ]גלה קאם לקבלה וב[ע]א[ ] פפו[רא טבא
גברא טבא עבד [עבידת מלכו]תא מה אעבד לכה

There is among your servants a Judean, one of the notables of (the tribe of) Benjam[in], an exile; he stands before you ... He is a good man, a good servant, [he serves for the King]dom What can I do for you?

There are two important parallels to Esther here. First, the question, "What can I do for you?," can be linked to Ahasuerus' question to Esther (cf., Est. 5:3 מה לך "What is it?"; Est. 5:6; 7:2, מה שאלתך "What is your request?"). Though the identity of the person asking the question in 4Q550 is unknown, it is clear that the inquirer is a male based on the subsequent lines, and the "you" is a female. The phrases are not identical, but as Crawford (1996a, 33) has observed, "There are no other scenes in biblical or Second Temple literature, to my knowledge, which are set at a court, in which a powerful male, a king, asks his female companion what he may do for her, outside of the *Esther* story." Second, the man is described as someone in exile, a leader or noble who is a Judean and a Benjaminite, and Est. 2:5-6 describes Mordecai in much the same way: "There was in the citadel of Susa a Jew of the tribe of Benjamin by the name of Mordecai son of Jair ... who had been carried off into exile."¹⁷ This description, coupled with Milik's reconstruction of Patireza as the son of Jair, has obvious connections to the Esther story.

In sum, the names and details in the story of the extant fragments of 4Q550 bear striking resemblances to the book of Esther: Something upsets King Ahasuerus (Xerxes), and he demands that the "books of his father," Darius, are read to him. In the books, the protagonist, Patireza (possibly the son of Jair), who had some conflict with Saphra, is rewarded for his faithfulness. Patireza appears to be rewarded by Ahasuerus. Someone is then punished, and Haman's name is mentioned. Someone else, perhaps Patireza, is described as a faithful servant to a

---

15. The LXX, AT, OL, and Josephus all read that God made the king unable to sleep. See Crawford (1996b, 310–11) and Talmon (1995, 253) for more on how the story of the temper of the king might have developed in subsequent versions.

16. The Greek witnesses to Esther all identify the king as either Artaxerxes I (465–423 BCE) or Artaxerxes II (404–358 BCE).

17. Translation mine.

female character, most likely a royal figure. Someone in exile, possibly Patireza, is described as a Benjaminite from Judah. The question is then asked, "What can I do for you?," and we are told that a Cuthite man, presumably an enemy, is responsible for something. A person is then elevated to a high position.[18]

The parallels to the book of Esther in 1Q20, the "Genesis Apocryphon," and 4Q550, "Proto-Esther," confirm two things: (1) the authors of these texts were, at the very least, familiar with the story of Esther and Mordecai or a story like it; and (2) there are some correlations between these texts and the various Esther traditions (MT, LXX, AT, Proto-AT, the "Additions," and the daughter versions).[19] However, the consensus among scholars is that 1Q20 and 4Q550 are not sectarian texts and therefore reveal nothing about what the conveners at Qumran knew. As Talmon (1995, 256) put it, these texts do not "exhibit any characteristic traits of the *Yaḥad's* intellectual world. Rather, they are part of an all-Israelite fundus of literary traditions of the late Second Temple period." We know very little about the provenance and authorship of 1Q20 and 4Q550; and the fact that they were found in the Qumran repositories does not prove that the conveners knew of the book of Esther. The absence of any religious or intellectual views unique to the Qumran community should not necessarily rule out a Qumran origin, especially with texts that fall in the genre of "rewritten bible," such as the Genesis Apocryphon; but I agree with Talmon that it is impossible to ascertain the provenance of 1Q20 and 4Q550.

Esther in the Sectarian Texts

In recent years, scholars have sought to demonstrate knowledge of the book of Esther by identifying rare expressions and *hapax legomena* in MT Esther that also occur in the sectarian texts at Qumran, texts that reflect the conceptual world and social order of the conveners.[20] For example, in 4Q267, a copy of the Damascus Document, it has been argued that a scribe accidentally wrote מיום ליום ו[מחדש לחדש], "every day and every month," a phrase that is meaningless in the context of the Damascus Document but is found in Est. 3:7. Ben-Dov (1999, 282–4) argues that the scribe's "acquaintance with the Book of Esther must have been so profound that characteristic words from its text occurred in his mind while copying other compositions." Another example is the expression בקש לשלח יד "seek to harm someone [lit., stretch out a hand]," which only occurs

---

18. See Crawford (1996b, 315) for a helpful summary of the similarities and differences between 4Q550[a-c] and the book of Esther.

19. See Crawford (1996b, 323–5), for a plausible theory on how 4Q550 was as an earlier story that eventually developed into the MT and Proto-AT versions.

20. The first *hapax legomenon* is the lone example that does not occur in a sectarian text. In fact, Talmon expanded on Finkel's most convincing example from 1Q20, the expression בוץ וארגמן.

twice in the Bible: in Est. 2:21 and 6:21. The exact expression also occurs in the Psalms Pesher and may be a conscious allusion to Esther (Katzin 2004, 139–40):

4Q171 ii 18-19

פשרו על רשעי אפרים ומנשה אשר יבקשו לשלוח יד בכוהן ובאנשי עצתו

Its interpretation concerns the wicked of Ephraim and Manasseh who *will attempt to lay hands* on the Priest and the member of his council.

By far, the most important study on whether or not the Qumran conveners knew Esther was undertaken by Shemarayahu Talmon. Talmon (1995, 256) identified several *hapax legomena* in Esther that also occur in sectarian texts at Qumran, which "confirm the thesis that the authors of these texts knew the Esther story, and that some of them were actually familiar with the biblical Book of Esther." I will briefly summarize some of his examples.

The phrase איש וָאִישׁ, where the word איש is repeated in a conjunctive structure with the definite article, is attested only in Est. 1:8: כי כן יסד המלך על כל רב ביתו לעשות כרצון איש וָאִישׁ, "for the king had ordered that all stewards of his palace should comply with *everyone's* wishes." Talmon argued that this particular grammatical formula is unique to Esther in the Bible and is used not as a distributive, as is usually the case, but to express inclusivity.[21] The phrase איש וָאִישׁ is found in at least three sectarian texts: 1QS 9:12 (Manual of Discipline), 4Q177 f1 4:11 (Catena A), 4Q418 11 (Instruction), and, possibly, the parallel text, 4Q416 f1:5 (Instruction).[22]

The *hapax legomenon* תר followed by the repeated nouns נערה ונערה is an expression found only in Est. 2:12: ובהגיע תר נערה ונערה. The word תר is used twice in important Qumran texts on community life:

1QS 6:10-11

אל ידבר לפני תכונו הכתוב לפניו האיש הנשאל ידבר בתרו

No (man) shall speak before one who is registered in rank before him. The man who is asked shall speak *in his turn*.

CD 14:10-11

על פיהו יבאו באי העדה איש בתרו

According to his (the overseer) instruction, the members of the congregation shall come, each man *in his turn*.

---

21. The same formula occurs many times in Esther with other words: כל מדינה ומדינה (Est. 1:22; 3:12, 14; 4:3; 8:9, 13, 17; 9:28); כל איש ואישה (Est. 4:11); עם ועם (Est. 8:9); עיר ועיר (Est. 8:11; 9:28); בכל שנה ושנה (Est. 9:21, 27); and יום ויום (Est. 2:11; 3:4). A brilliant example of this grammatical structure is the concatenation of four consecutive examples: דור ודור משפחה ומשפחה מדינה ומדינה ועיר ועיר (Est. 9:28).

22. Another possible occurrence that Talmon does not mention is 4Q259 3:8 (Rule of the Community). The text is damaged where איש ואיש might have appeared, but this is based on context and reconstruction.

Another example is the idiom איש יהודי, which occurs only twice in the Hebrew Bible: Zech. 8:23 והחזיקו בכנף איש יהודי, "they will take hold one Jew by the corner (of his cloak)," and Est. 2:5 איש יהודי היה בשושן הבירה, "a Jew lived in the fortress, Shusan." Talmon argued that its use in Zech. 8:23 is a general term to distinguish Jew from non-Jew, whereas its use in Est. 2:5 introduces Mordecai as a man of elite status at the court of King Ahasuerus. In other words, the expression is used in Esther as a title of honor, which is how it is employed in the texts at Qumran. For example, it is attested in 4Q333 f2:1 אחד] איש יהודי, a fragment from what appears to list a rota of priestly watches in the Temple.[23] Related to this is the Aramaic equivalent גבר יהודי found in 4Q550 (Proto-Esther): לכא]גבר יהודי מן רברבני מ, "a Jew, one of the nobles of [the king."[24]

The formulaic expression שאלתי...ובקשתי "(my) wish ... and (my) request," which occurs only in the book of Esther, also occurs in 11Q5 24:4 (Psalms A): הט אוזנכה ותן לי את שאלתי ובקשתי אל תמנע ממני, "Give ear and grant *my plea*; *my request* do not without from me." Though this extra-canonical song is a sectarian text, Talmon argued that the psalms in this scroll were most likely used as liturgy in the prayer services of the community and would have been known to the redactor or scribe who selected, compiled, and copied them.[25] Other examples include the word-pair אורה ושמחה, "light and gladness," which is attested only in Est. 8:16. Talmon identified two texts where this phrase occurs in Qumran, 4Q431 f2:3 and 1QM 17:7.[26] He also linked the concatenation of the lexemes אכל, יגון, שמח, and הפך in Est. 9:22 to 4Q166 2:17 (Hosea Pesher): נהפכה להם לאבל [שמחתם], "[joy] will be changed into mourning for them."[27]

Conclusion

The allusions to Esther in 1Q20, "The Genesis Apocryphon," and similarities with the Esther story with the names, details, and plot in 4Q550, "Proto-Esther," suggest

---

23. See also 4Q300 8:8 לאיש יה]ודי.

24. See also 4Q424 יהודי [גבר] והוא.

25. This same argument could be made for the parallels between Esther and 1Q20 (The Genesis Apocryphon) that Finkel identified and Talmon rejected. Talmon acknowledged that the author of 1Q20 knew Esther but maintained that this does not prove that the conveners knew of the book of Esther, as 1Q20 does not reveal anything about the beliefs or customs at Qumran. However, if 1Q20 is to be categorized as "rewritten scripture," a genre akin to the Targum or Midrash, it would have been a document that was read publicly, studied carefully, and perhaps even imitated. If Talmon's example from 11Q5 is to be accepted, one must also consider the parallels in 1Q20 as evidence for knowledge of the book of Esther.

26. It is likely that this phrase is also used in 4Q427 f7 2:4 [מחה]הופיע אור וש.

27. From a methodological standpoint, this example is not convincing. As Talmon himself notes, these four lexemes appear together in Jer. 31:13, and one could argue that there is more thematic correspondence between the Hosea Pesher (4Q166) and Jeremiah than with Esther. In other words, it is possible this is an allusion to Jeremiah 31.

that, at the very least, the story of Esther was known by the time of Qumran. Textual evidence from the LXX, its daughter versions, the AT, Josephus, and possibly even Ben Sira[28] add weight to the theory the book of Esther was known and perhaps even circulated in the Second Temple period. Even if these manuscripts were not composed at Qumran, it is likely that they were read, studied, copied, and even recited by the conveners.

The parallels to Esther in 1Q20 and 4Q550 alone do not prove that they knew of the book of Esther. The definitive proof in identifying conscious parallels and allusions to Esther by the Qumran conveners is found in the sectarian texts at Qumran, and at least ten *hapax legomena* and unique phrases from Esther have been identified in the sectarian texts.[29] If there were only one or two examples, one could justifiably conclude that the similarities were simply coincidental or that the evidence was inconclusive, but there are several compelling cases that leave little doubt that the book of Esther was known and used by those at Qumran.

---

28. For connections between Esther and Ben Sira, see Leiman (1976, 151 n. 139), who quotes Eberharter as an advocate for Esther in Ben Sira.

29. Brief mention should also be made of a parallel between the "Temple Scroll" and the book of Esther. The provenance of this text and its use at Qumran are highly contested matters and there is no consensus. E.g., Schiffman (1994, 54) said "the *Temple Scroll* could not simply be identified as a document of the Qumran sect." However, this view has been challenged in recent years. De Troyer (2000, 412–18) has proposed an interesting parallel that adds to Talmon's examples: 4Q524 f14:3 יתלו אותו העץ, "they shall hang him on a tree," and Est. 9:13 ואת עשרת בני המן יתלו על העץ, "let the ten sons of Hama be hanged on a tree." It should be noted, however, that the expression תלה + העץ is not unique to Esther (cf., Josh. 8:29).

Chapter 12

READING JOSEPHUS READING ESTHER

Paul Spilsbury

Flavius Josephus, one of our most important literary sources for the history of Jews and Judaism in the first century CE, is known to us from four major works.[1] The largest of these, the *Jewish Antiquities*, is a sweeping history of the Jewish people from the biblical creation of the world down to the mid-first century and the buildup to the Judean war (i.e., Josephus' own time). The first half of this work is in effect an idiosyncratic paraphrase of the narrative parts of the Hebrew Bible; and it is here that we find Josephus' extensive retelling of the story of Esther and Mordecai (*Ant.* 11.184–296), which is the focus of the current chapter.

In his introduction to the *Antiquities*, Josephus informs his readers that his work is an exact translation of the Hebrew text that sets forth "the precise details of what is in the Scriptures" (τὰ ... ἀκριβῆ τῶν ἐν ταῖς ἀναγραφαῖς). He assures us that nothing is either added or omitted (*Ant.* 1.17; see also *Apion* 1.42). The named historical precedent for his project is none other than the Septuagint, which venerable work Josephus claims to have superseded by covering not only the five books of Moses but the rest of the Jewish Scriptures as well (*Ant.* 1.10–12). We soon discover, though, that Josephus' work is nothing like a literal translation of the Hebrew Bible. For one thing, it covers only the narrative sections (except for some summaries of the laws in *Ant.* 3.91–294 and 4.196–301). More significantly, not only does he omit large sections of the original storyline and add material of his own despite his promise to do neither, even where he does follow the biblical story fairly closely, he adapts, shapes, and colors the material in ways that have long been the subject of extensive and detailed study (e.g., Feldman 1998a, 1998b; Spilsbury 1998, etc.). Broadly speaking, Josephus' biblical paraphrase is like other examples

---

1. For a general introduction to Josephus' works, see Chapman and Rodgers (2015). The standard edition of the complete works of Josephus in English is the Loeb edition (Thackeray et al. 1926–65). More recently, the Brill Josephus Project (Mason 1999) to date provides a new English translation along with full commentary for about half of Josephus' works, including *Jewish Antiquities* 11, which contains Josephus' paraphrase of the book of Esther (Spilsbury and Seeman 2017). Translations of Josephus in this chapter are taken from the Brill volumes.

of "rewritten" Bible in Jewish antiquity such as *Jubilees*, the *Genesis Apocryphon*, and Pseudo-Philo's *Biblical Antiquities*. While scholars debate the definition and intentions of these works, it is generally understood that they were attempts to adapt and apply the Scriptures to the realities of the writers' own circumstances by incorporating within the retold stories the interpretive insights drawn from the exegetical tradition based on those texts (Alexander 1988; Vermes 1973). Josephus' *Jewish Antiquities*, including the retelling of the Esther story, certainly fits this definition, thus giving us the opportunity to observe the dynamics of a first century CE Jew adapting and repurposing the Scriptures for a new setting. While the impetus for Josephus' work is often described in terms of "apologetic," we will see that there are other elements in play as well.

Josephus takes the story of Esther very seriously. Not only does it address life and death issues, but it allows Josephus to offer a kind of blueprint or manifesto for Jewish flourishing in the Diaspora (see also Kneebone 2013). Not only does he regard Esther as one of the books of the prophets (*Apion* 1.40; Spilsbury 2016), but it is a book that powerfully validates the central thesis of *Antiquities* as a whole, namely, that

> those who comply with the will of God and do not venture to transgress laws that have been well enacted succeed in all things beyond belief and that happiness lies before them as a reward from God. But to the extent that they dissociate themselves from the scrupulous observance of these laws the practicable things become impracticable, and whatever seemingly good thing they pursue with zeal turns into irremediable misfortunes. (*Ant.* 1.14)

All the way through the *Antiquities* we find Josephus emphasizing this point, and nowhere more so than here in his recounting of the story of Esther. Erich Gruen (2002, 137–48) is no doubt correct to say that the book of Esther has functioned since ancient times as a parody written partly to poke fun at a ridiculous fictional king (Artaxerxes in Josephus' retelling, as in LXX) and his hateful vizier; but for Josephus this story is no joking matter. For him it is a historical episode that serves as a vehicle to speak plainly both to fellow Jews and to hoped-for gentile readers about what it means to live and even thrive as a minority community in a sometimes hostile and always constrained environment.

Josephus' Biblical Text

One of the pertinent critical questions within Josephus scholarship is the question of which biblical texts he may have used as the basis for his biblical paraphrase. Any attempt to answer this question is hampered by the degree to which Josephus' creative and paraphrastic rewriting of the biblical texts obscures his source from view. In effect, it is practically impossible to determine with any confidence what his textual sources may have been. Having said that, the scholarly consensus regarding the book of Esther is that, because Josephus makes use of all but the first and the last of the additional passages found only in the Greek versions, he must have used one or other, or both, of the Greek texts (e.g., Feldman 1970, 526 n. 22; Motzo 1928; Seyberlich 1964; Spilsbury and Seeman 2017, 52–3), though there may be instances where direct use of a Hebrew text is indicated. This view has recently been challenged by Étienne Nodet (2018), who argues on the basis of the colophon to LXX Esther that the additional passages found in the Greek versions are in fact based on lost Hebrew originals (see also Bickerman 1944), which he argues Josephus used for those passages as well. Nodet's thesis—which argues that Josephus used only a Hebrew text for the entire biblical section of the *Antiquities*— is yet to receive wide support, however; and one is reminded of Rajak's (2009, 252) perceptive comment that it is surely inconceivable that Josephus would have been able to complete a project of such mammoth proportions had prior Greek translations of the Bible not already existed. Further, for the purposes of this study it is perhaps enough to note that what Josephus has provided is a colorful retelling of the dramatic story of Esther that fits perfectly within his own wider agenda for the writing of the *Antiquities*.

The Story of Esther

Josephus was a storyteller. Admittedly, the *Antiquities* is inordinately long and can be tedious at times, but where his source material allowed, Josephus was more than capable of seizing the opportunity to spin a good yarn. The story of Esther is such an opportunity, and Louis Feldman (1970) has provided the classic account of the many ways that Josephus colored his version of the Esther story for a Hellenized audience, with more recent and more nuanced analyses being provided by Swart (2006) and Kneebone (2013). As noted by Feldman, one of the ways that Josephus enhanced the story of Esther was by heightening the sensuous and erotic elements within the story. Thus, we find that both principal women are described as being surpassingly beautiful. In the case of Vashti, Josephus exceeds the biblical descriptions of her by asserting that the king wished to demonstrate to his gathered vassals that his wife "surpassed all women in beauty" (*Ant.* 11.190; cf., Est. 1:11; *B. Meg.* 12b); and Esther, for her part, "surpassed all in beauty, and the grace of her countenance attracted the stares of all who saw her" (*Ant.* 11.199; cf., Est. 2:7, 15). Josephus also takes time to emphasize the sumptuous cosmetic treatment (*Ant.* 11.200; cf., Est. 2:12) of the four hundred virgins prepared for the king's sexual perusal. No such number is provided in the biblical texts. In Josephus' description, the king is said to be utterly besotted, first with Vashti then with Esther. Regarding the former, Josephus says that even though the king was "in love" (διακείμενος δὲ πρὸς αὐτὴν ἐρωτικῶς) with her and could not bear to be separated from her, he was nevertheless forbidden by Persian law from being reconciled with her (*Ant.* 11.195). Regarding Esther, Josephus says that when she went to the king "he was pleased with her" and "having fallen in love" (πεσὼν ... ἐις ἔρωτα) with her, promptly married her (*Ant.* 11.202; cf., Est. 2:17). The king is thus presented as driven by desire, unlike Mordecai whose affection for Esther is purely filial (*Ant.* 11.204). Ultimately, the king's excessive desire is constrained by the requirements of law, which is another crucial motif for Josephus.

One not so constrained is Haman, who in the dramatic climax of the story throws himself on Esther in a desperate and ill-fated plea for clemency only to create the illusion of trying to violate her (*Ant.* 11.265). The irony of this scene, of course, is that the vile man is not actually guilty of the crime in this case, yet the truth of his evil character is exposed. Indeed, the formerly duped king finally speaks truth when in Josephus' version he declares Haman the "worst of all men" (ὦ κάκιστε πάντων ἀνθρώπων; *Ant.* 11.265). This is not the first time he was been thus identified, for Mordecai had called him that much earlier in the story even though the king thought of him as a man of "faithfulness and steadfast good will" (*Ant.* 11.217). In that case too, though, there was an element of profound irony, because Mordecai had mistakenly thought Haman was mocking him when he was required by the king to present Mordecai with the reward for his loyalty (*Ant.* 11.257). In fact, Josephus revels in the dark humor of the story on many levels and goes so far as to present God mocking (καταγελάω) Haman's intention to "crucify" Mordecai, and "knowing what would happen, [God] was delighted (τέρπω) by what would come about" (*Ant.* 11.247). This theme is reminiscent of Esther's earlier prayer in the Greek version of the story, in which she pleads with God not to let their enemies "laugh at our downfall" (LXX Add. Est. C:22; AT 4:23 has "rejoice"). Further, the reversal theme, which would have been familiar to Josephus' Greek readers and is already a key theme in the biblical book (Winitzer 2011), is of course part of Josephus' central contention regarding the fate of those who fail to live up to the just requirements of God's law (*Ant.* 1.14). Going further, Josephus claims to be amazed at the reciprocity (Swart 2006, 57) of God's wisdom and justice whereby Haman's evil plan is not only checked but meted out on him instead, providing thereby "for others to learn that whatever a person prepares against another he is unwittingly preparing first against himself" (*Ant.* 11.268; see also 11.286).

Conflicting Laws

The heightened eroticism and dark irony of the story, powerful though they are, are balanced for Josephus by another important theme, namely the interplay of conflicting laws (Chalupa 2016; Kneebone 2013, 168–74). Right from the beginning of the story, the characters are embroiled in the complexity of competing customs and legal constraints. Vashti, for example, refuses the authority of the king—and thus forfeits her position as queen—because of her regard for the laws of the Persians "that forbid women to be seen by strangers" (*Ant.* 11.191). This explanation of Vashti's behavior is Josephus' own addition to the story. While it fails to explain why neither the king nor his advisors seem to have acknowledged that law (in order to thus exonerate the queen), it serves to highlight one of Josephus' own interests throughout the story. The king, after all, had himself set aside a customary norm of the Persians by the way he gave leeway to the serving and imbibing of alcohol (*Ant.* 11.188). And later in the story, at the dramatic moment when Esther enters the king's presence unbidden and then faints under the extreme duress and terror of the moment, Ahasuerus assures her that the law was aimed at the king's subjects, so that she as his coruler "had no need to fear" (*Ant.* 11.238). In this extra-biblical detail, Josephus is following the Greek versions, which include the statement (not in the Hebrew text), "Take heart! You shall not die, for our ordinance is only for the common person" (LXX/AT Add. Est. D:8-9/5:8-9). Josephus goes beyond the Greek versions, though, with a personal editorializing comment to the effect that "I think" the king changed his mind because of the will of God (*Ant.* 11.237). One cannot help but recall that in Josephus' version, Esther had prayed before entering the king's presence that God would make her appearance even "more beautiful than before" (*Ant.* 11.232). That Esther was forced to rely on her beauty in such a perilous situation is made more dramatic by Josephus' novelistic description of the king as surrounded by men with axes (πελέκεις, *Ant.* 11.205).

For Josephus, the tension is all the more real because of immovable laws that catch individuals and whole communities in impossible binds. In such cases it is only counter-laws (or divine intervention) that can save the day. Thus, according to Josephus, it is Mordecai's wisdom and scrupulous adherence to "his native law" (τὸν οἴκοθεν αὐτοῦ νόμον) that land him and the whole nation of the Jews in the calamitous crisis that forms the central crux of the story. Haman's lofty status, on the other hand—whereby he could expect all and sundry to make obeisance to him—was undergirded by a royal decree. Later in the story, Josephus follows the Greek versions by inserting a prayer in which Mordecai confesses to God that he would not bow to Haman, because he could not abide the thought that "the honour that I habitually give to you should be given to this man" (*Ant.* 11.230; cf., LXX/AT Add. Est. C:7/4:15).

In addition to the various royal subjects (Vashti, Esther, Mordecai) who are under the rule of law, the king himself is subject to the law as well, though somewhat inconsistently. Not only does Josephus go beyond the biblical versions to emphasize that his marriage to Esther was "lawfully" (νομίμως) contracted, but even before that, it is the inviolability of Persian law that had made reconciliation with Vashti impossible (*Ant.* 11.195; cf., Est. 1:19). Throughout the story, though, it is above all the Jewish people (as represented primarily by Esther and Mordecai) who are truly law abiding. Thus, in Mordecai's prayer for salvation from Haman's plot, he reminds God that his people are those who "do not transgress your laws" (*Ant.* 11.230). And in the same context, Esther scrupulously adheres to "ancestral law" in her manner of mourning, fasting, and petitionary prayers (*Ant.* 11.231). Of course, Esther also shows the depth of her courage by determining to approach the king on this throne despite the law prohibiting it (*Ant.* 11.228). This ties in with Josephus' emphasis on the "virtues" of all his protagonists all through the biblical paraphrase (see, e.g., Feldman 1998a and 1998b) and contrasts strongly with the presentation of Haman as an evil man, as noted above. At one point, Haman promises to pay the king 40,000 silver talents (an exorbitant sum) for any loss of tribute revenue incurred because of the destruction of the Jewish community (*Ant.*

11.214), which gives the impression that Haman's standing with the king is bought rather than based on character as is Mordecai's.

Josephus' emphasis on law within the story draws our attention to two other important features as well, namely, the introduction of God into the narrative and the formulation of Haman's charges against the Jews. We now turn to each of these in turn.

The Introduction of God

As we have noted already, Josephus follows the Greek versions by regularly introducing God into the story (*Ant.* 11.227, 229, 232, 234, 237, 247, 259, 279, 280, 282, 294).[2] The first of these instances occurs when Mordecai counsels Esther not to shirk her responsibility in the face of Haman's threat to her people. Should she do so, Mordecai warns, not only would help come from God but she and her paternal house would ultimately be destroyed by the Jews themselves (*Ant.* 11.227). Incidentally, Josephus' introduction of God in no way diminishes the responsibility placed on Esther's shoulders, as Swart (2006, 58) has shown. In the next scene, both Mordecai and Esther fast and pray to God, confessing the historic sins of the people and pleading for God's intervention. Josephus' version of Esther's prayer strikes quite a different tone than the Greek versions, where she prays for courage and eloquence (LXX/AT Add. Est. C:23, 24/4:25) while also confessing the sins of the nation and affirming her trust in God. Greek Esther goes on, however, to refer scathingly to the idol-worship of the Persians (LXX/AT Add. Est. C:19-20, 22/4:22) and to insist that she hates "the bed of the uncircumcised and of any foreigner," and that she abhors "like a menstrual cloth" the crown on her head, which she wears in public but never in private (LXX/AT Add. Est. C:26, 27/4:26). All of this is far too inflammatory for Josephus, who has Esther ask simply for God to have pity on her, "so that when the king saw her pleading, her speech might seem persuasive to him and her appearance more beautiful than ever before" (*Ant.* 11.232), and that the king might by this means come to hate the Jews' enemies instead. While Josephus has no intention of presenting Esther as one who hates non-Jews, he does not shy away from portraying her as vengeful at the end of story, by requesting the crucifixion of Haman's ten sons (*Ant.* 11.289). Presumably, Josephus thought such a response to be perfectly justifiable within the context of the attempted genocide—and, presumably, he thought his readers would agree.

Josephus' God, finally, not only oversees and protects his people (represented in this story by Esther and Mordecai), but he oversees and grants the power of

---

2. It should be noted that while Josephus follows the Greek versions by inserting God into the narrative, he chooses not to include the first and last of the additional passages that portray the conflict between Haman and Mordecai as a cosmic conflict between apocalyptic forces (Spilsbury and Seeman 2017, 52).

empire to the king himself—a point Josephus' Artaxerxes explicitly recognizes (*Ant.* 11.279) and that fits neatly into Josephus' overall vision of the rise and fall of nations (Spilsbury 2003).

Haman's Charges and Their Remedy

Josephus follows the biblical versions in making the standoff between Mordecai and Haman the centerpiece of the story. While Mordecai is introduced as possessed of innate wisdom (*Ant.* 11.210), Haman "the Agagite" (Est. 3:1) is identified as an Amalekite (*Ant.* 11.209). Josephus is thus the first extant exemplar of a line of interpretation later found also in the Rabbis (cf., B. Meg. 13a; Est. Rab. 3:2; 7:4) when he states that "by nature [Haman] hated the Jews because the race of the Amalekites, from which he himself came, had been utterly destroyed by them" (*Ant.* 11.211). In Josephus' retelling, Haman hates the Jews not because of ethnic or religious disdain but because of an historic grievance—a grievance that Josephus does not dispute. Josephus then follows and expands the biblical accounts' rendition of Haman's slanders to produce "one of the most all-encompassing anti-Jewish statements to have come down to us from antiquity" (Spilsbury and Seeman 2017, 54). In Est. 3:8 Haman's calumny to the king reads as follows:

> There is a certain people scattered and separated among the peoples in all the provinces of your kingdom; their laws are different from those of every other people, and they do not keep the king's laws.

Josephus, for his part, relates that Haman brought an accusation to the king,

> saying that scattered throughout the world ruled by him was an evil nation, unsociable, exclusive, having neither the same worship as others nor using the same laws, but hostile in both its customs and its practices to [his] people and to all humanity. (*Ant.* 11.212)

In both the biblical and Josephan accounts the Jews are characterized as a "scattered" people, but now in addition they are vilified as evil (πονηρόν), unsociable (ἄμικτον), and exclusive (ἀσύμφυλον). The biblical characterization of the Jews as having unique laws is retained, along with the addition of charges of insubordination and hostility to all humanity. Josephus then provides a tight paraphrase of the LXX's Addition B, in which the king is made to repeat Haman's slanders in official form, including the characterization of the Jews as "a hostile nation mixed in with all humanity, with strange laws and insubordinate to kings and having peculiar customs and hating monarchy and disaffected by our government" (*Ant.* 11.217).

In both Josephus and the Greek versions, Haman forges a link between uniqueness or particularity on the one hand and a threat to the imperial order on the other. He equates strangeness with hostility, peculiarity with insubordination, and disaffection with a hatred of monarchy (Spilsbury and Seeman 2017, 54–5).[3] The remedy for Haman's slanders is not only the overthrow of Haman himself, along with the repudiation of his person—and delighting in the reversal of his fortune and the destruction of his sons—but, even more importantly, the official publication of the king's rescript (*Ant.* 11.273–83; Add. Est. E:1-24/7:22-32), which asserts the opposite of Haman's slanders as forcefully as possible. In Josephus' retelling, Haman's "false accusations and slanders ... against those who had done no wrong" were motived by "personal hatred" (μῖσος ἴδιον). Haman, we now learn, in addition to being an Amalekite and "a stranger to Persian blood," failed to deal properly with his good fortune (a trope familiar to readers of Greek tragedy) and proved unable to manage his prosperity with "sound reason" (*Ant.* 11.276; cf., 8.251; 9.122). The Jews, by contrast, "are not evil, but live under the best kind of government and rely on the God who guarded the kingdom for me and our ancestors" (*Ant.* 11.279). They are now to be shown "every honour," and the imperial decree declaring that the Jews are to be allowed "to live in peace according to their own laws" is to be displayed prominently throughout the kingdom (*Ant.* 11.281; cf., Add. Est. E:19/7:29).

I have pointed out elsewhere (Spilsbury and Seeman 2017, 58) that Josephus' close paraphrase of the edicts offered in the Greek versions reveals something of the seriousness with which he regarded all official and bureaucratic decrees, edicts, official letters, and legal rulings of all kinds that, no matter how disparate, might contribute to a cumulative case for the recognition of Jewish claims to their place within whatever society they found themselves (cf., *Ant.* 14.185–267, 305–22; 16.160–78). The overall impact of such material, as Tessa Rajak (2009, 178) has demonstrated, was to create an impression of "enduring official respect" for Jewish communities shown by various gentile jurisdictions and authorities in cities around the world. While the specific terms and details of this respect varied from jurisdiction to jurisdiction, the import for Josephus is that the Jews should be allowed to live unmolested according to their own laws and customs. At the end of one series of citations he notes,

> Now it was necessary for me to cite these decrees ... in order to show that in former times we were treated with all respect and were not prevented by our rulers from practicing any of our ancestral customs but, on the contrary, even had their cooperation in preserving our religion and our way of honoring God. (*Ant.* 16.174)

Josephus' inclusion of the text of the king's rescript in the Esther story may be seen in light of this statement, with the sense that it gives of the Jewish community's hopes

---

3. For similar accusations in antiquity, see Hecataeus of Abdera (cited in Diodorus Siculus 40.3.4), Manetho (cited in Josephus, *Apion* 1.73–91, 227–50), Apollonius Molon (cited in Josephus, *Apion* 2.148), Cicero (*Flac.* 67, 69), Juvenal (*Sat.* 14.103–104) and Tacitus (*Hist.* 5.5.1).

and aspirations. By citing these kinds of imperial decrees, and by emphasizing the Jews' adherence to law, Josephus seeks to mitigate the sense of difference between the Jews and others, and any implication that there may be anything inappropriate or unseemly about the Jewish way of life (Chalupa 2016, 148–9).

Diaspora Complexities

Josephus introduces his retelling of the Esther story by announcing that it relates to a time during the reign of the Persian king Artaxerxes, when "the whole Judean nation along with their women and children was in danger of being utterly destroyed" (*Ant.* 11.184). Thus, he foreshadows the crisis created by Haman's hatred that runs throughout the story and is only relieved in the final scenes of celebration at the very end of the story. Emily Kneebone (2013) has demonstrated that the Esther story allowed Josephus to explore the extraordinary challenges that faced Jewish communities living in Diaspora contexts (also Frilingos 2009). The excellence of the Jewish constitution—one of Josephus' central claims in both the *Antiquities* (1.5) and *Against Apion* (2.178)—is proven by the mettle of Esther and Mordecai and is eventually even asserted by the king himself (*Ant.* 11.279). In communities far away from the natural protections afforded by one's own homeland, Diaspora Jews were constantly in danger of the kinds of threats represented by Haman. Nevertheless, Josephus refuses to retreat into a purely defensive mode. Rather, he presents his protagonists as living confident and successful lives within foreign empires.

Josephus thus avoids the impression of Diaspora life as inferior to an imagined ideal homeland. At the conclusion of the Esther story we find the Jews celebrating the inaugural feast of *Purim* with Mordecai "great and illustrious in the eyes of the king," and the affairs of the Jews "better than all hope" (*Ant.* 11.295–96). More subtly, Josephus draws attention to Diaspora dynamics by the way he structures the post-destruction sections of his biblical paraphrase. Josephus' retelling of the specifically biblical part of his history concludes without comment at *Antiquities* 11.296, which is also the end of the Esther narrative. From that point till the end of Book 11, Josephus narrates a series of stories associated with late Persian-period Judah, including, most famously, the account of Alexander's interactions with the Jews in and around Jerusalem. This completes a pattern of alternating stories from the Diaspora and the land of Israel throughout his account of the period from the fall of Jerusalem in the latter stages of Book 10, all the way through to the end of Book 11. Thus, he concludes Book 10 with a retelling of the book of Daniel (set in Babylon). Then, for the first half of Book 11 he offers a rewriting of the narratives from the biblical books of Ezra and Nehemiah, which focus on the return of the exiles to the province of Judah. At regular points along the way he includes episodes set in Babylon or Persia: the story of Zerubbabel (*Ant.* 11.33–63), the introduction of Ezra (*Ant.* 11.120–33), and the story of Nehemiah the cupbearer (*Ant.* 11.159–67). These stories serve to keep us in touch with a sense that while the main narrative is unfolding in the land of Israel, there is a parallel story involving faithful Jews in Mesopotamia. The story of Esther, then, takes its place at the end of this chain of Diaspora stories, before Josephus brings us back to the main Judah story, set in and around Jerusalem to conclude Book 11.

I will pause here to note that this sense of parallel "spheres" of Jewish life is also maintained in Josephus' well-known definition of the term Ἰουδαῖοι, which pops up unexpectedly in his retelling of the story of Nehemiah:

> And the *Ioudaioi* [he writes] … were called by this name from the days when they went up out of Babylon, after the tribe of Judah, which was the first to come into those places; so that both they and the country share the designation. (*Ant.* 11.173)

Josephus has been using the term Ἰουδαῖοι throughout the *Antiquities*, so it is not entirely clear why he pauses to make this clarification here; but we may note simply that Josephus chooses to define the term *Ioudaioi* in a context where there is both a homeland and a Diaspora—and that the term applies equally to the communities in both places. A similar dynamic may be discerned in *Antiquities* 11.133, in which Josephus explains that despite the permission given to Persian Jews by Xerxes in the time of Ezra, "the people of the Israelites as a whole" (ὁ … πᾶς λαὸς τῶν Ἰσραηλιτῶν) remained where they were. He then continues to explain that this is the reason that there are two tribes of Jews in Asia and Europe, while the remaining ten tribes "are still beyond the Euphrates till now—countless myriads unable to be known by number." This is critical for his presentation of the Esther material. The story of Jews in the Persian Empire is not a side story, as it were. It is as much at the heart of what it means to be a Jew as any other part of his narrative of Jewish history and identity.

Despite this reality, Esther still feels compelled to hide her national identity (*Ant.* 11.203; cf., Est. 2:10, 20), even though she is "a Judean woman of royal descent" (*Ant.* 11.185). Thus, it is only Mordecai, "one of the prominent men among the Judeans," who is targeted by Haman. Clearly, though, it is Jewish identity and all that it entails for Esther and Mordecai that bring their lives, and indeed those of the whole Jewish community, to the brink of calamity. For Josephus, the point of the story is to demonstrate that those detractors and haters who take Jewishness to be a cause for malice are profoundly misguided and foolish.

Conclusion

In his description of the immediate aftermath of the fall of Jerusalem in 70 CE Josephus includes an account of the fortunes of the Jews in Antioch (*War* 7.41–111), which bears comparison to the perilous situation recounted in the book of Esther. Here too, Josephus tells us, "the Jews were subject to accusations which put them in danger of genocide" (ὄλεθρος).[4] The cognate term ὀλέθριος appears in *Antiquities* 11.282, where it is used by Artaxerxes near the conclusion of his edict

---

4. Trans. Hammond (2017).

declaring the 13th of Adar to be a day of salvation rather than one of "destruction" as Haman had intended. As in Persia, so in Antioch the gentile ruler (Titus on this occasion) decides in favor of the Jews, refusing to disregard or set aside certain bronze tablets, "on which the rights and privileges of the Jews were inscribed" (*War* 7.110). What this incident reveals is that the danger portrayed in the book of Esther is still utterly real in the lived experience of Jews, not only in the immediate aftermath of the war but well into the late first century as well (Barclay 2005; Goodman 2007, 428–47; Schäfer 1997, 180–95) when Josephus was writing his various tomes. And the lessons of Esther still pertained. By retelling this story along with other Diaspora stories Josephus was able to project a realistic and yet hopeful picture of the possibilities for Jewish existence in a world dominated by foreign rulers and hostile detractors. Ultimately, Josephus presents a world in which Diaspora Jews can establish legally protected communities in which flourishing meant the ability to live peaceably according to their own customs. Perhaps Josephus saw his own work in Rome as contributing in some material way to this outcome.

Chapter 13

ESTHER IN DIALOGUE WITH MARK: POWER, VULNERABILITY, AND KINGSHIP

Kara J. Lyons-Pardue

Attentive reading of stories of kings and the machinations of powerful people, especially biblical ones, must take note of who *actually* holds the power in a particular situation and what they do with the authority with which they are entrusted. Across the biblical witness, the common aphorism "Might makes right" is rejected again and again. This critique of power's misuse extends both to foreign powers lording it over the Hebrew people (e.g., Exod. 1:8-22; 5:1-9, 15-19) and to Israel's own kings and leaders (e.g., 1 Sam. 8; 2 Sam. 12:1-15). The traditions and texts conveying the stories of Esther—and the gentile king Ahasuerus (MT)/Artaxerxes (LXX)[1]—add an additional layer of complexity to the portrayal of power: the impact of gender. Fascinatingly, those intersecting dynamics and their complexity seem to be understood, or at least reflected, in a passage found in the Gospel that was likely the earliest written. Mark relates the story of Herod Antipas, his aristocratic dinner guests, his wife Herodias, her daughter, and their devastating interactions with Jesus' prophetic forerunner John. In doing so, the Evangelist uses one of his most overt intertextual allusions.[2]

Within Mark's Gospel, the story of John the Baptist's beheading is exceptional in several ways. First, the series of courtly encounters is lengthy and related in great detail, despite Jesus being entirely absent from the scene. The gruesome

---

1. While LXX Esther is the text in reference most frequently throughout (illuminating connections to the Greek text of Mark), the versification follows MT Esther for ease of reference in translated versions, though the LXX and MT may differ. Throughout, I designate the king in reference in the book of Esther, the Persian king commonly called Xerxes I, as "Artaxerxes" (Ἀρταξέρξης), his name in the main text in reference, the Septuagint (LXX). The king's name in the Hebrew and in many English versions of Esther is *Ahasuerus* (אֲחַשְׁוֵרוֹשׁ; See NRSV, KJV, CEB, ESV; contra "Xerxes" used in the NIV, CEV, NLT, and NIRV).

2. Mark's use of Scripture in allusive ways—in comparison, e.g., to the direct citation formulas found in Matthew—is well established (see Hays 2016, esp. 97–103; Marcus 1992; Watts 1997). Of course, there are direct quotations of OT passages in Mark, but often the scriptural undercurrent of Mark's narration is seen more in whispers than shouts, so to speak.

tableau—replete with several manipulative and violent episodes—exists as an aside. The narrative flashback scene is, ostensibly, an explanation of Herod Antipas' reaction to Jesus' spreading renown (6:14-16). The catastrophic backstory plays out entirely off the Christocentric stage of Mark's Gospel, contained in a royal courtly environment into which Jesus never sets foot. The omniscient narrator relates the motivations and intentions of his aristocratic subjects.

Mark's is a narrative in which female figures (primarily anonymous ones) seem to receive a higher percentage of Jesus' scant approval than do his named male followers. In that light, the second aspect that makes the pericope relating John's beheading unusual within the Second Gospel is that, in it, one of the women is named and both are identifiable by their associations with well-known ruling men. Other than Jesus' mother Mary (6:3) and the women named within the passion and tomb narratives (15:40, 47; 16:1 [9]), this is the only other occurrence of a named woman in Mark's Gospel. Typically, women are distinguished by connections to male relatives,[3] maladies from which Jesus heals them (5:25-34; 7:25, 30), or some aspect of their life-circumstances (7:24-30; 12:42-44). In Mk 14:3-9, the woman who anoints Jesus at Bethany—to whom Jesus pays extra attention and about whom he institutes a sweeping statement ensuring that she be memorialized (v. 9)—fits the pattern as anonymous, but departs from it as the narrator identifies her by her actions and their location alone. Herodias, then, as a woman who is named, elite, and famous, is quite unlike the other female characters to which Mark devotes narrative interest.

Third, the Herodian women in Mk 6:14-29 are not presented as sympathetic characters, or even neutral ones, at least on an initial reading. The mother and daughter pair seem to orchestrate the grisly death of Jesus' forerunner, John. As the only female villains in a story otherwise absent of them,[4] it is clear that there is something out of the ordinary being conveyed in the thirteen verses that comprise the story of John's death. Just as John's death portends something ominous about the trajectory of Jesus' own ministry, the story surrounding his death may provide

---

3. The women identified by family relation include: Simon's mother-in-law (1:30-31); initially, Jesus' mother (3:31-35) and, quite possibly, female siblings among his "brothers" (οἱ ἀδελφοὶ αὐτοῦ in 3.31; οἱ ἀδελφοί μου in 3:33, 34), as a seeming textual addition (not found in the very earliest codices) in 3:32 makes clear ("Your mother and your brothers [and your sisters] are seeking you outside"; ἡ μήτηρ σου καὶ οἱ ἀδελφοί σου [καὶ αἱ ἀδελφαί σου] ἔξω ζητοῦσίν σε); Jesus' female siblings are mentioned without a doubt—but also without names—in 6:3 and metaphorically in 3:35; Jairus' daughter (5:22-24a, 35-43) and her mother (5:40); the slave girl of the high priest (14:66, 69). Arguably, women who are mentioned in theory, either in teaching or dialogue, tend to be denoted through relationship, wives, mothers, widows, and the pregnant or nursing mothers of infants (see 10:2, 4, 7, 29-30; 12:19-23, 40; 13:17). Even when women are named, they can be further specified by relationship, as in the case of Mary the mother of James and Joses (15:40, 47; 16:1). Here and throughout, all translations are the author's own, unless otherwise noted.

4. The slave girl of Mk 14:66, 69 certainly has an antagonistic part to play. But Simon Peter, whom she confronts, is certainly the "bad guy" of the pericope (see 14:72).

illumination for other aspects of Jesus' interactions. The connections and implications a reader should draw from the episode, however, deepen and shift somewhat when read in light of their primary intertextual allusion to the story of Esther.

Mark 6:17-29 deserves a closer reading, to which we will turn, but it is important to establish the connection between the bold promises made by Herod Antipas to Herodias' daughter (6:22b-23) and the favor the king vows to Esther (5:3; 7:2). Common between them is the careless offer of a substantial portion of the kingdom entrusted to each leader's care to a woman within his sphere. The episodes diverge in important ways in the relationships between the ruler and the woman to whom he promises such a significant portion of authority, in the events that precipitate the pledge, and in outcome. Nevertheless, Herod Antipas' rash promise that leads to John the Baptist's execution carries with it a set of intertextual associations to Esther that are worth investigating.

Table 13.1 highlights vocabulary common between Esther's and Mark's narratives.[5] Each king (ὁ βασιλεὺς) speaks directly to a female (e.g., σου, σοι) and offers her a nearly open-ended promise of favor, in both cases "up to half" of his kingdom (ἕως [τοῦ] ἡμίσους τῆς βασιλείας μου). In each instance, the powerful man does not give instructions to the female recipient of his favor regarding what she should request. He asks *what* (τί) she wants. Of course, favor bestowed so capriciously might well be taken away with as little warning,[6] so caution is warranted.

There is sufficient coherence—including word-for-word parallels—to assume Mark's dependence upon the Esther story, or, at a minimum, a purposeful allusion. Indeed, Mark's use of the term the "king," that is, βασιλεὺς,[7] for Herod is inaccurate for his actual position, but likely chosen strategically to intensify the allusion to Esther. The most profound verbal connection is quite obvious in the scale and extravagance of the offer: "up to half my kingdom" (ἕως [τοῦ] ἡμίσους τῆς βασιλείας μου; Est. 5:3; Mk 6:23).

The power imbalance between Queen Esther and her king Artaxerxes (LXX) does not, initially, seem as profound as that between Herod Antipas and the stepdaughter Mark refers to as a "little girl" (κοράσιον; 6:22, 28). Yet the narrative of the book of Esther demonstrates King Artaxerxes to be both impulsive (Est. 1:10-12) and able to be swayed by male courtiers (e.g., 1:13-22; 2:4; 3:8-11). Nevertheless, he is immersed in a culture of absolute kingly sovereignty (4:11).[8]

---

5. Bolded terms in Greek indicate verbal connections between LXX Esther's terminology and Mark's.

6. See, e.g., Vashti's former position (1:9-12) and John the Baptist's previous favor, even if only as a curiosity or amusement to Herod Antipas (6:20).

7. Although Mark calls Herod Antipas "king" (ὁ βασιλεὺς) his actual role was tetrarch. See references to him as τετραάρχης in Mt. 14:1 and Lk. 3:19; 9:7.

8. That kingly sovereignty is intended to extend to all male–female relationships, at least marital ones, as per the royal dictate of Est. 1:17-22. Meredith J. Stone (2018, 144) describes the decrees as "seeking to stabilize hegemonic masculinity." As such, patriarchy in localized households is intended to reflect the king's (recovered) sovereignty in his (143).

Table 13.1 Promised Favor in LXX Est. 5:3, 6; 7:2; 9:12, and Mk 6:22b, 23

FIRST OCCURRENCE IN LXX ESTHER
LXX Est. 5:3 (King Artaxerxes to Esther)
καὶ **εἶπεν ὁ βασιλεύς** Τί θέλεις, Εσθηρ, καὶ τί σού ἐστιν τὸ ἀξίωμα; **ἕως τοῦ ἡμίσους τῆς βασιλείας μου** καὶ ἔσται **σοι**.

And the King said, "What do you want, Esther, and what is your petition? Up to half of my kingdom and it is yours."

REPETITIONS OF PROMISE IN LXX ESTHER (intensifications underlined)[a]
LXX Est. 5:6 (King Artaxerxes to Esther)
ἐν δὲ τῷ πότῳ εἶπεν **ὁ βασιλεὺς** πρὸς Εσθηρ Τί ἐστιν, βασίλισσα Εσθηρ; καὶ ἔσται **σοι** ὅσα ἀξιοῖς.

Now, while they were drinking, the King says to Esther, "What is it, <u>Queen</u> Esther? And it will be yours <u>as much as [you deem] worthy</u>."

LXX Est. 7:2 (King Artaxerxes to Esther)
εἶπεν δὲ ὁ βασιλεὺς Εσθηρ τῇ δευτέρᾳ ἡμέρᾳ ἐν τῷ πότῳ Τί ἐστιν, Εσθηρ βασίλισσα, καὶ τί τὸ **αἴτημά σου** καὶ τί τὸ ἀξίωμά σου; καὶ ἔστω **σοι ἕως τοῦ ἡμίσους τῆς βασιλείας μου**.

Now the King said [to] Esther on the second day while drinking, "What is it, Esther <u>Queen</u>, and <u>what is your request</u> and what is your petition? <u>And let it be yours</u> up to half of my kingdom!"

LXX Est. 9:12 (King Artaxerxes to Esther)
… τί οὖν ἀξιοῖς ἔτι καὶ ἔσται **σοι**;

… Therefore, what [do you deem] worthy <u>still</u> and it will be yours.

FIRST PROMISE IN MARK'S ACCOUNT
Mk 6:22b (King Herod Antipas to Herodias's daughter)
εἶπεν ὁ βασιλεὺς τῷ κορασίῳ· **αἴτησόν** με ὃ ἐὰν θέλῃς, καὶ δώσω **σοι**·

The king said to the little girl, "Ask from me for whatever you might want, and I will give to you!"

REPETITION OF PROMISE IN MARK'S ACCOUNT (intensifications underlined)
Mk 6:23 (King Herod Antipas to Herodias's daughter)
καὶ ὤμοσεν αὐτῇ [πολλά] ὅ **τι** ἐάν με **αἰτήσῃς** δώσω **σοι ἕως ἡμίσους τῆς βασιλείας μου**.

<u>And he swore</u> to her [<u>many times</u>], "Whatever you might ask from me, I will give to you <u>up to half of my kingdom</u>."

---

[a] While some of the stories' intensifications are preserved in the Greek translation (relying on Rahlfs–Hanhart edition of the LXX), both Est. 5:6 and 9:12 are far more emphatic and intensified in the Hebrew (as modern English translations, e.g., the NRSV, reflect well). The LXX seems more apt to streamline the effusiveness of the king's promises, while retaining each repeated occurrence.

Those factors, comingled with the plentitude and apparent disposability of courtly women (2:2-4, 14) and even the queen, as Queen Vashti[9] experienced (1:19; 2:17), makes Esther's position anything but secure, even before the revelation of her Jewish identity (2:10; 4:10-17).

---

9. The LXX gives the name of the queen as Αστιν (1:15), but because English readers are more familiar with the name Vashti (וַשְׁתִּי), the transliteration of the MT name will be preferred (following Stone 2018, 117 n. 50).

Throughout the narrative, it is reinforced that King Artaxerxes does as "pleases" (ἀρέσκω)[10] him again and again (e.g., 1:21; 2:4)—a disposition reflected in his lackey, the story's villain Haman, as well (5:13-14)—which conveys both sovereignty and also extreme pliability. The account demonstrates that the king's "pleasure" is too often rash and susceptible to the schemes of others, whether advisors (1:19-21), Haman (3:9-11), or, in the end, Esther (7:3; 8:5-8; 9:13-14).[11] On the other hand, "pleasing" onlookers is what secures Esther's influence in the royal household (2:9) and then with the king himself through "finding favor" (2:17; cf., 7:3; 8:5). It is, after all, the bestowal of favor that introduces the major plot twists in the narrative.[12]

Allusively, Mark's account evidences conceptual and terminological overlap with the precedent of the Esther narrative, in terms of pleasure and granting favor. In 6:22, the young girl who dances pleases (ἀρέσκω) Herod and his banquet guests.[13] It is then that he bestows carelessly a great deal of favor on Herodias' daughter, echoing the promise Artaxerxes makes to Esther. Perhaps readers are intended to hear the echo, while noting both its congruence and dissonance. For while the narrative of Esther demonstrates the fickle favor—with dramatic consequences—of Artaxerxes' pleasure, the result is favorable for Esther, his queen, and her people. Herod's conduct is even more fickle: he bestows up to half

---

10. I highlighted this Greek verb because of its use in Mk 6:22. However, while the Hebrew typically conveys the sense that something "seems pleasing" with similar vocabulary—a conditional phrase "if it should [seem] pleasing …" (e.g., here "to the king": אִם־עַל־הַמֶּלֶךְ טוֹב; 3:9) or that something or someone "pleased" (e.g., וַיִּיטַב; 2:9) the king or other in control—the Greek uses a wider range of expressions. Primarily, the LXX alternates between two main verbs—ἀρέσκω and δοκέω—to convey the volition and shifting wishes of the king and others in position of authority. See LXX Esther's use of δοκέω here: 1:19; 3:9; 5:4; 8:5 and 8. The other term, ἀρέσκω, is utilized only slightly more often; see: 1:21; 2:4 (twice), 9, 17; and 5:14. In the Greek, there are other terms enlisted to convey shifting wishes (e.g., ὡς βούλει; 3:11).

11. Obviously, the book expresses the irony that a woman who receives her position of honor as a result of a series of actions that seek to enforce the cultural ideal that the kingdom's women should be subject to their husbands (1:19-22; 2:1, 16-17) is the one able to persuade her husband, the king, to alter one of his "irrevocable" official decrees (8:3-8; cf., 3:14-15).

12. Beyond Esther's place in King Artaxerxes' household (see 2:9, 17), the king's affirmative responses to requests—"if it pleases the king"—afford Haman his growing influence (3:9) and, conversely, Esther the opportunity at a banquet to undo Haman's influence (5:4). In 7:3, however, Esther leverages explicitly the favor received from the king to protect herself and her people (Heb: אִם־מָצָאתִי חֵן בְּעֵינֶיךָ הַמֶּלֶךְ/"If I have won favor in the king's sight"; LXX: Εἰ εὗρον χάριν ἐνώπιον τοῦ βασιλέως/"If I found favor before the king"). A similar conditional phrase is repeated in 8:5.

13. Note that Herod Antipas had listened formerly *with pleasure* (καὶ ἡδέως αὐτοῦ ἤκουεν) to John (6:20).

his kingdom on a young girl (κοράσιον; 6:22), his wife's daughter, not on a loyal queen. For both Artaxerxes and Herod, it is likely that readers are to imagine an evening fueled by food and drink contributed to the laxity of judgment and rash promises.[14] While Esther's precarious hold on the king's favor and pleasure extends over a period of time,[15] the young girl's dance sparks a spontaneous offering from Herod (Mk 6:22). The result of Herod's impulsivity is decidedly negative within the Evangelist's purview.

In terms of congruence with Esther's story, security of position is, of course, the main thing at stake for Herodias. Her relationship with Antipas has been called into question by the meddlesome prophet John (Mk 6:18-20). In both stories, royal women are vulnerable to the whims and preferences of royal men. In Esther's case, however, the vulnerability extends beyond Esther and her relative Mordecai, to the members of her people, the Jews, throughout Artaxerxes' kingdom (Est. 3:6; 4:3). There is no broader reach, beyond protection of herself and her daughter, for Herodias, as far as the reader is aware. The self-risking bravery of Esther on behalf of a broader community (4:9-17) predisposes most readers to cheer on Esther's securing of her position. Readers of Mark are likely indifferent to or skeptical of Herodias' position.

In terms of audience perspectives, when most readers encounter Mark's tale of Herodian courtly intrigue, any vulnerability on the part of Herodias or her daughter is easy to miss (6:17-29). While the machinations and power imbalances in the Herodian court are patent, it is the mistreatment and unjust death of John that garners the reader's interest. Yet those very same forces, the unstable and shifting favor of the king and his unchecked power, place Herodias and her daughter (θυγατρὸς) in the mode of reliance and contingency. Further, Mark describes Herodias' daughter as a κοράσιον—a little girl—which demonstrates that she is far more susceptible than powerful.[16]

---

14. In Mk 6:21, all that we are specifically told is that Herod throws himself a birthday banquet and invites elite officers and Galilean aristocrats. The invited guests of Herod include military officers (χιλιάρχοις), which bear a marked similarity to the guests at Artaxerxes' earliest banquet in Est. 1:3 (MT: חָיִל). Although we may assume that excesses in food and drink were part of celebratory occasions—among those who could afford it—in the Esther account, both the Hebrew and Greek versions identify drinking (Heb: בְּמִשְׁתֵּה הַיַּיִן; LXX: ἐν τῷ πότῳ) as the activity during which the initial two promises take place (5:6; 7:2).

15. Esther's own favored status was far from guaranteed. Her note to Mordecai makes clear that she remained cognizant of the passage of time between her audience with the king (thirty days, in this instance), keeping tabs vigilantly on her status (4:11). The totality of time in which Esther was said to be Artaxerxes' favored consort is unclear, but the banquets extended at two days (7:2) and subsequent requests extended beyond that (see 8:9-12).

16. The diminutive κοράσιον does not convey a precise age range, but likely an age prior to standard marrying ages (childhood through early teenage years). In Mark, in the other instance of the term's use, κοράσιον refers clearly to a female child still under the protection of her parents (5:41-42). In addition to κοράσιον, Jairus' daughter is also called

It is worth noting that Herod Antipas' devotion was already being tugged between Herodias, his wife (6:17-19), and the bold prophet John the Baptist (v. 20) well in advance of any "opportunity" (εὔκαιρος) that allowed Herodias to secure her position.[17] The child becomes entangled in her mother's deadly intrigue; indeed, her own vulnerability is wrapped up in and amplified by her mother's. Repeated deference to her mother illustrates the girl's family loyalty as well as her role as a dependent (6:24, 28). It requires consultation (v. 24) after Herod vows to bestow on the girl "whatever you might wish" (vv. 22-23) before she recognizes what "she" wants. She absorbs her mother's suggestion as her own wish ("I want" [θέλω]; v. 25). The reward Herodias' daughter receives for dancing passes along to the person who actually requested it, Herodias (v. 28). The girl is left no better off than when the scene opened, when she could have been granted up to half of the kingdom (v. 23).

The young girl is plunged into violent and "mature" circumstances, replete with political and interpersonal landmines. The girl's request both echoes her mother's suggestion and seems to intensify it and add details in a distressing way.[18] Herodias' daughter demands that Herod behead John "at once" (ἐξαυτῆς). Yet Mark includes clues in his narration that show that the girl remains a vulnerable, dependent child, being used by both parental figures. Herod takes pleasure from her dance. Many commentators read the pleasure of Herod and his guests in sexual terms, even as the lecherous exploitation of a minor and a stepdaughter.[19] But many interpreters (sometimes the same ones who note her exploitation) also place responsibility on the girl for the eroticism of her dance itself.[20] The narrator states only that by dancing she "pleased" Herod and his guests; pleasure remains within their perception of the dance.

θυγάτριόν by her father (5:23). That diminutive is used by the narrator in the story of the Syrophoenician mother's advocacy for her "little daughter" as well (7:25).

17. Herodias' posture toward John the Baptist is called ἐνέχω in 6:19. The term can indicate *entanglement in* a situation. Although it may not be obvious to modern readers, Herodias was subject to the decisions of her (second) husband, which seemed to waver based on his susceptibility to others' opinions. In this instance, it was John's preaching that drove her to seek a more secure footing in the royal household. Although triangulated relationship dynamics make it difficult to detect, Herod was actually the cause of Herodias' vulnerability. The obstacles the ruler presented, however, were not as easily swept aside as John's objections. Herodias' situation was a precariously entangled one.

18. Compare Herodias' simple statement—"The head of John the Baptist" [τὴν κεφαλὴν Ἰωάννου τοῦ βαπτίζοντος] in 6:24—to her daughter's: "I wish that you should give to me now upon a platter the head of John the Baptist" [θέλω ἵνα ἐξαυτῆς δῷς μοι ἐπὶ πίνακι τὴν κεφαλὴν Ἰωάννου τοῦ βαπτιστοῦ] in v. 25. Joel Marcus (1992, 402) calls it her "own macabre touch."

19. E.g., Marcus (1992, 396, 401). Likewise, lechery seems to be the impulse behind the royal summons to Vashti in Est. 1:10-12.

20. See, e.g., Marcus (1992, 397).

We learn that the king feels regret after his demonstrative promise. But he grants the request, thinking not of the girl whose dance brought him pleasure, nor of the prophet he used to take pleasure in hearing, but of maintaining his honor before his guests (6:26). The girl's mother thinks about her grudge, not the blood-soaked request she implants in her daughter's mouth. Mark uses the diminutive κοράσιον two times in v. 28: the "little girl" receives the platter holding the decapitated head of John and the "little girl" delivers her gruesome prize to her mother. Herodias' daughter takes center stage in the narrative, with little evidence that she exercised her own volition throughout the ordeal. Neither of the adults on whom she relies seem to consider her needs, her traumatization, nor her protection.[21]

Here, Mark's "soundtrack" for this grisly sequence of events features melodies taken from the Esther story. Perhaps other harmonies are at work as well; recognizing this can press us to return to Esther's own bloody episodes (e.g., 7:10; 8:11-12; 9:6-16).[22] There is an upbeat tone in recounting the Purim origin story, at least superficially, and perhaps a "happily ever after" vibe to the fairytale elements of the narrative (9:24-28; 10:1-3). However, Mark's use of the story might indicate that he sees past those things and finds more in common between the vulnerable and misused daughter of Herodias and the seemingly adored Queen Esther. The latter is enlisted in a battle taking place outside the castle walls where she has been cloistered, a battle with potentially dire consequences for her people, her guardian Mordecai, and herself (4:9-17). In risking her life, the narrator makes clear that Esther adopts as her own a plan that she did not devise. Fidelity to Mordecai persuades her to take on the dangerous plot. It is when Mordecai enters the scene with greater prominence (8:1-2) that her role turns from protector to avenger (8:3-12). The bloody slaughter of enemies, or potential enemies, may well have been coerced. Esther is used: it is up to the reader to determine whether that use is for good or ill.

I have argued elsewhere that Mark arranges this unusual episode in a way that implicitly contrasts Herodias' role as mother unfavorably with that of parents of

---

21. Again, within the explicitly patriarchal society in which Herodias herself operates, it deserves mention that one should suppose that Herodias' own actions and manipulation of her daughter's actions strive only to secure their place in Herod's good graces. They would be seeking, then, the ongoing protection of her daughter. Women, even aristocratic ones, existed in some ways subject to the desires of the men in their lives (e.g., Suetonius, *Nero* 34). Whatever "protection" Herodias may have understood herself to be granting her daughter required her to leverage her daughter's body in dancing and to subject her to potential traumatization in the violence that ensued.

22. The numbers of those reported to be killed in self-defense across the provinces are extreme: ultimately, more than 75,000 (9:16). Even when viewed as hyperbole in a mythic fiction, the numbers are shocking. As Stone (2018, 295) remarks, in the contest between Esther's God and Artaxerxes, God seems to win, but "the existence of domination is only perpetuated in mimicry and ambivalence as violence becomes a hallmark of God's victory."

daughters elsewhere in Mark (5:21-43; 7:24-30; Lyons-Pardue 2020). The recurring use of the diminutive (whether "little daughter" or "little girl") presses a reader to consider that Mark is concerned with repudiating Herodias' manipulation and overexposure of her "little" daughter, particularly in contrast to the extreme care exercised by Jairus and the Syrophoenician woman regarding their daughters. But, within the pericope itself, it is clear that Herodias' own position is subject to the king's shifting allegiances and whims.[23] Something similar may be argued for Mordecai's position as a member of a threatened ethnic minority. With the Esther/Artaxerxes parallel at the forefront, the vulnerability of all (even those with seemingly greater power, like Herodias, Esther, or Mordecai) to the king is on full display. In the present study, this focus highlights a different contrast in Mark's Gospel: Jesus' treatment of those in his sphere of influence, particularly the vulnerable people he encounters, in juxtaposition to those of ruling figures.

The flippancy of the kingly figure—whether Artaxerxes or Herod Antipas—regarding his territory, subjects, and the life-or-death impact of his whims stands in stark contrast to Jesus' regard for the supplicants he encounters. Despite having ostensibly insignificant political power relative to either Artaxerxes or Herod, Mark has established Jesus' potential power and public sway (e.g., 1:35-39; 4:41).[24] Each ruling figure is easily swayed by those in his proximity, whether for good or ill. Jesus, however, seems to persist along "the way" (ἡ ὁδὸς) in a manner that resists either establishing a sphere of influence or being beholden to the influence of adherents (e.g., staying in Capernaum, 1:37-38). When he pauses to teach or heal, it is not his own gratification or the impulse of projecting power that governs his actions, but at several junctures Mark notes compassion (σπλαγχνίζομαι) as the cause (1:41; 6:34; 8:2).

The ways in which Jesus interacts with children are demonstrated in Mark's narrative with comparative frequency (5:22-24a, 35-43; 7:25-30; 9:17-29, 36-37; 10:13-16).[25] Children are never merely pawns, pushed and prodded to bring about Jesus' desired outcomes. Further, in contrast to Herod's rash vow, any promise Jesus makes he intends to keep (e.g., 9:23). Even when an initial tone of dismissiveness mars the pericope from the outset (7:27), the child benefits from her mother's

---

23. One supposes that Herodias' machinations seek to protect her place in Herod's household, which would imply the perpetual security of her daughter, as well.

24. In the pericopae immediately following the beheading of John in the Herodian palace, Mark records Jesus' feeding of the 5,000 and walking on water (6:30-52), dramatic demonstrations of power.

25. It is possible that the person who was paralyzed, whom Jesus healed, was a young person, as Jesus addresses him as "child" (τέκνον; 2:5). However, this term could also bespeak affection or a parental sense of care, evidenced when Jesus uses the same term of his disciples in 10:24: τέκνα. He also addresses as "daughter" (θυγάτηρ) a mature woman whose uncontrollable menstrual hemorrhage had afflicted her for twelve years (5:34).

encounter with Jesus (v. 30). The same is sadly untrue for the daughter of Herodias in the traumatic events into which she is drawn as a puppet.

The women Jesus encounters are not reduced to objects of pleasure or convenience. While seldom stated explicitly—perhaps because of implicit Christological assumptions regarding Jesus' celibacy—the beauty (or lack thereof) of any woman he encounters as well as any descriptions of appearance are entirely absent in Mark. Esther's natural beauty and its enhancement in the harem (Est. 2:2, 7, 12) is the implied, or perhaps required, catalyst for all the subsequent plot developments. When Jesus recognizes and praises the women with whom he comes into contact, it is for their faith (5:34), speech (7:29), generous giving (12:43-44), and good work (14:6).

It is worth reflecting further on how Mark reappropriates the crucial kingly vow, which was repeated multiple times within Esther's narrative and the one which brings about the essential plot twist in Esther's favor. Evidently, Mark receives and echoes that essential story element and places it in a scene in his Gospel in which it can only be viewed negatively. This demonstrates a first-century reception of the heroic Esther story that is nuanced. Mark's allusive use of the Esther story, including the aspects of violence and power imbalance within it (many of which inflict a disparate cost along gendered lines), was not necessarily naively accepted or ignored by ancient readers. In Mark, a king like Artaxerxes is shown misusing power—or perhaps exposed as not truly powerful at all—even as the innocents in the interaction, a young girl and a godly prophet, become victimized by the careless use of power. Perhaps engaging with Mark's reuse of the Esther tradition can drive readers to reconsider further Esther's own victimization and the ways that she both resisted and participated in the violent system in which she was entangled. Whatever the outcome, Mark's Christology is evidently apophatic in relation to this story: Jesus is, most decidedly, a king *unlike* Artaxerxes or Herod Antipas.[26]

---

26. Although the term "king" is not used for Jesus widely throughout Mark, its recurrence in key moments of the Passion account indicate that it is critically important to Mark's Christology: Mk 15:2, 9, 12, 18, 26, 32 (cf., 11:10 as well). Certainly, Jesus' frequent teaching about God's "kingdom" (ἡ βασιλεία τοῦ θεοῦ) and his role in it extends the metaphor throughout the Gospel (see 1:14-15; 4:11, 26, 30; 9:1, 47; 10:14-15, 23-25; 12:34; 14:25).

Chapter 14

READING ESTHER IN DIALOGUE WITH THE RABBIS

Jonathan Grossman

One of the commonest ways in which the rabbis read the Bible was through the lens of analogy (Bruns 1987; Fishbane 1986). Sometimes they state the analogy explicitly, and sometimes they present its results and the reader must uncover the analogy on which the midrash is based (Grossman and Sasson 2007, 2010). Such midrashic readings developed in a particular way due to the univocal approach to the Bible, leading to the possibility of conversation between different books and different authors (Frenkel 1991, 163-80, 1996, 161-96; Heinemann 1954, 56-7). The book of Esther has a special place of honor in this connection: Various midrashim suggested various readings of the book against the background of other biblical stories, of prophecy, and especially of wisdom literature (not merely in the introductions, as is usual in the midrash, but also in that the story of Esther reflects the principles of wisdom literature). From this perspective, it is possible that the rabbis already felt that there was something in common between the basic idea of the book of Esther, according to which the wicked fall by the same means with which they sought to bring down others (Haman's being hanged on the same gallows that he prepared for Mordecai), and wisdom literature, a view that some modern scholars share (Bachmann 2014; Gordis 1981; Talmon 1963).

The intertextual reading of Esther by the rabbis can be divided into four basic models. I will discuss them briefly and then focus on a single midrash that demonstrates some of the challenges that accompany an investigation into literary analogy in rabbinic literature.

An Analogical Reading within the Book Itself

Before we examine rabbinic intertextual reading between Esther and other biblical books, it should be noted that analogies between scenes even within Esther itself are widespread in rabbinic literature. In this respect, the midrash matches the design of the book itself: The parallels between various scenes within the book of Esther are well known. The motif of reversal is one of the most basic motifs of the story, and so the story makes fun of Haman's fate, which flipped over onto his own head. Various midrashim point to this reversal, but other midrashim point to an implicit dialogue between scenes that do not express reversal but reward, resulting naturally from a deed and reward nexus. So, for example,

> R. Jacob b. Aha said: God said to him: "You have inquired of the welfare of one person, to know how Esther did (Est. 2:11); I swear that in the end you will seek the welfare of a whole nation"; and so it says, "Seeking the good of his people and speaking up for the welfare of all his seed" (Est. 10:3). (*Est. Rab.* 6:8; Tabory-Atzmon 117 f.)[1]

The word שלום ("welfare"), which forms the basis of the connection between these two scenes, occurs in Esther in one additional place (9:30), and it therefore appears that it is not only the shared word that led the rabbis to create a connection between them but also the course of the plot and the nature of the character. In both episodes, Mordecai is concerned about the welfare of others—at first, Esther's welfare; eventually, the welfare of all his nation. The rabbis see in this a development and interpret the second mention of "inquiring about the welfare" as a reward that Mordecai had earned for his original concern about Esther's welfare. Since in the prevailing biblical conception עם refers to an ethnic group and is to be considered an extended family (Block 1997; Grossman 2016, 50–9; Speiser 1960), the basis of the midrash gets an additional anchor: at first Mordecai was concerned about his cousin alone; eventually he was concerned about all his nation and his "seed."

Linguistic Allusions

Connecting distant texts by means of shared language is widespread in the midrash. With great interpretive courage, the rabbis saw in this literary method a tool that could escape the bounds of narrative and be employed as well with practical legal implications. The *gezerah shavah* or analogy based on linguistic similarity is in fact a model of allusion that made it possible to transfer laws from one legal realm to another. In the halakhic midrashim, such dialogues have legal implications, and in the aggadic midrashim such dialogues bring the entire Bible into conversation. One word shared between two stories is enough for the sages to imply a dialogue between stories that are quite different.

In the book of Esther many linguistic links were exploited to construct midrashim and surprising analogical readings of other books of the Bible. A striking example of this is the following midrash:

---

1. I would like to thank Dr. Gilad Sasson of the Department of Talmud at Bar-Ilan University for his comments on this chapter.

Citations from Esther Rabbah are taken from the Soncino translation; additional page references are to the 2014 Hebrew edition of Tabory and Atzmon.

BUT IT SEEMED CONTEMPTIBLE IN HIS EYES TO LAY HANDS ON MORDECAI ALONE (Est. 3:6). He was a contemptuous man like his ancestor before him. Elsewhere it is written, So Esau despised his birthright (Gen. 25:34), and here it is written, IT WAS CONTEMPTIBLE IN HIS EYES. (*Est. Rab.* 7:10; Tabory and Atzmon 2014, 129)

According to this midrash, Haman is a descendant of Amalek, the grandson of Esau (Gen. 36:12). The comparison between these words about Haman and the words about Esau is therefore also a comparison between an ancestor and a descendant ("a contemptuous man like his ancestor before him"). It is noteworthy that the form ויבז occurs in the Bible nowhere but in these two verses, so it is possible that this allusion leaves the realm of midrash and can be seen as intentional, in which case it should be considered part of the straightforward sense, intended by the author of the story ("deliberate authorial intertextuality").[2] In some of the parallel midrashim the midrash is also connected to Obad. 1:2, "See, I will make you small among the nations; you will be utterly despised [בזוי]."[3] Thus is created a conversation between three texts, all of which describe Esau and his descendants as "contemptible." Note that both Esau and Haman are described as actively *expressing* contempt; this does not prevent the interpreter from applying the adjective *contemptible* to them.

The creator of this midrash does not himself develop the meaning of the analogy between Haman and Esau, and we may wonder whether he indeed saw a real meaning to this analogy or whether he simply wished to point to a similarity between the two characters and thereby to describe a kind of "family behavior." The family connection between Haman and Esau comes up in additional midrashim (e.g., *Est. Rab.* 7:4), and it provides fertile soil for the linguistic allusion of ויבז, which equates the two characters, to flourish. Note that we are not speaking here about an analogy that relies on the plot; the linguistic link is enough to set the two characters side by side.

Such midrashim are quite common in rabbinic readings of the book of Esther,[4] but it is especially worth mentioning the surprising midrash of R. Akiva in *Est. Rab.* 1:8. That passage explains that when R. Akiva saw his students drowsing, he

---

2. On these two fundamental positions about this literary technique, see Tull (2000); Miller (2011).

3. See the notes in Tabory and Atzmon (2014). Bible translations outside Esther Rabbah are taken from the NIV 2011, with slight alterations when necessary to make the linguistic point clear.

4. E.g., the connection between Memucan's suggestion to give Vashti's royal position "to someone else who is better than she" (Est. 1:19) and Samuel telling Saul that his kingship has been given "to someone else, who is better than you" (1 Sam. 15:28) (*Est. Rab.* 4:9). So too "the wise men who understood the times" mentioned in Est. 1:13 are, in the midrashic view, the sons of Issachar, of whom we are told in 1 Chron. 12:33 that they were "men who understood the times" (*Est. Rab.* 4:1); there are many such examples.

suggested to them that Esther had been found worthy of ruling over 127 provinces through her being a descendant of Sarah, who lived for 127 years. It is hard to know whether the midrash intends to suggest a serious analogy between Esther and Sarah (Heinemann 1954, 66), or whether the setting of the midrash—a way to wake up the students—hints that it is merely meant as a joke (Tabory and Atzmon 2014, 85). If we follow the first theory, we find that the midrash is ready to make an analogy between two stories even because of the existence of an identical number in both. Perhaps it was this unusual number, not recorded in any other biblical text, that led R. Akiva to create his midrash. It is also noteworthy that other traditions about the Persian Empire tell of 120 provinces (e.g., Dan. 6:2)—a more elegant and appropriate number—by which it would appear that the number 127 mentioned at the beginning of our story was deliberately chosen. In any case, it was not the plot that led R. Akiva to suggest this midrash (despite the fact that it is possible to find similarities in what happened to Sarai in Pharaoh's palace and what happened to Esther in the palace of the king).[5] The shared number was enough for him to point to a dialogue between the two stories.

Developed Plot Analogy

Sometimes the midrash presents an analogy that goes beyond a single picture and develops along with the plot through several scenes. The most noticeable example in Esther—which was not missed by the rabbis—is the link between the story of Esther and Mordecai and that of Joseph:

AND IT CAME TO PASS, AS SHE SPOKE TO JOSEPH DAY BY DAY, etc. (Gen. 39:10). R. Judan said in the name of R. Benjamin b. Levi: The sons of Rachel underwent trials of equal severity and attained to equal greatness.

They underwent equal trials:
- And it came to pass, as she spoke to Joseph day by day (Gen. 39:10) = Now it came to pass, when they spoke unto him day by day (Est. 3:4);
- That he harkened not unto her (Gen. 39:10) = And he hearkened not unto them (Est. 3:4.).

They attained to equal greatness:
- And Pharaoh took off his signet ring from his hand, and put it upon Joseph's hand (Gen. 41:42) = And the king took off his ring, which he had taken from Haman, and gave it unto Mordecai (Est. 8:2);
- And arrayed him in vestures of fine linen, and put a gold chain about his neck (Gen. 41:42) = And Mordecai went forth from the presence of the king in royal

---

5. Such an analogy has been suggested in modern scholarship. See, e.g., Zakovitch (1995); Grossman (2011, 38–9, 68).

apparel of blue and white, and with a great crown of gold, and with a robe of fine linen and purple (Est. 8:15);
- And he made him [Joseph] to ride in the second chariot which he had (Gen. 41:43) = And cause him [Mordecai] to ride on horseback through the street of the city (Est. 6:9);
- And they cried before him [Joseph]: Abrech (Gen. 41:43) = And proclaimed before him [Mordecai]: Thus shall it be done unto the man, etc. (Est. 6:11). (*Gen. Rab.* 87:6)

The midrash focuses on the story of Mordecai and parallels it to the story of Joseph. The analogy is based first and foremost on both being "sons of Rachel"—again the comparison is based on a family connection. Haman (like Esau) is a contemptible man who is the son of a contemptible man; equally, the descendants of Rachel both achieve greatness. One might add to the comparison the rise of Esther herself (the Hebrew girl) to royalty, so reminiscent of the rise of Joseph (the Hebrew boy) to the position of viceroy. But the midrash ignores Esther and focuses on Mordecai alone. Perhaps this stems from the assumption that a stable analogy is one that follows a particular character and does not jump between characters (as Noble 2002 thinks); perhaps also the analogy is based specifically on linguistic allusions and not on plot materials unsupported by linguistic similarity. But the most reasonable possibility for ignoring Esther is that the writer wants to focus on the experience of Mordecai and his reward; widening the analogy would create a second focus for the midrash.[6]

This last possibility can clarify an omission even more surprising than the other components of the comparison between the characters. Esther Rabbah contains an additional analogy to the story of Joseph (already mentioned in *B. Meg.* 13b), according to which there is a similarity between the Bigthana and Teresh scene and the story of the two officers of the king who are confined to the prison in Genesis 40:

> R. Berekiah said in the name of R. Levi: It is written, Come, behold the works of the Lord, who hath made desolations in the earth (Ps. 46:9). He made servants wroth against their master in order to confer greatness on the righteous, as it says, BIGTHANA AND TERESH WERE WROTH, etc.—to bestow greatness on Mordecai. He also makes masters wroth with their servants [as, for instance], to confer greatness on Joseph, as it says, Pharaoh was wroth with his servants, etc. (Gen. 41:10). (*Est. Rab.* 6:13; Tabory and Atzmon 2014, 120–1)

The midrash sets the two officers in Genesis in antithetic parallelism to the two eunuchs of the king in Esther. Pharaoh, the king of Egypt, "was angry" at two of his officers, just as the two eunuchs "became angry" at their king. In both these episodes there is "anger," whose role in the plot is to further the goals of the hero

---

6. On the rabbis' widespread use of analogy to indicate reward presented via literary technique, see Heinemann (1954, 64–8).

of the story, or, in the words of the midrash, "to confer greatness on the righteous." Though the midrash is aware of this link, it is not integrated into the structure of comparison between Mordecai and Joseph. Considering our hypothesis that the rabbis are focusing only on comparative materials that are relevant to their purpose, this omission can be understood. If the purpose was indeed to highlight the reward received by the characters who stood up to the test (they "underwent trials of equal severity and attained to equal greatness"), they prefer to focus on what happened to these particular characters and not any others. In this respect, midrashic intertextuality differs from that accepted in modern scholarship. Interpreters do not assemble all the connections and then judge their meaning; instead, they choose from the wider analogy the elements that focus on their midrashic purpose.

Formal Structural Analogy

Building an analogy based on a shared formal structure demands real sophistication and literary sensitivity. The rabbis do pay attention to these aspects—even if one may doubt whether we are talking about analogy or just an indication of a repetitive writing style. One example of "delayed exposition" will suffice.[7] The expository data that presents Mordecai to us (Est. 2:5-7) is inserted in the story *after* we have already been told that the king has decided to seek a new wife for himself (Est. 2:1-4). On this structure, the midrash comments:

> And let the maiden that pleaseth the King. etc. (2:4). Who was the right man for this occasion? Mordecai; and the text continues, There was a certain Jew in Shushan the castle, whose name was Mordecai.
>
> Similarly we read, And God saw the children of Israel, and God took cognizance of them (Exod. 2:25). Who was the right man for this occasion? Moses; [and so it goes on], Now Moses was keeping, etc. (3:1).
>
> Similarly, And Samuel said unto the men of Israel: Go ye every man unto his city (1 Sam. 8:22). Who was the right man for this occasion? Saul; and it goes on, Now there was a man of Benjamin, whose name was Kish, etc. (1 Sam. 9:1).
>
> Similarly, And when Saul and all Israel heard those words of the Philistine, they were dismayed, and greatly afraid (1 Sam. 17:11). Who was the right man for this occasion? David; and it goes on, Now David was the son of that Ephrathite, etc. (1 Sam. 17:12) ...
>
> He mightily oppressed the children of Israel (Judg. 4:3) ... Who was the right person for this occasion? Deborah; and so the text goes on, Now Deborah, a prophetess, the wife of Lappidoth, etc. (Judg. 4:4). (*Est. Rab.* 5:4; Tabory and Atzmon 2014, 108)

---

7. The coinage is that of Meir Sternberg (1978, 8–14).

All these are cases of delayed exposition, which creates a special awareness—the reader already knows when the character is presented, what that character is destined for, and what will happen to the character as the plot moves along. As noted, the midrash does not indicate a dialogue between the stories that is formulated by their identical structure; it only points to the use of delayed presentation in all these stories (and in two others omitted here). I have discussed the possible connections between the characters mentioned in this midrash elsewhere (Grossman 2011, 61–71, 2015, 328–30), but even without developing the analogy between the stories, the indication of the recurrent literary structure itself demonstrates literary sensitivity.

Mordecai as Moses

Two basic questions accompany the discussion in research into the rabbis' awareness of literary analogies, and I intend to present them via a study of a single midrash taken from Esther Rabbah (6:2). The midrash presented there suggests that we view Mordecai against the background of Moses:[8]

THERE WAS A MAN, A JEW IN SHUSHAN THE CASTLE.
The word MAN here tells us that Mordecai in his generation was equal to Moses in his; for of Moses too it is written, Now the MAN Moses was very meek (Num. 12:3).
Just as Moses stood in the breach, as it is written, Therefore He said that He would destroy them, had not Moses His chosen stood before Him in the breach (Ps. 106:23), so did Mordecai, as it is written, Seeking the good of his people and speaking peace to all his seed (Est. 10:3).
Just as Moses taught Israel Torah, as it is written, Behold, I have taught you statutes and ordinances (Deut. 4:5), so did Mordecai, as it is written, And he sent letters... with words of peace and truth (Est. 9:30), [and truth means Torah], as it is written, Buy the truth, and sell it not (Prov. 23:23). (Tabory and Atzmon 2014, 111)

The midrash depicts Mordecai's leadership as resembling that of Moses and focuses on two things—both characters defended their people from disaster, and

---

8. Modern scholars too have suggested reading Esther against the background of the Exodus story and putting Moses and Aaron parallel to Mordecai and Esther. See especially Gerleman (1973, 11). He notes principally the following connections: a Jewish man is introduced into the palace of the non-Jewish king; the existential danger to the nation of Israel; Israel's victory over their enemies; a festival for all generations that is established in the wake of the victory. Still, we may wonder whether these connections indicate an intentional parallel. See also Loader (1980, 148–51).

Table 14.1 Comparison of Moses and Mordecai

The Greatness of Moses (Exod. 11:3)	The Greatness of Mordecai (Est. 9:3-4)
The LORD gave the people favor in the sight of the Egyptians …	And all the nobles of the provinces, the satraps, the governors and the king's administrators helped the Jews, because fear of Mordecai had seized them.
… and Moses himself was a man highly regarded in the land of Egypt, in the sight of Pharaoh's officials and in the sight of the people.	Mordecai was prominent in the palace; his reputation spread throughout the provinces, and the man Mordecai became more and more powerful.

both taught Torah to the people.[9] Another text that presents this midrash (*Panim Aherim*, version B) adds that both of them understood seventy languages.

The sole linguistic link in the midrash is found at the very beginning—both characters are called "man." The rest of the comparisons are not based on linguistic similarity but on plot materials that the midrash connects.

This midrash brings up two basic questions that accompany the discussion of the use the rabbis make of analogies in the Bible. The two questions are related to what is not explicitly written and to the demand placed on the reader of the midrash to broaden the scope of the analogy beyond what is explicitly mentioned, and this from two different perspectives.

First (as I noted above with regard to Bigthana and Teresh), there is a real link between the characters being discussed, which for some reason the midrash does not mention, though it is hard to believe it went unnoticed:[10]

Since the midrash connects Mordecai and Moses by the designation "man" that they share, one might expect this to be based on the description of Moses' greatness in the sight of the Egypt, where he is also called "a man." The allusion appears to be a genuine one, and it seems that the description of Mordecai as "prominent in the palace" is dependent on the parallel description of Moses. In addition to the clear linguistic link, in both stories the description of the characters' greatness is presented doubly: with regard to the palace and with regard to the public.[11] Moreover, beside the "greatness" of these two "men," both descriptions also mention the Gentiles' favorability toward the entire Jewish people; there may

---

9. Isaac Gottlieb has shown that the goal of the midrash is to present the level of holiness of the book of Esther as comparable to that of the Pentateuch, and as part of that goal the writing of the scroll is equated to the giving of the Torah and Mordecai is equated to Moses (Gottlieb 2008).

10. In modern research several scholars have noted this connection, e.g., Levenson (1997, 121); Berlin (2001, 84).

11. On the absence of Pharaoh himself from the list of those in whose sight Moses was great, see the suggestion of Carol Meyers: "the unnamed Egyptian ruler has become a parody of a powerful sovereign, isolated in his adherence to a misguided and doomed policy" (2005, 92).

be a connection between the greatness of these characters and this supportive relationship. In Exodus too it is possible to understand that the people found greater favor in the sight of the Egyptians on account of the fact that Moses "was a man of great [גדול] importance in the land of Egypt,"[12] just as the author of the book of Esther describes all the officials of the provinces as supporting the Jews because "Mordecai was prominent [גדול] in the palace."

As noted, the rabbis based the link between the two characters on the fact that both are called "man," but to prove that Moses is also called "man" they had to go all the way to Num. 12:3, where Moses is called "a very humble man." A much simpler link would have been the comparison between "Moses himself was a man of great importance" and "the man Mordecai grew more and more powerful," two verses that both describe the special status of the two "men"—which would be more appropriate to the subject of the midrash.

What explains the omission of such basic components in the structure of the comparison? A priori, there are three possibilities:

1. A failure of recognition: The rabbis did not recognize the link that they did not mention.
2. Deliberate omission: The rabbis deliberately omitted the link that they did not mention. Perhaps they found it not persuasive enough, or perhaps—as we saw above in the discussion about Bigthana and Teresh—it did not mesh with the purpose of the midrash. Perhaps also the omission had a polemic basis, of one kind or another.
3. Partial mention: The rabbis put only some of the components of the comparison into the midrash, letting them point the way to a broader comparison.

In the case before us, it is difficult to decide among the three possibilities: Theoretically, it is possible that the creator of this midrash did not notice the link with Exodus 11 (possibility 1), and it is also possible that he meant to feature Moses' good qualities and thereby to preach to his listeners about the quality of humility that befits a leader. And perhaps he did not want his listeners to pay attention to the success of the characters among the non-Jews as much as the way they led Israel (possibility 2). But we cannot rule out the third possibility, and this has important implications for the way in which we must read the intertextual remarks in the midrash. It seems that sometimes the analogy in the midrash opens a window to a broader comparison between the stories, which the midrash makes no pretense of presenting fully.

Beside this question, the midrash raises an additional basic methodological question, also connected to what is not mentioned explicitly in the midrash, one

---

12. Cassuto (1967, 132) preferred to phrase it the opposite way: Since the people found favor in the sight of the Egyptians, Moses felt comfortable speaking more forcefully to Pharaoh.

much more difficult to settle. Every literary analogy or allusion, by forging an opening to a story, makes it possible to look through the opening to the parallel story. These two openings face each other, but each story has a complete literary structure of its own that is perfectly good. Working through the analogy creates a dilemma: How far should we push the view through the opening into the structure that is hiding behind it? In our case, the midrash is comparing the Moses who "stood in the breach" to Mordecai, who similarly "stood in the breach." In general, these two characters defended their people against the troubles that beset them, but a further look at the connection that is forged makes the comparison somewhat uneasy. The argument that Mordecai was concerned for the welfare of his people rests on the verse that ends the book of Esther: "Mordecai the Jew was second in rank to King Ahasuerus, preeminent among the Jews, and held in high esteem by his many fellow Jews, because he worked for the good of his people and spoke up for the welfare of all the Jews" (Est. 10:3). True, Mordecai and Esther succeeded in fending off Haman's decrees, and at the end of the story Mordecai continues to defend his people. But the argument that Moses was concerned for the welfare of his people and stood firm in the face of disaster depends on a midrash on Psalm 106, which describes Israelite history:

> At Horeb they made a calf and worshipped an idol cast from metal. They exchanged their Glory for an image of a bull, which eats grass. They forgot the God who saved them, who had done great things in Egypt, miracles in the land of Ham and awesome deeds by the Red Sea. So he said he would destroy them—had not Moses, his chosen one, stood in the breach before him to keep his wrath from destroying them. (Ps. 106:19-23)

The verse that was chosen to teach about Moses repelling the disaster threatening Israel describes God's anger at the people because of the sin of the Golden Calf. The "breach" in Ps. 106:23 was a danger not from an enemy of flesh and blood but from God's anger. This is a quite surprising choice on the part of the midrash. Mordecai having stood up to Haman and defeated him, we might expect that the midrash would describe Moses defeating the Egyptians who were threatening Israel and seeking their welfare in this way.

However, such distinctions do not always say "Expound me." The rabbis may take a verse from here and another verse from there and fashion a midrash that depends on a partial analogy, but in this case the comparison of Mordecai to Moses—that both of them stood up to an enemy of Israel—is what was wanted. The most basic component in the comparison of Moses' and Mordecai's leadership was their success in thwarting the desire of the enemies of the Jews to destroy them. What led the rabbis to set up God as someone Moses had to stand up to?

Actually, that the midrash turned to Psalm 106 is surprising. This is a historical psalm, dedicated entirely to Israel's ingratitude toward God. The psalm opens with a warning—"We have sinned, even as our ancestors did; we have done wrong and acted wickedly" (Ps. 106:6)—which accompanies the psalm throughout. Israelite history is presented in the psalm as a series of junctions that mark the people's sins, starting with the exodus from Egypt and going all the way to their taking possession of the land, and the corresponding response of God—now with compassion, now with punishment.[13] As part of this difficult historical description, Moses and Phinehas are introduced, whose deeds and prayers defended Israel from God's wrath.

The surprising inclusion of Psalm 106 in the midrash comparing Mordecai to Moses is so strange that for this very reason it would appear not to be coincidental. Mordecai, who defends Israel against the decrees of Haman, is compared to Moses, who defends Israel against God's wrath.

It seems that precisely through this imbalance the midrash is hinting at a subversive reading that is hiding beneath the surface. The analogy between the two leaders hints at a criticism of their people without having to say so explicitly. By comparing Mordecai to Moses, who prays to God not to destroy the people, the midrash paints the Jews in the story of Esther in the same colors as Israel in Psalm 106, thus indicating their bleak situation. The book of Esther does not describe the story of a miraculous, glorious rescue but the situation of Diaspora Jewry, which did not return to the land of Israel after the proclamation of Cyrus but remained in exile until Haman arose against them and sought to destroy them. According to the midrash, Haman was none other than the anger of the Lord that was sent forth against the Jews, and Mordecai, by managing to overcome Haman, in fact managed to propitiate God and assuage God's anger.

Note that when the midrash cites the verse describing Moses "standing in the breach," it ends with the Hebrew word וגומר, "etc." (i.e., it is up to the reader to finish the verse, which has not been cited in its entirety). This is quite different from "etc.," which implies that the continuation is unimportant to the argument. In rabbinic literature, the argument quite frequently depends precisely on the part of the verse that is not cited explicitly.[14] In our case, the verse continues this way: "had not Moses, his chosen one, stood in the breach before him to keep his wrath from destroying them," and the subsequent verse describes what happened to Israel later, after the sin of the spies: "Then they despised the pleasant land; they did not believe his promise" (Ps. 106:24). That is, it is not merely the general description in the psalm of the sins of the people by which the midrash hints at criticism of the Jews of Persia but specifically the sin of the spies, which comes directly after the verse cited in the midrash. Can it be possible that the midrash was hinting that the Jews living in Persia and invited to the king's feast could be

---

13. In this respect Psalm 106 differs from the preceding Psalm 105. In Psalm 105's description of history, God's kindness is prominent, and there is no mention of the sins of the people. This contrasts, as already noted, with the primary aim of Psalm 106. The creator of the midrash could easily have relied on the optimistic Psalm 105, but he chose to use Psalm 106, which is highly critical of Israel.

14. "With biblical verses, the writer relies on the reader's expertise, and therefore finds it sufficient to cite just the beginning of the verse" (Sharvit 2008, 38).

understood to have "despised the pleasant land" as their ancestors did?[15] Was the midrash hinting that Jewish history as reflected in the book of Esther was a continuation of the bleak history reflected in Psalm 106, and that what is said at the end of the psalm could be said as well of the Jews in the story of Esther?

> Therefore the LORD was angry with his people and abhorred his inheritance. He gave them into the hands of the nations, and their foes ruled over them. Their enemies oppressed them and subjected them to their power. Many times he delivered them, but they were bent on rebellion and they wasted away in their sin. Yet he took note of their distress when he heard their cry; for their sake he remembered his covenant and out of his great love he relented. (Ps. 106:40-44)

In light of this possibility I would like to pose a question that is inescapable in the study of rabbinic intertextual readings: Does the interpreter who lays bare a link between two passages intend for the reader to study both passages in their entirety, in that way alone giving the analogy its full meaning? If so, sometimes the point is precisely that which remains unsaid explicitly in the midrash. This question is equally inescapable in the study of intertextual reading that occurs in a halakhic context. When the rabbis compare, for example, the festival of Sukkot to the installation of Aaron and his sons as priests—because both passages use the word תשבו ("you shall dwell," B. Suk. 43b)—are they assuming that there is an essential similarity between the week in which the Tabernacle was inaugurated (with its extra eighth day) and the seven days of the festival of Sukkot (with its own extra eighth day, Shemini Atzeret)? Or is the comparison about a precise linguistic similarity and nothing more? This is a matter of scholarly disagreement; some prefer to see such allusions as linguistic links, unburdened with any rational basis (Liberman 1994, 60), while others argue that it is possible to see a development in rabbinic literature: Originally, the *gezerah shavah* was perceived as a basic method of logical analysis that should be considered a genuine literary analogy, but eventually some midrashim came along in which the *gezerah shavah* reflects no more than a localized linguistic equivalent (Gilat 1992, 373).

I am inclined to see at least in some of these linguistic links, at least in some of the cases, an opening for a broader analogy, and in our midrash, as noted, such a conclusion leads to dramatic results. Beside the explicit statement glorifying Mordecai as the equivalent of Moses is hidden an implicit intertextual reading through which the midrash hints also at criticism of the Jews of Shushan.

It is difficult to pin down this suggestion, let alone to prove it, but the question of opening up the original story on which the rabbis make the later story depend is a dramatic question of interpreting the analogy in the midrash and of unpacking the potential hidden in literary analogies of this kind. In every analogy there is a kind of winking at the reader, and it is precisely through this literary technique that an

---

15. On the possibility that the book of Esther itself implicitly criticizes the Jews who did not return to Israel, see Stern (2010); Grossman (2018).

author can conceal criticism of a character that he does not want to express openly, or to hint at other polemical messages. In our case, we are not dealing with the author himself but with an interpreter who uncovers an analogy but nonetheless works in similar fashion: He points to an opening through which one can enter the passage as a whole, and when all of it is visible, the reader can interpret in full the meaning of the analogy, even what has not been stated explicitly in the midrash.

Chapter 15

HUMAN NATURE AND POLITICS: A MODERN POLITICAL-THEORETICAL READING OF ESTHER

Kyong-Jin Lee

In international political theory, classical realists believe that national and international actors are bound to pursue their self-interest and concomitant political and economic goals. This time-tested and unchanging nature of politics is a view articulated by countless political philosophers, who have typically rendered a negative assessment of human nature over the course of history. In the view of the Realist School, an incessant drive for power is inherently rooted in human nature.[1] This view was first popularized in the Western world through the seventeenth-century English philosopher Thomas Hobbes (1588–1679) and his famously dark characterization of politics:

> And because the condition of Man ... is a condition of Warre of every one against every one; in which case every one is governed by his own Reason, and there is nothing he can make use of, that may not be a help unto him in preserving his life against his enemyes; It followeth that in such a condition, every man has a Right to every thing; even to one another's body. (Hobbes 1996, 91)

Thus the realist theory of international relations tends to operate on the presupposition that pervasive evil resides in human nature and political interaction. In the Hebrew Bible, the question of human nature and morality in political dynamics is prominently featured in the book of Esther through its illustration of an imperial organization in which the legal system of checks and balances is simply a flamboyant formality and statewide decisions are reduced to *arbitrary*, private, and *subjective* judgments. This comedic novella of political and moral limitations urges a theoretical reflection on the meaning of a key concept that underlies the biblical writer's scrutiny and critique of power and authority—the implication of human nature in politics.

---

1. For classical works on the principles of political realism stemming from a pessimistic view of human nature, see Morgenthau (1946, 1954).

The present discussion is an interdisciplinary and intertextual conversation, which attempts to elucidate the biblical author's political thought on human nature by applying the works of two of the twentieth century's most notable political theorists—Carl Schmitt (1888–1985) and Friedrich A. Hayek (1899–1992). Schmitt's insight from constitutional philosophy and Hayek's from political economy will show how hermeneutical tools from non-Jewish texts can contribute to a fruitful study of the book of Esther and Jewish diaspora life. Indeed, Jewish philosophical discourse has long been in conversation with the non-Jewish world, demonstrating how much the Jewish and non-Jewish philosophical traditions have shared historically in their concerns for the purported purposes of politics. Non-Jewish political–philosophical works here will provide pertinent theoretical tools to unlock the political thought in this diaspora literature. This will stimulate ideas and interests that will articulate the political philosophy of Esther and contribute to a constructive reevaluation of the relationship between morality and political dynamics.

The German jurist Schmitt and the British economist Hayek endeavored to diagnose and lay out intelligibly the fundamental problems of political liberalism. Both sought to unravel complex questions on the political quality of liberalism in the modern age of pluralism. For a modern political community, the possibility of combining and maintaining a balance between the Enlightenment's two principal ideals—liberty and equality—seems further out of reach than ever before in this age of global, transnational reality. This complex balancing act frames Hayek's and Schmitt's explorations of the links among law, politics, and liberalism, and their resulting incisive articulations on human nature. In order to understand better their positions on human nature, it is important to preface that both political theorists denounced liberalism for taking its cue from its intellectual predecessor, the European Enlightenment, in its unquestioning faith in rationality to guide politics (Hayek 1978, 2001; Schmitt 1996, 2008). Schmitt and Hayek coincided in their observation that the core problem of liberalism is its failure to recognize that reason is not an antidote to human self-interest and selfishness. In their view, liberalism's fundamental flaw is its conceptual indeterminacy, which is incompatible with the real world where conflicting ideals, interests, and identities compete for attention and resources. Both consistently demonstrate how the concept of human nature as a standard is impossible to dispense with in critical moral and political discourse and insist that human rationality has been exaggerated by modern science and industry.

Hayek and Schmitt reject the notions that rationalism anchors morality and that societies can find the path to an orderly existence chartered by reason. Their definitions of the role of the state, their critiques of liberalism, and their views on individual rights stem from exasperation with a blind faith that a society can be organized rationally and scientifically. Both sternly warn against the unwarranted illusion that the state can rally its citizens purposefully as they are persuaded with reason. Reason is limited in its moral application. Schmitt's main criticisms of liberal political theory is that it does not acknowledge this condition, but on the contrary rests upon an idea of rational reasoning and the belief that conflicts of interest can be solved through rational discussion. To Schmitt this is a dangerous illusion that does not take into account the fact that sudden human conflicts are of a fundamentally antagonistic nature and cannot be solved through rational discussion. (Thomsen 1997, 11)

Hayek in answering questions regarding the virtue of markets, on the one hand, and Schmitt establishing the legitimacy of sovereign authority, on the other, concede that the quest must begin with a comprehensive outlining of the state of human nature. Hayek maintains an optimistic view on society's ability to overcome the flaws of human nature, recognize the fallacy of reason, and guide its political action with historically and socially constructed attitudes and values—informal institutions. But he warns against the Enlightenment-driven belief that civilization's achievements are a product of reasoning. He asserts the unique power of informal institutions when he highlights how traditional ideals and norms tend to govern conduct throughout society. Hayek writes, "Institutions and practices which have not been designed in this manner can be beneficial only by accident. Such became the characteristic attitude of Cartesian constructivism with its contempt for tradition, custom, and history in general. Man's reason alone should enable him to construct society anew" (Hayek 1978, 11). Hayek, continuing a natural-law tradition, believed that collective economic and political life had its internal control mechanisms; thus artificial contrivances such as political policies could not successfully regulate the social or market behavior. The general welfare of the society was best left to the natural process of spontaneous evolution.

These sobering views on the egoistic nature of human beings and modern society's exaggerated confidence in reason and technology dovetail with the biblical writer's critique on the Persian Empire's glorification of power without a corresponding ethical framework as illustrated in Esther. In this biblical account, power and authority rest on an autocratic leader who governs a vast number of imperial subject peoples in consultation with seven aristocratic dynasties.[2] In the fifth century BC, the Achaemenids ruled over the largest empire that history had ever witnessed. Most historians today estimate a population of around fifty million. That means that between one-half and one-third of the world's population at the time lived within the borders of the Persian Empire. The Bible describes Ahasuerus as the ruler of every nation stretching from India to Ethiopia—in all 127 provinces. Even if the biblical author was exaggerating greatly, Ahasuerus's historical counterpart Xerxes I (r. 486–465 BC) ruled over an expansive territory and corresponding number of ethnic groups and nations. Against this historical

---

2. "Then the king consulted the sages who knew the laws (for this was the king's procedure toward all who were versed in law and custom, and those next to him were Carshena, Shethar, Admatha, Tarshish, Meres, Marsena, and Memucan, the seven officials of Persia and Media, who had access to the king, and sat first in the kingdom)" (Est. 1:13-14 NRSV).

backdrop, the book of Esther tells a suspenseful account of a minority people living in the shadow of an empire trying their best to raise their young and prosper in society as exemplified in the story of an ordinary Jewish man, Mordecai (Est. 2:5-7, 10-11).

The relevance of the book of Esther in today's world can be found in its critique of secular government as seen in the human effects of hegemonic power and the limitations of corporate morality exemplified in normative law and formal institutions. A commentary on the dynamics of power and ethics in the Persian Empire shares obvious parallels with and offers a valuable commentary on today's globalizing and therefore increasingly pluralistic world in ways that parallel Hayek's and Schmitt's critiques. In the biblical account, one cannot infer whether Ahasuerus, Haman, or the nobles who issue the royal decree ordering the annihilation of the Jewish people statewide knew anything about the people whose fate they decided. Based on the contemporary Achaemenid royal inscriptions and other surviving historical documents, the province of Yehud, Mordecai's ancestral land, and its people did not figure among prominent vassal nations under the Persian hegemony (Cameron 1965; Herrmann 1989; Lerner 1991; Poebel 1933; Schmitt 1999). Mordecai and his fellow Babylonian Jews' quotidian life is upended at the whim of a single individual, Haman: second-in-command in the Persian Empire. Haman is displeased when Mordecai will not do obeisance to him. Thus, upon learning of Mordecai's Jewish origin, the prime minister decides to request permission from the king to annihilate an entire people group.

> Then Haman said to King Ahasuerus, "There is a certain people scattered and separated among the peoples in all the provinces of your kingdom; their laws are different from those of every other people, and they do not keep the king's laws, so that it is not appropriate for the king to tolerate them. If it pleases the king, let a decree be issued for their destruction, and I will pay ten thousand talents of silver into the hands of those who have charge of the king's business, so that they may put it into the king's treasuries." (Est. 3:8-9 NRSV)

Despite the biblical writer's caricature of his clumsiness, Haman's indictment of the Jews shows that the Persian prime minister was an adroit politician. His description of Mordecai's people contains pivotal elements typically featured in discourses and debates on the idea of nationalism. Haman describes the Jews as one people/nation (עַם־אֶחָד), whose collective identity is presumably identifiably distinct among the many ethnicities, nations, and languages who inhabit the Persian Empire. This notion of "one people," which stresses the unique and incommensurable identity of each cultural entity, has been articulated widely throughout history. For example, German thinker Johann Gottfried Herder (1744–1803) focused on culture, rather than politics, when proffering his widely discussed conceptualization of nationalism. In the Hebrew Bible the term עַם (also גּוֹי), which is used to describe the Hebrews, Israelites, and Jews, "comes rather close to the modern definition of 'nation'" (Speiser 1960, 160). Theorists of nationalism typically agree that "the nation concept is fundamentally about distinguishing us from them" (Scott,

Carter, and Drury 2019, 35).³ A historical survey on attitudes and actions around nationalism and nationhood may show that notions of peoplehood and nationhood are inherently attached to value-laden perspectives. A discussion on the moral dimension of the phenomenon of nationhood and nationalism is beyond the scope of this chapter, but Haman's characterization of the Jewish people as a single unified entity is a well-documented rhetorical device often utilized by instigators of ethnic conflict to stoke tensions between inclusivity and exclusivity in a diverse society. Thus, Haman's deliberate choice of language can be interpreted as questioning the political legitimacy and self-determination of Mordecai's people. Haman highlights their geophysical situation, describing Mordecai's people as diffuse and decentralized because they live in all the provinces of the vast empire (מְפֻזָּר וּמְפֹרָד בֵּין הָעַמִּים בְּכֹל מְדִינוֹת מַלְכוּתֶךָ). One may suggest that Haman's comment seeks to delegitimize the Jewish peoplehood because they do not meet typical conditions to claim nationhood but still aspire to sovereignty, *ethnic recognition*, and *land* tenure— typical legitimizing elements of nationalism. In fact, in the ancient Near East "many peoples could cope with the idea of being a nation through the preservation of their religion and culture without being within the framework of an independent state of their own" (Mendels 1992, 15). More recently, sociologist Émile Durkheim (1858–1917) famously espoused the similar view that a nation includes customs, traditions, and beliefs derived from a common history; thus each nation has its own soul and unique characteristics (Durkheim 1986). The Achaemenid Empire encompassed many peoples who possessed their own religion and customs and were considered legitimate and autonomous nations within the imperial system so Haman's accusation that "their laws are different from those of every other people, and they do not keep the king's laws" may be interpreted as saying that though they do not all reside in one location, Jews stand out in their subversion of and aversion to imperial rule by insisting on a distinctive set of customs, religion, and law— דָּת. The aspects of Jewish life in the diaspora against which Haman raises accusations constitute the very vision of Jewish political order that the Hebrew Bible consistently heralds: Israel as one people who share a common history, solidarity, and fate, governed by one political system under one God.⁴

Readers are naturally disturbed when they note that Ahasuerus does not respond to Haman's sensational allegations. The king does not ask for any clarification or deliberation. Nor does he object to the proposal to wipe out an entire people across the empire. As seen above, such incendiary characterization of the Jews was often

---

3. Also see Ozkirimli (2010).

4. The Sabbath liturgy refers to the Jews as "*one nation* in the land" (italics mine). The Passover *Haggadah* quotes the credal statement from Deut. 26:5 when the Israelites bring their first fruits in recognition of the fulfillment of YHWH's promises. וַיְהִי־שָׁם לְגוֹי גָּדוֹל עָצוּם וָרָב (Foer 2012, 39). The fact that Israel's existence as one people could not be contained within the confines of a single geographical location was a testimony to the fulfilment of YHWH's promise to Abraham to make of his descendants a great nation, powerful and numerous. For an alternate treatment of Haman's depiction of the Jews, see Firth (1997).

used as a political weapon to undermine Jewish aspiration for self-determination in antiquity. The king's silence beckons the readers' attention. The writer of Esther deploys the rhetorical tool of silence in order to invite the reader to fill in implicitly a moral gap that is conspicuously open in Ahasuerus' profile. "[T]he fact that the narrator does not deal with the 'why or how . . .' of the actions of characters, hardly means he is not interested in character" (Dickson and Botha 2000, 164). Ahasuerus is not as blatantly immoral as Haman, though silence and ambiguity have replaced the king's moral dicta. Frederic Bush (1996, 387) comments,

> Ahasuerus does not respond to this incredible proposal with even a question or a comment, let alone an objection. He simply gives Haman his signet, which empowers him to act fully in his name and authority, with the casual and offhand comment "Do with the people and the money as you please." This response reveals that he doesn't care whether this people is destroyed or not. The whole matter is too insignificant a concern to occupy his time or attention. Haman is unmitigated evil, but the king is dangerous indifference personified.

Other commentators have characterized the Persian king as an egomaniacal buffoon.[5] Ahasuerus is the antithesis of the predecessors of the historical Xerxes whom scholars believe he represents. Historically, Persian rulers erected sumptuous monuments for the purpose of royal propaganda, promoting their moral and political legitimacy by projecting the image of a king who embraced the highest royal ideals: justice, liberty, and benevolence.[6]

Readers have noticed Haman's cunning (Aronowicz 2008; Fox 2010, 183; Glickman 1999; Harvey 2003, 186). "There was never another slanderer as skilled as Haman."[7] In his proposal to the king "Haman reveals himself as a shrewd, clever, and malignant slanderer" (Bush 1996, 386). The imbalance of power and morality exposes the vulnerability that one powerful man's flaws can inflict upon a sophisticated legislative system and centralized government. Once the plot is hatched by Haman and authorized by Ahasuerus, "The couriers went quickly by order of the king, and the decree was issued in the citadel of Susa. The king and Haman sat down to drink; but the city of Susa was thrown into confusion" (3:15). Ahasuerus and his political entourage commanded a political system that recognized no limits to its authority and possessed a legislative institution that controlled the vast empire efficiently. Yet they did not know about the history, identity, or life of the people who lived in Susa, at the center of the empire. Citizens reacted to the royal edict with confusion, perplexity, and agitation

---

5. See, e.g., Whedbee (1998, 184–8); Feinstein (2014, 40–53).

6. The Behistun Inscription is one of the most sumptuous examples. See Cameron (1951, 47–54); Vogelsang (1998, 195–224). Also see Enenkel and Pfeijffer (2005).

7. Rava (Rabbi Abba ben Joseph bar Ḥama) said, "There was never another slanderer so skilled as Haman." *Bavli, Mo'ed, Megillah* 13b. English translation from Fox (2010, 47). Also see Epstein (1948).

(נְבֻכָה), "wandering aimlessly" in the absence of moral leadership.[8] This situation parallels today's global, transnational political and economic decision-making practices, which increasingly concentrate power and influence in the hands of a few who determine the fate of the remote faceless masses. It also reveals that a sophisticated and efficient system of law in the possession of a hegemonic power is not impermeable to human prejudice and passion.

The legislative powers of the imperial administration are featured as an effective medium for consolidating the *Pax Persica*. In 1:13-22, when Queen Vashti refused to heed to the king's summons, the king and his counselors consulted sages who knew the laws of the Persian Empire, and eventually proposed that a royal edict be issued to the laws of the Persians and the Medes so that it could never be altered and Vashti could never again come before the king. Royal writs were sent to every province in its own script and to every people in its own language. Historically, Achaemenid legislative action was broadly attested as a strategic instrument for ruling over the many vassal territories. The Persian Empire's use of the construct of law in its diplomatic dealings with the local leadership is known by scholars as Imperial Authorization (*Reichsautorisation*; Frei 1984, 8–43, 2001, 1–40). This theory explains how the Achaemenids consolidated and maintained their imperial authority over subject peoples for the sake of long-lasting dominion, and how they ordered their working relationships with local administrations through a skillful knowledge and tactical maneuvering of local society's normative codes. Still, in both instances in the story of Esther above, legal strictures were incapable of breaking arbitrary and selfish wielding of power and authority. In fact, legal backing legitimized the Persian authority's plan to destroy an entire ethnic group. Hayek comments on the independence, impartiality, and integrity of law, "General rules, genuine laws as distinguished from specific orders, must therefore be intended to operate in circumstances which cannot be foreseen in detail, and therefore, their effect on particular ends or particular people cannot be known beforehand. It is in this sense alone that it is at all possible for the legislator to be impartial" (Hayek 2001, 79–80). It is true that individual prejudice cannot be eradicated from legislative action, but the spontaneous ordering of social structures can offer collective guiding principles and accountability mechanisms to benefit the social system (Hayek 1978, 46–7).

Schmitt's viewpoint on the role of law is pertinent here. Schmitt, like Hobbes, thinks that human beings are not naturally suited for peaceable collective living. Hobbes adopted a grim position on the state of nature in surmising that the human condition prior to the institution of government was a state of constant war.[9] The competitive nature of mankind drives him to seek an advantage

---

8. "Pharaoh will say of the Israelites, 'They are wandering aimlessly (נְבֻכִים) in the land; the wilderness has closed in on them'" (Exod. 14:3 NRSV).

9. "In [the state of nature] there is no place for industry, because the fruit thereof is uncertain, and consequently no culture of the earth, no navigation nor use of the commodities that may be imported by sea, no commodious building, no instruments of moving and removing such things as require much force, no knowledge of the face of the

over his fellows socially, economically, and politically. Schmitt calls attention to the fact that the effective functioning of the legal norms presupposes a general condition of social normality. In reality, unexpected circumstances often arise and not all the right conditions for an effective expression of legality may take place. Observing the subjective character of law, Schmitt notes that "natural law is unstable, being sometimes juristic and other times moral. This instability infects rule of law itself, with moral claims often generating novel prosecutions, therewith increasing the number of acts criminalized" (McAleer 2014, 68). Put another way, legal norms alone can neither foresee nor determine society's social or moral relationships. The function of law as seen in the book of Esther precisely illustrates this phenomenon. Unlike normative laws and formal institutions, time-tested informal social rules are not as susceptible to individual whim, prejudice, and subjectivity (Schmitt 2007, 72). Schmitt's work is greatly influenced by that of the French philosopher Baron de Montesquieu (1689–1755). Montesquieu's best-known work *The Spirit of the Laws* (1748) is often referenced for its contribution to the question of liberty under law. As one of the first of the Enlightenment philosophers to propose the notion of both universal and specific laws to individual societies and their governments, Montesquieu laid down the foundation for political liberalism when he outlined his well-known doctrine of the distribution of powers as necessary condition for political liberty. His theory of the state demonstrates his recognition of the general shortage of the necessary social virtue for a moral and logical functioning of society. Montesquieu famously declared, "It is present only when power is not abused, but it has eternally been observed that any man who has power is led to abuse it; he continues until he finds limits. Who would think it! Even virtue has need of limits. So that one cannot abuse power, power must check power by the arrangement of things" (Montesquieu 1989, XI, 4).

Given that Schmitt's expertise in constitutional law was used to defend the Nazi regime's totalitarian agenda, it is paradoxical that Schmitt wrote in defense of individual liberty that trumps legal rights. His conception of basic rights does not square with the liberal concept of universal human rights, but his realist theory of law proves to be more reasonable and fair-minded than his opponents make it out to be. Schmitt points to the illogical aspect of constitutionalism in which individual liberty may be subsumed by the legal principle of the "rule-of-law" (*Rechtsstaat*). He contends that liberal constitutional provisions hamper freedom—a general human right. Schmitt elevates the significance of basic rights above that of legal rights, averring that nothing trumps freedom. A basic right is not simply a state-endowed legal entitlement: private property, security, and freedom of conscience fall within the domain of basic rights—they are not granted

---

earth; no account of time, no arts, no letters, no society, and, which is worst of all, continual fear and danger of violent death, and the life of man solitary, poor, nasty, brutish, and short" (Hobbes 1996, 89).

by the modern-bourgeois *Rechtsstaat*. The state has the obligation to uphold and protect these fundamental existential rights (Schmitt 2008).

When this "obligation" is in the hands of a leader such as Ahasuerus who has absolute dominion, power and authority can be devoid of the moral call to ensure that human interaction is cooperative and orderly. Thus, Hayek rightly warned that strong political institutions, even when armed with positive laws, yet devoid of moral obligation or religious considerations, cannot guarantee the establishment or preservation of a humane and cohesive society.

> [T]he interests of those who bring about the required adjustments to changes, namely those who could improve their position by moving from one group to another, are systematically disregarded. So far as the group to which they wish to move is concerned, it will be its chief aim to keep them out. And the groups they wish to leave will have no incentive to assist their entry into what will often be a great variety of other groups. Thus, in a system in which the organizations of the existing producers of the various commodities and services determine prices and quantities to be produced, those who would bring about the continuous adjustment to change would be deprived of influence on events. (Hayek 1978, 92)

The biblical author's critique of power in its analysis of political process in the Persian Empire diagnoses a fatal flaw when the moral authority of the ruler and his counselors is assumed as a power resource within the imperial administration. It warns against an instinctive and unconditional bestowal of authority without a clear moral framework around the power structure. Moral authority has long been considered a foundation of political legitimacy and expected of political authority, as exemplified by the royal propaganda of the Persian Empire. In an absolutist system sovereign authority is vested in a single individual as morally legitimate political authority. Esther shows how conflation of hierarchical status with moral legitimacy in political process can be an effective tool for sovereign influence over the people. Thus in the Hebrew Bible, intervening mechanisms must be in place in order to curb royal power. Such a view is evident in Deut. 17:14-20, which famously limits royal power in a stark recognition of the negative tendency of uncontrolled human political rule. In order to prevent human nature from taking full control over power, authority, and autonomy of the monarchic office, the king's reach must be mitigated through balance and moderation practiced between the king's bodily and emotional needs and his rights and duties. The royal office is bound by the authority of the Torah and the people of Israel are the king's brothers. Institutions such as the priesthood and prophecy can supersede royal authority and censure it when the king's negative tendencies of human nature manifest themselves. 1 Sam. 8:11-17 articulates the consequences of political power when negative tendencies of human nature go unchecked—expropriation of one's land, production, labor, and even children.[10] In a similar vein, Montesquieu also noted

---

10. For an informative presentation on medieval and Renaissance Jewish political philosophy, see Melamed (2012).

that "unlike physical laws, which are, instituted and sustained by God, positive laws and social institutions are created by fallible human beings who are subject ... to ignorance and error, [and] hurried away by a thousand impetuous passions" (Montesquieu 1989, I, 1).

As seen above, neither the Persian imperial administration's carefully choreographed and reasoned propaganda of moral authority nor its sophisticated legislative apparatus could curtail the negative impacts of selfish human nature on power. The tension posed by rationalism's confidence in human nature's ability to recognize and do the good on the one hand, and the belief that only the elite few actually possessed the superior moral capacity and political acumen to act on the other, was rampant in the Enlightenment movement and critiqued by the biblical author in the portrayal of an absolutist regime headed by Ahasuerus and Haman.[11] Despite a rhetoric that liberalized reason, in large measure the Enlightenment thinkers also reaffirmed the traditional belief that hierarchy in the social, economic, and political realm was natural and necessary. Schmitt's and Hayek's works point out that the social ordering proposed by the liberal political scheme, despite its heavy emphasis on science and reason, actually lacks the intellectual coherence and human affect necessary for implementation (Hayek 1945, 1952). They observe that the predominant model of liberal democratic institutions postulates answers to questions regarding the role of the state, individual liberty, and justice, which by nature cannot be helped by a definite scientific treatment. Hayek's conception of liberty regularly stresses the fundamental importance of moral content in a society's efforts to assess the powers and limitations of its social doctrines.

The book of Esther offers a valuable commentary on today's globalizing world. Transnational political and economic interdependence generates uncertainty and confusion similar to what the citizens of Susa experienced. Esther serves as a careful warning against the consolidation and integration of powers that is vulnerable to ethical insensitivity. Transnational consolidation of financial, technological, and political life is today's reality. Political and social theorists often speak of the modern world's characteristics in terms of intensified interdependence between far-flung nations and peoples.[12] The likelihood of one's life being ruled by decisions made in another jurisdiction, detached from social solidarity, and desensitized to humanity is among the real effects of globalization. Thus, each society's predilections and interests must engender the collective moral content that best represents and empowers its members, allowing them to command their own destiny. "In our predilections and interests we are all in some measure specialists. And we all think that our personal order of values is not merely personal, but

---

11. Oscar Kenshur (2003, 228) writes, "The tension in Shaftesbury between a secular morality that democratized human nature by universalizing the capacity to know what is good and to practice the best kind of behavior and, on the other hand, his insistence on the superiority of a political and cultural elite reflected a larger tension that permeated Enlightenment thinking about human nature."

12. See, for instance, Nagel (2010); Miller (2002).

that in a free discussion among rational people we would convince the others that ours is the right one" (Hayek 2001, 57). Empirical innovations, over time incorporated into informal institutions, diffuse throughout a social group that learns collectively. When the definition of "moral" is left to a totalitarian authority, the actions engendered from it are not guaranteed to be moral. Thus, although Hayek (2001, 80-5) may offend our sensibilities, he is painfully correct when he reminds us,

> The state ceases to be a piece of utilitarian machinery intended to help individuals in the fullest development of their individual personality and becomes a "moral" institution—where "moral" is not used in contrast to immoral but describes an institution which imposes on its members its views on all moral questions, whether these views be moral or highly immoral. In this sense the Nazi or any other collectivist state is "moral," while the liberal state is not.

Chapter 16

READING ESTHER INTERTEXTUALLY AFTER THE SHOAH

Marvin A. Sweeney

Introduction

Protestant Christian readers have struggled to read Esther as a theological book from the very outset of the Protestant Reformation. Martin Luther expressed his hostility to the book of Esther and raised questions concerning its canonicity largely because the Hebrew version of the book does not mention G-d at all, although he does not attempt to remove it from the Protestant canon despite his claims that it is less worthy than other books that he hates. He states in his *Tischreden* (47:156), "I am so hostile to the book (2 Maccabees) and to Esther that I wish they did not exist at all; for they Judaize too much and contain much heathen perverseness."[1] Nevertheless, he does not miss an opportunity to express his virulent anti-Semitism by claiming falsely in the same passage that the Jews revere Esther more than the Prophets.[2] Even in the immediate aftermath of the Shoah, some interpreters, such as Robert Pfeiffer (1948, 743) and Bernard W. Anderson (1950), continued to express their own hostility to the book by decrying its alleged Jewish nationalism and animosity toward Gentiles while ignoring the fact that the book is fundamentally concerned with an attempted genocide against the Jews. Old Testament theologians, such as Walter Eichrodt (1961-7) and Gerhard von Rad (1962-5), gave Esther scant treatment in their own work.

Nevertheless, Esther is a quintessentially theological book, particularly in the aftermath of the Shoah, insofar as it raises the question of how we humans are to respond to gross injustice in the world even when G-d does not act.[3] Indeed, the question of divine absence is a key theological motif in books such as Isaiah and

---

1. Cited in Anderson (1950, 33). See also Bardtke (1964, 72-3).

2. On Luther's anti-Semitism, see now Kaufmann (2017).

3. For my earlier writings on Esther, see Sweeney (2000, 264-75, 2008, 219-22, 2012, 441-7). For recent studies and commentaries on Esther, see Beal (1999); Berlin (2001); Craig (1995); Fackenheim (1990, esp. 60-2); Fox (1991b); Hazony (2016); Levenson (1997); Stewart (2014); Walfish (1993).

Psalms, the canonicity of which are never questioned.[4] Even if G-d is presumed to be present in the world, there are times at which G-d does not act, generally for reasons that are not clear to us, and Esther is a book that addresses this issue. The Bible at large presumes the human responsibility to act in the world in order to observe the covenant with G-d, and Esther is no exception. Interpreters have already noted the intertextual dimensions of Esther, viz., its relationship with the narratives concerning Saul in 1 Samuel, particularly his failure to observe YHWH's command to destroy Agag and the rest of the Amalekites, who were condemned in the Pentateuch as a quintessential enemy of Israel for their attempt to destroy Israel in the Wilderness (1 Samuel 15; cf., Exod. 17:8-16; Deut. 25:17-19). The book of Esther identifies Mordecai and Esther as descendants of Saul's father, Kish, and Haman as a descendant of Agag in an effort to portray what needs to be done when an enemy comes to destroy Israel and G-d remains absent, that is, it counsels the need for human action, even if one is of questionable religious observance. In portraying such a situation, Esther also interrelates intertextually with the Former Prophets (Joshua–Kings) and the Chronicler's History in 1–2 Chronicles, both of which presume divine involvement throughout Israel's history, by positing that there may be times when G-d does not act, leaving humans alone to exercise responsibility to do so.

This chapter therefore presents an intertextual reading of Esther in an effort to demonstrate its inherently theological character in the aftermath of the Shoah.[5] Its theological significance becomes clear when one considers its intertextual dialogue concerning the questions of divine presence and righteousness in the face of the threat of genocide against the Jewish people. It proceeds first with detailed treatment of the intertextual relationship between Esther and 1 Samuel 15, in which Saul is rejected as king for failing to kill Agag, and the accounts of Israel's encounter with Amalek in Exodus 17 and Deuteronomy 25. It then turns to the dialogue established between Esther and the Former Prophets and Chronicles, both of which posit divine presence and power, whereas Esther does not.

The Intertextual Relationship between Esther and 1 Samuel 15

The intertextual relationship between Esther and the Saul narratives of 1 Samuel 1–15, especially the account of Saul's failure to kill Agag, King of the Amalekites, has been recognized since antiquity as well as in early-modern critical scholarship (Paton 1908, 166–72). Nevertheless, the full dimensions of this literary relationship are not always adequately explored, in part due to misguided attempts to prove the historicity of the book. There has never been a documented attempt by the Achaemenid Persian Empire to exterminate its Jewish population, nor have many of the characters in the Esther narrative, such as Esther herself, Mordecai, Haman,

---

4. See esp. Balentine (1983); Berkovits (1973); Braiterman (1998).
5. For discussion of intertextual theory, see esp. Newsom (2003); Mandolfo (2007).

and Vashti, among others, ever been adequately verified. Scholars generally place the composition of Esther between the fourth and second centuries BCE in the aftermath of the emergence of hostility against Jews in late-fifth-century Egypt and subsequently in the Hellenistic world (Moore 1992, 633–43, esp. 641; cf.. Schäfer 1997). But it appears that Esther would have been read especially in relation to the Jewish revolt against Seleucid Syria led by the Hasmonean family of priests in 167–142 BCE. Indeed, Esther is a fictional narrative, typical of the time, that was read to address the problem of divine absence and human responsibility to act at a time of paramount national crisis for the Jewish people, for example, during the Hasmonean revolt against the Seleucid Empire when the practice of Judaism was proscribed upon pain of death. It teaches that everyone, even a nonobservant Jewish girl who attains high position by virtue of her morally questionable actions in sleeping with and marrying a Gentile king, must act in the face of existential crisis for their people, particularly if they are in an exclusive position to do so.

The intertextual relationship between Esther and the Saul narratives is signaled at the outset of the book in Est. 2:5-6 when Mordecai, one of the major protagonists of the narrative, is identified as the son of Jair ben Shimei ben Kish, a Benjaminite Jew exiled from Jerusalem during the reign of King Jeconiah (Jehoiachin) of Judah by King Nebuchadnezzar of Babylon. Est. 2:7 also introduces the other major protagonist, Hadassah, also known as Esther, the daughter of Mordecai's uncle who came under Mordecai's care following the death of her parents. Mordecai's pedigree as the great grandson of Kish would also apply to his cousin, Esther.

The identification of Kish as the great grandfather of both Mordecai and Esther should not occasion any particular notice when read in and of itself. Mordecai and Esther are fourth-generation descendants of Kish, which means that Kish would have lived perhaps a century prior to the destruction of Jerusalem if Esther were an historical narrative. But the fact that Mordecai and Esther live during the reign of King Ahasuerus of Persia, generally identified as King Xerxes I, 486–465 BCE, should indicate the fictional character of the narrative, insofar as Xerxes ruled Persia beginning one hundred years following the fall of Jerusalem when Mordecai was exiled.

The full significance of the identification of Kish as the ancestor of Mordecai and Esther only becomes apparent when Est. 3:1 introduces Haman ben Hammedatha the Agagite as the antagonist of the narrative. Haman is thereby identified as a descendant of Agag, the King of the Amalekites whom King Saul of Israel failed to kill as instructed by YHWH through the prophet Samuel in 1 Samuel 15 and therefore lost his right to serve as Israel's king. Because Saul is identified as the son of Kish in 1 Sam. 9:1, the identification of Mordecai and Esther as descendants of Kish then takes on intertextual importance insofar as it suggests the relationship between the Esther and Saul narratives. This identification can in no way be considered historical as Saul's father is identified as the son of Abiel ben Zeror ben Becorath ben Aphiah of Benjamin, who would have lived in the pre-monarchic period some five-hundred years prior to the fall of Jerusalem to the Babylonians. But the point is not to establish a verifiably historical relationship between the protagonists and Kish; rather, it is to establish a literary relationship that would thereby call to mind to the reader, presumably one familiar with the Saul narratives, that Saul's failure to kill Agag and the consequences that would derive therefrom is signaled in the Esther narrative.

The reader must ask why such an identification is important to the Esther narrative. According to 1 Samuel 15, YHWH commanded Saul, King of Israel, through the prophet, Samuel, to attack Amalek and proscribe or put to death all that belongs to Amalek, including men, women, children, and infants, as well as their cattle, sheep, camels, and asses. The reason for this command is given in 1 Sam. 15:2 as YHWH's punishment against Amalek for what they did to Israel during the wilderness journey of Israel following the Exodus from Egypt. 1 Samuel 15 narrates that Saul destroyed all Amalek from Havilah to Shur near Egypt, and that he put to death all the people of Amalek as instructed, except that he spared Agag, King of the Amalekites, as well as the best of the sheep, the cattle, the second born, the lambs, and everything of value. They only destroyed the animals and property that were considered worthless and despised. When Samuel appeared to find Agag and the best of the animals alive, he upbraided Saul for disobeying the command of YHWH, killed Agag, and declared that YHWH had rejected Saul as King of Israel despite his attempts to explain his failure to execute YHWH's commands fully.

The narrative in 1 Samuel 15 portrays YHWH's command to commit genocide against the Amalekites. If read in isolation, such a command would seem immoral, but 1 Samuel 15 must be understood intertextually in relation to Exodus 17 and Deuteronomy 25, both of which discuss the Amalekite attack against Israel in the wilderness. Exodus 17:8-16 depicts the Amalekite attack against Israel at Rephidim.[6] Israel won the encounter, but the narrative does not explain the full circumstances of the attack. Nevertheless, YHWH declares that Amalek must be entirely destroyed and that YHWH will be at war with Amalek for all time. It is left to Deut. 25:17-19 to explain the reason for YHWH's declaration, viz., Amalek ambushed Israel on the road when the people were hungry and weary, and they cut down all the stragglers at the rear of the Israelite column in a bid to destroy them. Essentially, YHWH calls for the destruction of Amalek because of their attempt to destroy Israel. Amalek then becomes the symbol of an unrelenting enemy in Jewish tradition that must be destroyed lest it return and destroy all Israel itself.

The Amalek narratives teach that Israel is obligated to defend itself against an unrelenting enemy that seeks its destruction. The failure to destroy such an enemy thereby entails that such an unrelenting enemy will come back and try again. That is the issue at stake in 1 Samuel 15 in YHWH's command to kill Agag and the best of their cattle and property together with all the people. And that is also the issue in the book of Esther.

---

6. For commentary on 1 Samuel 15, see esp. McCarter (1980, 258-71); Campbell (2005, 151-61); Tsumura (2007, 387-409). For commentary on Exod. 17:8-16, see Meyers (2005, 133-5); Coats (1999, 140-4); Dozeman (2009, 391-8). For commentary on Deut. 25:17-19, see Tigay (1996, 235-7).

Indeed, the book of Esther portrays what might happen when such an enemy as the Amalekites returns to destroy Israel in the future. In this case, Haman ben Hammedatha the Agagite emerges in a later generation as the agent of destruction. Biblical narrative does not explain how a descendant of Agag could exist after Saul allegedly killed all the Amalekites and Samuel killed Agag according to 1 Samuel 15, but Rabbinic tradition steps in to provide an answer by claiming that Saul's delay in killing Agag provided Agag with the opportunity to become the ancestor of Haman on the day prior to his death at the hands of Samuel. As a result, a descendant of Agag was born who would then become the ancestor of Haman, thereby enabling Haman to attempt to destroy the Jewish people as his Amalekite ancestors through Agag had attempted.[7]

The plot is relatively simple. Haman throughout the narrative is described as the enemy of the Jews: צוֹרֵר הַיְהוּדִם (Est. 3:10; 8:1; 9:10; cf., 7:6). Mordecai was a Jew, living in the Persian capital at Shushan, who discovered a plot to assassinate the king, reported it, and saved the king's life. When Haman came to power, he was incensed because Mordecai would not bow down to him because Jews only bow down to G-d. Haman therefore plotted to destroy the entire Jewish people in the Persian Empire. The order was issued to execute all the Jews on the thirteenth day of the twelfth month (Adar). Mordecai approached Esther, the Queen, and convinced her to go to the king to expose Haman's plot. She was reluctant to do so because it meant death to appear uninvited before the king unless he approved, but Mordecai convinced her by stating that she herself would not be safe, and that "who knows if it was for a time like this that you have attained royal power?" (Est. 4:14; translation mine). Esther went to the king, was accepted, and invited him to a banquet with her and Haman. At the banquet, Esther revealed Haman's plot, prompting the king to order Haman's execution. Because the king's earlier order could not be rescinded, the Jews were allowed to defend themselves and did so by killing all of Haman's family, some 75,000 persons altogether, who would be obligated to avenge the death of their kinsmen in the ancient world. The deliverance of the Jews from Haman's plot would thenceforth be celebrated as the holiday of Purim.

When read intertextually in relation to 1 Samuel 15, the book of Esther functions as a form of commentary on the narrative concerning Saul's failure to kill Agag as instructed and the consequences that would follow from his failure to do so. Esther requires the reader to know the narratives about Amalek in Exod. 17:8-16 and Deut. 25:17-19, which explain the rationale for YHWH's order to exterminate Amalek as an unrelenting enemy that seeks Israel's destruction. Although the Esther narrative makes it plain that YHWH does not act to thwart Haman's plot, Mordecai's speech to Esther in Est. 4:12-17 hints that deliverance for the Jews might come from another quarter if Esther does not act. Esther does act, and, although she is not the traditional model of the Jewish hero or sage, succeeds in saving her people at a time when divine action is not apparent. The Esther

---

7. See Targum Sheni to Est. 4:13; *B. Meg.* 13a.

narrative thereby highlights the responsibility of Jews, viz., any and all Jews, to act at a time of crisis when it is not clear that YHWH will act on their behalf. In this sense, Esther functions as a key theological text calling on human beings to act in a time of crisis when G-d apparently does not.

The Intertextual Relationship between Esther and Chronicles

The motif of the absence of G-d in the narrative account of the deliverance of the Jews from attempted genocide in the Persian Empire leads to the second major dimension of intertextuality in this chapter. That dimension is the intertextual interrelationship between the portrayal of history in Esther and those of other narrative historical works in the Bible, specifically the Former Prophets and the Chronicler's History, which comprises the book of Chronicles. Whereas Esther does not mention G-d at all in the Masoretic Hebrew form of the book and thereby presents only human beings as the major actors in its account of history, both the Former Prophets and the Chronicler's History present YHWH as a major actor together with the people of Israel and Judah, as well as other human figures, in their respective accounts of the history of Israel and Judah. Although the Former Prophets and the Chronicler's History present somewhat similar accounts of history, they constitute very different accounts of that history and the role of YHWH within it. Consequently, the Former Prophets, the Chronicler's History, and the book of Esther constitute very distinctive theological understandings of history in the Hebrew Bible. They disagree with each other in many respects, especially concerning the role of G-d in history, and therefore must be considered within the context of the various canonical forms of the Bible to be in dialogue with each other. Such dialogue suggests a debate within the Jewish Bible concerning the nature of history and the role of G-d and human beings within it.

The Former Prophets recount the history of Israel from the conquest of Canaan under Joshua through the emergence of the Israelite and Judean kingdoms, the destruction of the kingdom of northern Israel by the Assyrians in 722–21 BCE, and the destruction of the southern kingdom of Judah by the Babylonians in 587–86 BCE and its aftermath. Modern scholarship, beginning especially with the work of Martin Noth (1981; German original, 1957), has recognized that there is a complex compositional history that has led to the formation of these books, but it has also recognized that there is a distinctive theological perspective that appears throughout the final form of these books (Römer 2007). That perspective entails considerable influence from the theological premises of the book of Deuteronomy, which holds that there is a covenant between YHWH and Israel that calls for YHWH to protect and ensure the welfare of Israel in return for Israel's recognition of YHWH as its exclusive G-d and its observance of YHWH's requirements as expressed in Deuteronomic law. In addition to Israel's exclusive adherence to YHWH, other major requirements include the establishment of only one major sanctuary for the worship of YHWH in the land, the condition that YHWH may punish the people should they fail to observe YHWH's requirements, prohibitions against the worship of other gods and intermarriage with the Canaanite nations lest they lead Israel to the worship of foreign gods, and permission to establish a king provided that he be from among the people of Israel and that he study YHWH's Torah under the supervision of the priests in order to ensure that he abides by YHWH's expectations.

The purpose of the history presented in the Former Prophets, known in modern scholarship as the Deuteronomistic History, is to explain why the people of Israel and Judah were exiled from their land despite having been promised that land by YHWH. The concern with the people's failure to abide by YHWH's covenant therefore plays a prominent role in the history insofar as the people's alleged sins provide the major means to explain their exile as punishment from YHWH for failing to observe the covenant. Throughout the history, the people of Israel and Judah are accused of having violated YHWH's expectations by failing to destroy the Canaanites entirely, thereby prompting YHWH to bring punishment against the people for allegedly following in the footsteps of the Canaanites by worshipping their foreign gods and engaging in practices forbidden in Deuteronomic law, such as the worship of idols, the establishment of foreign sanctuaries, the commission of murder and other wrongdoing forbidden by Deuteronomy.

The kings of Israel and Judah in particular are identified as major sources of wrongdoing in history. With regard to the northern kingdom of Israel, all of the northern kings are judged to be wicked, beginning with Jeroboam ben Nebat, the first king of northern Israel, due to their penchant for engaging in idolatry, the worship of foreign gods, and the building of illicit sanctuaries. Consequently, the northern kingdom of Israel is destroyed by the Assyrians in 722–721 BCE insofar as the history portrays Assyria as YHWH's agent of punishment. With regard to the southern kingdom of Judah, most of the kings of the house of David are considered wicked, including David and Solomon, although there are a number of righteous Davidic kings, such as Asa, Jehoshaphat, Hezekiah, Josiah, and others. Due to the wickedness of King Manasseh, who is charged with exceptional wrongdoing in killing his enemies and engaging in illicit worship, YHWH decides to destroy Jerusalem and Judah, and even the righteousness of Manasseh's grandson, King Josiah, cannot stop the punishment.

The focus on YHWH's punishment of Israel and Judah for failing to abide by the terms of the covenant points to a characteristic dimension of the understanding of sin and punishment in the Former Prophets, viz., Israel and Judah are punished for the sins of past figures, particularly the kings. Northern Israel is destroyed because the first King of Israel, Jeroboam ben Nebat, allegedly worshipped the golden calves that he established in the sanctuaries of Beth El and Dan, and all of his successors followed suit. It is doubtful that Jeroboam actually had worship of the golden calves as gods in mind; they appear to have been understood as mounts for YHWH akin to typical practice in the ancient Near Eastern world at the time and also akin to the role of the Ark of the Covenant as a throne for YHWH above which YHWH was understood to be seated (Sweeney 2007, 172–8). But nevertheless, the history accuses Jeroboam of idolatry and uses that as the basis for YHWH's decision to destroy the northern kingdom, even though

Jeroboam lived some two-hundred years before Israel was destroyed. Of course, his successors are charged with continuing in Jeroboam's sins, but Jeroboam is the instigator. An analogous scenario emerges for the southern kingdom of Judah as well, viz., King Manasseh's sins are presented as the cause of YHWH's decision to destroy southern Judah, even though Manasseh died in 642 BCE, some fifty-five or so years prior to the destruction of Jerusalem by the Babylonians in 587–86 BCE. Despite King Josiah's exemplary righteousness—indeed, Josiah is the ideal monarch of the house of David, even more so than David himself—Jerusalem is destroyed (Sweeney 2008, 72–81, 2007, 424–50).

Some interpreters might see that the Former Prophets' penchant for explaining disaster for both northern Israel and southern Judah by pointing to the sins of kings who died years before the disasters took place might be morally questionable. Indeed, such a scenario appears to be the case when the Chronicler's History is examined closely.

The Chronicler's History in the book of Chronicles received much less attention than the Former Prophets (or Deuteronomistic History) in large measure due to the priestly character of the Chronicler's work.[8] Many considered the Chronicler to be theologically biased because of its priestly perspective, whereas the Deuteronomistic History was taken to be a far more reliable historical source. But as research has progressed on the Former Prophets, the theological perspectives of these books have become more and more clear. Such recognition has attracted more attention to the Chronicler. Although the Chronicler often repeats narratives from the Former Prophets, oftentimes, almost word for word, close attention to the Chronicler's work demonstrates that it often serves as a corrective to the work of the Deuteronomistic History when it makes even small changes to the text of Kings, such as the portrayal of Jeroboam's return to Israel following the death of Solomon. Whereas 1 Kgs 12:2 states that Jeroboam "stayed" (וַיֵּשֶׁב) in Egypt until he was summoned to Shechem to lead northern Israel in its negotiation with Solomon's son, Rehoboam, to become the next King of Israel, 2 Chron. 10:2 states that Jeroboam "returned" (וַיָּשָׁב) from Egypt to lead the delegation. The change is minor insofar as it only entails the repointing of the same consonants, וישב, to read, "and he returned" (וַיָּשָׁב) in 2 Chron. 10:2 from "and he stayed" (וַיֵּשֶׁב) in 1 Kgs 12:2 along with other modifications. The change is nevertheless important in understanding the Chronicler's use of the Former Prophets text, viz., Chronicles corrects the Kings reading to produce a more coherent text.

Indeed, Chronicles employs not only minor changes but major ones as well, to articulate a distinctive theological viewpoint from that of the Former Prophets. As a priestly work, Chronicles is much concerned with the Temple and its role as the holy center of creation, and so Chronicles begins with creation itself with the genealogy of Adam, the first human from the time of creation, in 1 Chron. 1:1, whereas the Former Prophets begins with Joshua's conquest of Canaan

---

8. For discussion of the Chronicler's perspectives, see Sweeney (2011); cf. Klein (2012, 471–529).

following the portrayal of Moses's rehearsal of the revelation at Sinai in the book of Deuteronomy. Chronicles gives far greater attention to the role that David played in planning the Temple, Solomon's efforts at building it, and various Temple celebrations by righteous Judean kings, such as David's bringing the Ark to Jerusalem in 1 Chronicles 15; Jehoshaphat's establishment of the judicial system in 2 Chronicles 19; Hezekiah's Passover celebration in 2 Chronicles 30; and Josiah's celebration of Passover in 2 Chronicles 35, whereas Kings gives little attention to such events. Whereas Kings is concerned with the sins of Jeroboam and northern Israel, Chronicles pays little attention to them because Chronicles is concerned with Jerusalem and the Temple. Indeed, Chronicles is often more historically reliable than Kings, insofar as it notes Rehoboam's building of fortifications to protect Jerusalem and Judah in 2 Chron. 11:1-12 that have been confirmed archeologically, and 2 Chron. 32:1-8 recounts Hezekiah's rebuilding of Jerusalem's water system and fortifications, whereas Kings ignores the water system. 2 Chronicles 33 refrains from holding Manasseh as responsible for the destruction of Jerusalem insofar as he repented from his sins after having been dragged in chains to Babylon by the Assyrian king, apparently to witness the consequences of the Babylonian revolt against Assyria in 652–48 BCE.

Indeed, the Chronicler's treatment of Manasseh is key to understanding the Chronicler's understanding of sin and punishment in distinction from that of the Former Prophets. The Chronicler does not explain disaster by pointing to the sins of earlier kings or earlier generations. Instead, Chronicles corrects the problems with the assertions of the Former Prophets that Israel and Judah suffer for the sins of their ancestors and earlier kings. According to the Chronicler, those who suffer do so due to their own sins. Insofar as the destruction of Jerusalem took place some fifty-five years after Manasseh's death, he could not be held responsible for the disaster, and he is instead portrayed as initially sinful, but repentant, especially given the fact that he reigned for fifty-five years, longer than any other monarch of the Davidic line. The Chronicler revised its assessment of Josiah as well. According to 2 Kings 22–23, Josiah was one of the greatest and most righteous monarchs of the House of David. But Josiah's early death at the hands of Pharaoh Necho of Egypt demands explanation. According to 2 Kings 22–23, Josiah was granted the right to die in peace before seeing the destruction of Jerusalem due to Manasseh's sins. But according to 2 Chronicles 34–35, Josiah must have done something to deserve his early death at the age of thirty-nine. According to 2 Chron. 35:20-27, Josiah sinned by defying YHWH's will to allow Pharaoh Necho of Egypt to move his army to confront the kingdom that wars with him, that is, Babylon. Josiah does not die in peace but in battle with Pharaoh Necho, who is prevented from confronting Babylon, thereby enabling Babylon later to destroy Jerusalem. In the end, Josiah dies because of his own sin.

The Chronicler's concern to charge that those who are punished suffer because of their own sins is characteristic of the priestly viewpoint as expressed in Ezekiel 18, which holds that individuals are punished for their own sins, not for the sins of their ancestors. In the case of Jerusalem, 2 Chronicles 36 holds that Jerusalem is not destroyed because of the sins of Manasseh but because the officers of the priests and the people committed transgressions and thereby defiled the Jerusalem Temple as stated in 2 Chron. 36:14 (Sweeney 2008, 81–3; cf., Klein 2012, 540-1). In keeping with the priestly view that a defiled Temple must be purged and restored, Solomon's Temple is destroyed, but Chronicles concludes in 2 Chron. 36:22-23 with a brief account of the announcement by King Cyrus of Persia that the Jerusalem Temple would be rebuilt following the seventy years in which the land repaid its violated Sabbaths (2 Chron. 36:20-21).

Esther offers a third alternative to the understanding of history, even if its portrayal of the Persian attempt to destroy the Jewish people is fictional. Esther argues that G-d may not be involved at all—or perhaps may act only surreptitiously. Human beings must rise to the forefront to save Israel in a time of crisis, because G-d might not do so. But Esther's distinctive perspective is not limited only to the absence of G-d in the narrative. The human protagonists who rise to the occasion to save the Jewish people from attempted genocide are not the typical righteous heroes of the earlier historical accounts, such as Joshua or Josiah in the Former Prophets or David and Solomon in the Chronicler's History. Esther is a nonobservant Jewish woman who ignores Jewish teachings on intermarriage and sexual morality to enter a contest in which she sleeps with and ultimately marries the Gentile Persian king. Although Mordecai is righteous in his refusal to bow to anyone other than G-d, he allows Esther to engage in such activity in his role as Esther's surrogate father. But such portrayals serve Esther's theological viewpoint, viz., in a time of crisis when G-d does not appear to act, those in a position to do so must rise to the occasion, whether they are observant or not, to save the Jewish people from attempted genocide. Part of Esther's worldview is that, despite their limitations, Mordecai and Esther are the only ones in a position to do so. Esther thereby engages in intertextual theological dialogue with the Former Prophets and the Chronicler's History—and indeed, the Pentateuch and Ezra-Nehemiah might be added to Esther's intertextual dialogue partners within the Jewish Tanak—to offer a different perspective on Jewish history and the roles that G-d and human beings might play in it.

Conclusion

Altogether, intertextual study of the book of Esther demonstrates that Esther is indeed a theological book, with an important theological message, viz., G-d might not come to the rescue in times of mortal danger to the Jewish people. Such a contention does not entail that G-d does not exist or that G-d is somehow unable to act. The fact of the matter is that we humans do not always know what G-d might or might not do in any given situation. Furthermore, Esther contends that human beings must rise to the occasion to act when G-d fails to do so. In articulating this view of human responsibility in the world, Esther also contends that a potential hero or heroine does not need to be a religiously observant figure as other major historical works in the Bible might prefer to contend. Rather, the ability and power to act is the requirement for such action—and indeed, the ability and power to act functions as a moral imperative to do so in Esther and the Jewish tradition at large.

In the aftermath of the Shoah, when some six million Jews and some six million others were deliberately murdered by Nazi Germany and its collaborators, the theological character of the book of Esther takes on special importance. There are times in human history and life when G-d appears to be absent, powerless, disinterested, not engaged, or even immoral, and yet human beings—as partners with G-d in the completion and sanctification of creation—must be prepared to step up and confront evil. In the Esther narrative and in the world of the Second World War, there were no voices in the Persian or the German government—or elsewhere in the world for that matter—who were willing to speak up against the immorality of the decision to murder Jews. Esther teaches that in such an event, any individual, including women and those who are not religiously observant, must be prepared to stand up and say no to those who would commit the evil or with their silence allow it to take place. In the narrative world of the book of Esther, Esther was the one person in the world who had the ability to speak against the atrocity—and she had the obligation to do so, even if it might cost her life. That obligation—to G-d and to humanity at large—makes Esther a theological book in Judaism and Christianity as well as in the human world at large.

BIBLIOGRAPHY

Abernethy, Andrew T. 2014. *Eating in Isaiah: Approaching Food and Drink in Isaiah's Structure and Message.* BibInt 131. Leiden: Brill.

Abernethy, Andrew T. 2018. "Feasts and Taboo Eating in Isaiah: Anthropology as a Stimulant for the Exegete's Imagination." *CBQ* 80: 393–408.

Adelman, Rachel E. 2015. *The Female Ruse: Women's Deception and Divine Sanction in the Hebrew Bible.* Hebrew Bible Monographs 74. Sheffield: Sheffield Phoenix.

Aletti, Jean-Noël. 1977. "Séduction Et Parole En Proverbes I-IX." *VT* 27.2: 129–44.

Alexander, Philip S. 1988. "Retelling the Old Testament." Pages 99–121 in *It Is Written: Scripture Citing Scripture. Essays in Honour of Barnabas Lindars.* Edited by D. A. Carson and H. G. M. Williamson. Cambridge: Cambridge University Press.

Anderson, Bernard W. 1950. "The Place of the Book of Esther in the Christian Bible." *JR* 30: 32–43.

Anderson, Gary A. 1991. *A Time to Mourn, a Time to Dance: The Expression of Grief and Joy in Israelite Religion.* University Park: Pennsylvania State University Press.

Aronowicz, Annette. 2008. "The Downfall of Haman: Postwar Yiddish Theater between Secular and Sacred." *AJSR* 32.2 369–88.

Bachmann, Veronika. 2014. "Unterhaltung mit Tiefgang: Das Esterbuch (Teil 1)." *BL* 87: 50–5.

Bal, Mieke. 1988. *Death and Dissymmetry: The Politics of Coherence in the Book of Judges.* Chicago: University of Chicago Press.

Bal, Mieke. 1999. "Lots of Writing." Pages 212–38 in *Ruth and Esther: A Feminist Companion to the Bible, Second Series.* Edited by Athalya Brenner. Sheffield: Sheffield Academic.

Balentine, Samuel E. 1983. *The Hidden God: The Hiding of the Face of God in the Old Testament.* Oxford: Oxford University Press.

Balentine, Samuel E. 2006. "'I Was Ready to Be Sought Out by Those Who Did Not Ask.'" Pages 1–20 in *The Origins of Penitential Prayer in Second Temple Judaism.* Edited by Mark J. Boda, Daniel K. Falk, and Rodney A. Werline. Vol. 1 of *Seeking the Favor of God.* EJL 21. Atlanta, GA: SBL Press.

Barclay, John M. G. 2005. "The Empire Writes Back: Josephan Rhetoric in Flavian Rome." Pages 315–32 in *Flavius Josephus and Flavian Rome.* Edited by Jonathan Edmondson, Steve Mason, and James Rives. Oxford: Oxford University Press.

Bardtke, Hans. 1963. *Luther und das Buch Ester.* Tübingen: Mohr Siebeck.

Barthes, Roland. 2008. "Toward a Psychology of Contemporary Food Consumption." Pages 28–35 in *Food and Culture: A Reader.* Edited by Carole Counihan and Penny Van Esterik. 2nd ed. New York: Routledge.

Barton, John. 2013. "Déjà Lu: Intertextuality, Method or Theory?" Pages 1–16 in *Reading Job Intertextually.* Edited by Katharine Dell and Will Kynes. LHBOTS 574. London: Bloomsbury T&T Clark.

Beal, Timothy K. 1997. *The Book of Hiding: Gender, Ethnicity, Annihilation, and Esther.* Biblical Limits. London: Routledge.

Beal, Timothy K. 1999. "Esther." Pages ix–130 in *Ruth and Esther*. Berit Olam. Edited by David W. Cotter. Collegeville, MN: Liturgical Press.
Bechtel, Carol M. 2011. *Esther*. IBC. Louisville, KY: John Knox.
Ben-Dov, Jonathan. 1999. "A Presumed Citation of Esther in 4QD^b." *DSD* 6: 282–4.
Berg, Sandra Beth. 1979. *The Book of Esther: Motifs, Themes and Structure*. SBLDS 44. Atlanta, GA: Scholars Press.
Berg, Sandra Beth. 1980. "After the Exile: God and History in the Book of Chronicles and Esther." Pages 107–27 in *The Divine Helmsman*. Edited by James L. Crenshaw and S. Sandmel. New York: Ktav.
Berger, Yitzhak. 2010. "Esther and Benjaminite Royalty: A Study in Inner-Biblical Allusion." *JBL* 129.4: 625–44.
Berkovits, Eliezer. 1973. *Faith after the Holocaust*. New York: Ktav.
Berlin, Adele. 2001. *Esther: The Traditional Hebrew Text with the New JPS Translation*. Jewish Publication Society Bible Commentary. Philadelphia, PA: Jewish Publication Society.
Berman, Joshua. 2016. "Law Code as Plot Template in Biblical Narrative (1 Kings 9.26–11.13; Joshua 2.9-13)." *JSOT* 40: 344–9.
Bickerman, Elias J. 1944. "The Colophon of the Greek Book of Esther." *JBL* 63: 339–62.
Block, Daniel I. 1997. "Nations/Nationality." Pages 966–72 in *NIDOTTE*, vol. 4. Grand Rapids, MI: VanGemeren.
Block, Daniel I. 1999. *Judges, Ruth*. NAC 6. Nashville, TN: Broadman & Holman.
Boda, Mark J. 2006. "Confession as Theological Expression: Ideological Origins of Penitential Prayer." Pages 21–50 in *The Origins of Penitential Prayer in Second Temple Judaism*. Edited by Mark J. Boda, Daniel K. Falk, and Rodney A. Werline. Vol. 1 of *Seeking the Favor of God*. EJL 21. Atlanta, GA: SBL Press.
Boda, Mark J. 2012. "Lament, Mourning." Pages 473–7 in *Dictionary of the Old Testament Prophets*. Edited by Mark J. Boda and J. Gordon McConville. Downers Grove, IL: IVP Academic.
Boda, Mark J., Daniel K. Falk, and Rodney A. Werline, eds. 2006–8. *Seeking the Favor of God*. 3 vols. EJL. Atlanta, GA: SBL Press.
Börner-Klein, Dagmar, and Elisabeth Hollender, trans. 2000. *Der Traktat Megilla*. Vol. 1 of *Rabbinische Kommentare zum Buch Ester*. Leiden: Brill.
Botha, Phil J. 1995. "Ironie as Sleutel tot die Verstaan van Psalm 14." *SK* 16: 16–27.
Botha, Phil J. 2013. "Psalm 53 in Canonical Perspective." *OTE* 26: 583–606.
Braiterman, Zachary. 1998. *(God) After Auschwitz: Tradition and Change in Post-Holocaust Jewish Thought*. Princeton, NJ: Princeton University Press.
Briant, Pierre. 2002. *From Cyrus to Alexander: A History of the Persian Empire*. Translated by Peter T. Daniels. Winona Lake, IN: Eisenbrauns.
Brown, Jeannine K. 2016. "Metalepsis." Pages 29–41 in *Exploring Intertextuality: Diverse Strategies for New Testament Interpretation of Texts*. Edited by B. J. Oropeza and Steve Moyise. Eugene, OR: Cascade.
Brown, William P. 2002. "The Pedagogy of Proverbs 10:1–31:9." Pages 150–82 in *Character and Scripture: Moral Formation, Community, and Biblical Interpretation*. Edited by William P. Brown. Grand Rapids, MI: Eerdmans.
Bruns, Gerald L. 1987. "Midrash and Allegory: The Beginnings of Scriptural Interpretation." Pages 625–46 in *The Literary Guide to the Bible*. Edited by Robert Alter and Frank Kermode. Cambridge, MA: Harvard University Press.
Burnett, Joel S. 2010. *Where Is God? Divine Absence in the Hebrew Bible*. Minneapolis, MN: Fortress Press.

Bush, Frederic. 1996. *Ruth, Esther.* WBC 9. Nashville, TN: Thomas Nelson.
Cameron, George G. 1951. "The Old Persian Text of the Bisitun Inscription." *JCS* 5: 47–54.
Cameron, George G. 1965. "New Tablets from the Persepolis Treasury." *JNES* 24.3: 167–92.
Camp, Claudia V. 2000. *Wise, Strange and Holy: The Strange Woman and the Making of the Bible.* Sheffield: Sheffield Academic.
Campbell, Antony F. 2005. *1 Samuel.* FOTL 7. Grand Rapids, MI: Eerdmans
Carruthers, Jo. 2008. *Esther through the Centuries.* Oxford: Blackwell.
Cassuto, Umberto. 1967. *A Commentary on the Book of Exodus.* Translated by Israel Abrahams. Jerusalem: Magnes.
Cataldo, Jeremiah W., ed. 2019. *Imagined Worlds and Constructed Differences in the Hebrew Bible.* LHBOTS 677. London: T&T Clark.
Chalupa, Petr. 2016. "The Book of Esther in Josephus: Authority of Conflict-Causing Laws." Pages 139–50 in *The Process of Authority: The Dynamics in Transmission and Reception of Canonical Texts.* Edited by Jan Dušek and Jan Roskovec. DCLS 27. Berlin: de Gruyter.
Chapman, Cynthia R. 2004. *The Gendered Language of Warfare in the Israelite-Assyrian Encounter.* Winona Lake, IN: Eisenbrauns.
Chapman, Honora Howell, and Zuleika Rodgers, eds. 2015. *A Companion to Josephus in His World.* Oxford: Blackwell.
Cho, Paul Kang-Kul, and Janling Fu. 2013. "Death and Feasting in the Isaiah Apocalypse (Isaiah 25:6–8)." Pages 117–42 in *Formation and Intertextuality in Isaiah 24–27.* Edited by J. Todd Hibbard and Hyun Chul Paul Kim. AIL 17. Atlanta, GA: SBL Press.
Clines, David J. A. 1984. *The Esther Scroll: The Story of the Story.* JSOTSup 30. Sheffield: Sheffield Academic.
Coats, George W. 1999. *Exodus 1–18.* FOTL 2A. Grand Rapids, MI: Eerdmans.
Coetzee, Johan H. 1998. "Worstel met God: Argumenteringstrategiee en hul sosio-retoriese funksie in Psalm 13." *SK* 19: 544–53.
Collins, John J. 1975. "Court-Tales in Daniel and the Development of Apocalyptic." *JBL* 94.2: 218–34.
Coote, R. B. 1998. "Joshua." Pages 592–6 in *The New Interpreter's Bible.* Edited by L. E. Keck. Nashville, TN: Abingdon.
Craghan, John F. 1982. "Esther, Judith, and Ruth: Paradigm for Human Liberation." *BTB* 12: 11–19.
Craig, Kenneth. 1995. *Reading Esther: A Case for the Literary Carnivalesque.* Louisville, KY: Westminster John Knox.
Crawford, Sidnie White. 1989. "Esther: A Feminine Model for Jewish Diaspora." Pages 161–77 in *Gender and Difference in Ancient Israel.* Edited by Peggy L. Day. Minneapolis, MN: Fortress Press.
Crawford, Sidnie White. 1996a. "Has Every Book of the Bible Been Found Among the Dead Sea Scrolls?" *BRev* 12: 28–33, 56.
Crawford, Sidnie White. 1996b. "Has *Esther* Been Found at Qumran? 4QProto-Esther and the *Esther* Corpus." *RevQ* 17: 307–25.
Crawford, Sidnie White. 2003. "Esther and Judith: Contrasts in Character." Pages 61–76 in *The Book of Esther in Modern Research.* Edited by Sidnie White Crawford and Leonard J. Greenspoon. London: T&T Clark International.
Creach, Jerome F. D. 2005. "The Psalms and the Cult." Pages 119–37 in *Interpreting the Psalms: Issues and Approaches.* Edited by Philip S. Johnston and David G. Firth. Nottingham: Apollos.

Crenshaw, James L. 1969. "Method in Determining Wisdom Influence upon 'Historical' Literature." *JBL* 88.2: 129–42.

Davies, Philip. 2013. "Saul, Hero and Villain." Pages 131–40 in *Remembering Biblical Figures in the Late Persian and Early Hellenistic Periods: Social Memory and Imagination*. Edited by Diana V. Edelman and Ehud Ben Zvi. Oxford: Oxford University Press.

Davis, Barbara. 2011. "Psychodynamic Psychotherapies and the Treatment of Co-Occurring Psychological Trauma and Addiction." Pages 74–111 in *Psychological Trauma and Addiction Treatment*. Edited by Bruce Carruth. New York: Routledge.

Day, Linda. 2005. *Esther*. AOTC. Nashville, TN: Abingdon.

De Troyer, Kristin. 2000. "Once More, the So-Called Esther Fragments of Cave 4." *RevQ* 75: 401–22.

De Troyer, Kristin. 2003. "On the Help of God in the Old Greek of Esther." Pages 9–28 in *Rewriting the Sacred Text: What the Old Greek Texts Tell Us about the Literary Growth of the Bible*. TCSt 4. Atlanta, GA: SBL Press.

Dell, Katharine, and Will Kynes. 2014. *Reading Ecclesiastes Intertextually*. LHBOTS 587. London: Bloomsbury T&T Clark.

Dickson, Charles R., and Phil J. Botha. 2000. "The Role and Portrayal of the King in Esther." *OTE* 13.2: 156–73.

Douglas, Mary. 1966. *Purity and Danger: An Analysis of Concepts of Purity and Taboo*. London: Routledge.

Doyle, Brian. 2010. "Where Is God When You Need Him Most? The Divine Metaphor of Absence and Presence as a Binding Element in the Composition of the Book of Psalms." Pages 377–90 in *The Composition of the Book of Psalms*. Edited by Erich Zenger. Leuven: Peeters.

Dozeman, Thomas B. 2009. *Exodus*. ECC. Grand Rapids, MI: Eerdmans.

Dunne, John Anthony. 2014. *Esther and Her Elusive God*. Eugene, OR: Wipf & Stock.

Durkheim, Émile. 1986. *Durkheim on Politics and the State*. Edited by Anthony Giddens. Translated by W. D. Halls. Cambridge: Polity.

Duvall, J. Scott, and J. Daniel Hays. 2019. *God's Relational Presence: The Cohesive Center of Biblical Theology*. Grand Rapids, MI: Baker Academic.

Edenburg, Cynthia. 2010. "Intertextuality, Literary Competence and the Question of Readership: Some Preliminary Observations." *JSOT* 35: 131–48.

Efthimiadis-Keith, Helen. 2004. *The Enemy Is within: A Jungian Psychoanalytic Approach to the Book of Judith*. BibInt 67. Boston, MA: Brill.

Efthimiadis-Keith, Helen. 2014. "Genealogy, Retribution and Identity: Re-Interpreting the Cause of Suffering in the Book of Judith." *OTE* 27.3: 860–78.

Ego, Beate. 2010. "Mordecai's Refusal of Proskynesis before Haman according to the Septuagint: Tradition-historical and Literal Aspects." Pages 16–29 in *Deuterocanonical Additions of the Old Testament Texts: Selected Studies*. Edited by Géza G. Xeravits and József Zsengellér. Berlin: de Gruyter.

Ego, Beate. 2015. "Prayer and Emotion in the Septuagint of Esther." Pages 83–94 in *Ancient Jewish Prayers and Emotions: Emotions Associated with Jewish Prayer in and around the Second Temple Period*. Edited by Stefan C. Reif and Renate Egger-Wenzel. DCLS. Berlin: de Gruyter.

Eichrodt, Walther. 1961–7. *Theology of the Old Testament*. OTL. 2 vols. Philadelphia, PA: Westminster.

Eisenman, Robert H., and Michael O. Wise. 1992. *The Dead Sea Scrolls Uncovered*. Rockport, MA: Element.

Enenkel, Karl A. E., and Ilja Leonard Pfeijffer. 2005. *The Manipulative Mode: Political Propaganda in Antiquity: A Collection of Case Studies*. Leiden: Brill.
Epstein, Isidore, trans. 1948. *The Babylonian Talmud*. London: Soncino Press.
Fackenheim, Emil. 1990. *The Jewish Bible after the Holocaust: A Rereading*. Bloomington: Indiana University Press.
Feinstein, Edward. 2014. *The Chutzpah Imperative: Empowering Today's Jews for a Life That Matters*. Woodstock: Jewish Lights.
Feldman, Emanuel. 1977. *Biblical and Post-Biblical Defilement and Mourning: Law as Theology*. The Library of Jewish Law and Ethics. New York: Ktav.
Feldman, Louis H. 1970. "Hellenizations in Josephus' Version of Esther." *TAPA* 101: 143–70.
Feldman, Louis H. 1996. *Jewish Life and Thought Among Greeks and Romans: Primary Readings*. Minneapolis, MN: Fortress Press.
Feldman, Louis H. 1997. "Torah and Greek Culture in Josephus." *The Torah U-Madda Journal* 7: 41–87.
Feldman, Louis H. 1998a. *Josephus's Interpretation of the Bible*. HCS 27. Berkeley: University of California Press.
Feldman, Louis H. 1998b. *Studies in Josephus' Rewritten Bible*. Supplements to the Journal for the Study of Judaism 58. Leiden: Brill.
Finkel, J. 1961. "The Author of the Genesis Apocryphon Knew the Book of Esther." Pages 163–82 in *Essays on the Dead Sea Scrolls in Memory of E. L. Sukenik*. Edited by Yigael Yadin and Chaim Rabin. Jerusalem: Hekhal Ha-Sefer.
Firth, David G. 1997. "The Book of Esther: A Neglected Paradigm for Dealing with the State." *OTE* 10.1: 18–26.
Firth, David G. 2010a. "When Samuel Met Esther: Narrative Focalisation, Intertextuality, and Theology." *Southeastern Theological Review* 1: 15–28.
Firth, David G. 2010b. *The Message of Esther: God Present but Unseen*. The Bible Speaks Today. Nottingham: IVP Academic.
Firth, David G. 2017a. "Models of Inclusion and Exclusion in Joshua." Pages 71–88 in *Interreligious Relations: Biblical Perspectives*. Edited by Hallvard Hagelia and Markus Zehnder. London: T&T Clark
Firth, David G. 2017b. "Disorienting Readers in Joshua 1.1—5.12." *JSOT* 41: 413–30.
Firth, David G. 2019. *Including the Stranger: Foreigners in the Former Prophets*. New Studies in Biblical Theology. London: Apollos.
Fishbane, Michael. 1986. "Inner Biblical Exegesis: Types and Strategies of Interpretation in Ancient Israel." Pages 19–37 in *Midrash and Literature*. Edited by Geoffrey H. Hartman and Sanford Budick. New Haven, CT: Yale University Press.
Fitzmyer, Joseph A. 1971. *The Genesis Apocryphon of Qumran Cave 1: A Commentary*. BibOr 18A. Rome: Pontifical Biblical Institute.
Flesher, Leann S. 2007. "The Use of Female Imagery and Lamentation in the Book of Judith: Penitential Prayer of Petition for Obligatory Action?" Pages 83–104 in *The Development of Penitential Prayer in Second Temple Judaism*. Edited by Mark J. Boda, Daniel K. Falk, and Rodney A. Werline. Vol. 2 of *Seeking the Favor of God*. EJL 22. Atlanta, GA: SBL Press.
Foer, Johnathan Safran, ed. 2012. *New American Haggadah*. New York: Little, Brown.
Fox, Michael V. 1991a. *The Redaction of the Books of Esther: On Reading Composite Texts*. SBLMS 40. Atlanta, GA: Scholars Press.
Fox, Michael V. 1991b. *Character and Ideology in the Book of Esther*. Columbia: University of South Carolina Press.

Fox, Michael V. 1996. "Amon Again." *JBL* 115.4: 699–702.
Fox, Michael V. 2001. *Character and Ideology in the Book of Esther*. 2nd ed. Grand Rapids, MI: Eerdmans.
Fox, Michael V. 2010. *Character and Ideology in the Book of Esther*. Eugene, OR: Wipf & Stock.
Fox, Michael V. 2012. "Joseph and Wisdom." Pages 231–61 in *The Book of Genesis: Composition, Reception, and Interpretation*. Edited by Craig A. Evans, Joel N. Lohr, and David L. Petersen. Leiden: Brill.
Frechette, Christopher G., and Elizabeth Boase. 2016. "Defining 'Trauma' as a Useful Lens for Biblical Interpretation." Pages 1–23 in *Bible through the Lens of Trauma*. Edited by Elizabeth Boase and Christopher G. Frechette. SemeiaSt 86. Atlanta, GA: SBL Press.
Frei, Peter. 1984. "Zentralgewalt und Lokalautonomie im Achämenidenreich." Pages 5–132 in *Reichsidee und Reichsorganisation im Perserreich*. Edited by Peter Frei and Klaus Koch. Göttingen: Vandenhoeck & Ruprecht.
Frei, Peter. 2001. "Persian Imperial Authorization: A Summary." Pages 1–40 in *Persia and Torah: The Theory of Imperial Authorization of the Pentateuch*. Edited by James W. Watts. Atlanta, GA: SBL Press.
Frenkel, Yona. 1991. *Darkei ha-Aggadah ve-ha-Midrash*. 2 vols. Givatayim: Yad la-Talmud (Hebrew).
Frenkel, Yona. 1996. *Midrash and Hagada*. Vol. 1. Tel Aviv: Open University of Israel (Hebrew).
Frilingos, Christopher A. 2009. "'It Moves Me to Wonder': Narrating Violence and Religion under the Roman Empire." *JAAR* 77: 825–52.
Gan, Moshe. 1961. "Megillat 'Esther Be'aspaqlariyat Qorot Yoseph Be'misrayim." *Tarbiz* 31: 144–9.
Garrett, Duane A. 2020. *The Problem of the Old Testament: Hermeneutical, Schematic and Theological Approaches*. Downers Grove, IL: IVP Academic.
Gera, Deborah L. 2014. *Judith*. CEJL. Berlin: de Gruyter.
Gerleman, Gillis. 1973. *Esther*. BKAT. Neukirchen-Vluyn: Neukirchener Verlag.
Gilat, Yitzhak D. 1992. *Studies in the Development of the Halakha*. Ramat Gan: Bar Ilan University (Hebrew).
Gilmour, Rachelle. 2011. *Representing the Past: A Literary Analysis of Narrative Historiography in the Book of Samuel*. VTSup 143. Leiden: Brill.
Gitelman, Zvi. 2012. *Jewish Identities in Postcommunist Russia and Ukraine: An Uncertain Ethnicity*. Cambridge: Cambridge University Press.
Glickman, Elaine Rose. 1999. *Haman and the Jews: A Portrait from Rabbinic Literature*. Northvale: Jason Aronson.
Goitein, Samuel. 1957. *Bible Studies*. Tel Aviv: Yavneh (Hebrew).
Goldingay, John, and David Payne. 2006. *Isaiah 40–55*. Vol. 1. ICC. London: T&T Clark.
Goodman, Martin. 2007. *Rome and Jerusalem: The Clash of Ancient Civilizations*. New York: Knopf.
Gordis, Robert. 1981. "Religion, Wisdom and History in the Book of Esther—A New Solution to an Ancient Crux." *JBL* 100: 359–88.
Gottlieb, Isaac B. 2008. "The Opposite Happened (Est. 9:1): Midrash on Megillat Esther." *Studies in Bible and Exegesis* 8: 119–35.
Grohmann, Marianne, and Hyun Chul Paul Kim, eds. 2019. *Second Wave Intertextuality and the Hebrew Bible*. RBS 93. Atlanta, GA: SBL Press.
Grossman, Jonathan. 2009. "'Dynamic Analogies' in the Book of Esther." *VT* 59: 394–414.

Grossman, Jonathan. 2011. *Esther: The Outer Narrative and the Hidden Reading.* Siphrut 6. Winona Lake, IN: Eisenbrauns.
Grossman, Jonathan. 2015. *Text and Subtext: On Exploring Biblical Narrative Design.* Tel Aviv: Hakibbutz Hameuchad.
Grossman, Jonathan. 2016. *Abram to Abraham: A Literary Analysis of the Abraham Narrative.* Das Alte Testament im Dialog 11. Bern: Lang.
Grossman, Jonathan. 2018. "The Attitude toward the Diaspora in the Book of Esther." Pages 1–22 in *The Blessings of Avraham.* Edited by Yosef Kaplan. Jerusalem: The Israel Academy of Science and Humanities.
Grossman, Jonathan, and Gilad Sasson. 2007. "On Implicit Biblical Analogies in Midrashim of the Sages." *Megadim* 46: 17–42 (Hebrew).
Grossman, Jonathan, and Gilad Sasson. 2010. "More on Hidden Biblical Analogies in Rabbinic Midrashim." *Megadim* 51: 109–18 (Hebrew).
Gruen, Erich S. 2002. *Diaspora: Jews amidst Greeks and Romans.* Cambridge, MA: Harvard University Press.
Hagelia, Hallvard. 2003 "Meal on Mount Zion—Does Isa 25:6–8 Describe a Covenant Meal?" *SEÅ* 68: 73–95.
Hamley, Isabelle. 2018. "Dis(re)membered and Unaccounted For: Concubines in the Hebrew Bible." *JSOT* 42.4: 415–34.
Hamley, Isabelle. 2019. *Unspeakable Things Unspoken: Otherness, Gender and Victimisation in Judges 19–21.* Eugene, OR: Wipf & Stock.
Hammond, Martin, ed. 2017. *The Jewish War.* Oxford World's Classics. New York: Oxford University Press.
Hartenstein, Friedhelm. 2010. "'Schaffe mir Recht, JHWH!' (Psalm 7, 9): Zum theologischen und anthropologischen Profil der Teilkomposition Psalm 3–14." Pages 229–58 in *The Composition of the Book of Psalms.* Edited by Erich Zenger. Leuven: Peeters.
Harvey, Charles D. 2003. *Finding Morality in the Diaspora? Moral Ambiguity and Transformed Morality in the Books of Esther.* Berlin: de Gruyter. Repr., Berlin: de Gruyter, 2014.
Hatton, Peter. 2008. *Contradiction in the Book of Proverbs: The Deep Waters of Counsel.* Hampshire: Ashgate.
Hayek, Friedrich A. 1943. "Scientism and the Study of Society. Part II." *Economica, New Series* 10.37: 34–63.
Hayek, Friedrich A. 1945. "The Use of Knowledge in Society." *American Economic Review* 35.4: 519–30.
Hayek, Friedrich A. 1952. *The Sensory Order: An Inquiry into the Foundations of Theoretical Psychology.* Chicago: University of Chicago Press.
Hayek, Friedrich A. 1978. *Law, Legislation and Liberty.* Chicago: University of Chicago Press.
Hayek, Friedrich A. 2001. *The Road to Serfdom.* New York: Routledge.
Hayek, Friedrich A. 2011. *Constitution of Liberty: The Definitive Edition.* Edited by Ronald Hamowy. Chicago: University of Chicago Press.
Hays, Christopher B. 2011. *Death in the Iron Age II and in First Isaiah.* FAT 79. Tübingen: Mohr Siebeck.
Hays, Richard B. 1989. *Echoes of Scripture in the Letters of Paul.* New Haven, CT: Yale University Press.
Hays, Richard B. 2016. *Echoes of Scripture in the Gospels.* Waco, TX: Baylor University Press.

Hazony, Yoram. 2016. *God and Politics in Esther*. Cambridge: Cambridge University Press.
Heinemann, Isaak. 1954. *Darkhei ha-Aggadah*. 2nd ed. Jerusalem: Magnes Press (Hebrew).
Herrmann, Georgina. 1989. *Sasanian Rock Reliefs at Naqshi Rustam: Naqshi Rustam 6, The Triumph of Shapur I*. Berlin: Deitrich Reimer.
Ho, Peter C. W. 2019. *The Design of the Psalter: A Macrostructural Analysis*. Eugene, OR: Pickwick.
Hobbes, Thomas. 1996. *Leviathan*. Edited by Richard Tuck. Cambridge: Cambridge University Press.
Holm, Tawny. 2013. *Of Courtiers and Kings: The Biblical Daniel Narratives and Ancient Story-Collections*. Winona Lake, IN: Eisenbrauns.
Hornung, Gabriel. 2020. "The Theological Import of Esther's Relationship to Joseph." *CBQ* 82: 567–81.
Hoschander, Jacob. 1923. *The Book of Esther in the Light of History*. Philadelphia, PA: Dropsie College.
Humphreys, W. Lee. 1973. "Life-style for Diaspora: A Study of the Tales of Esther and Daniel." *JBL* 92: 211–23.
Irigaray, Luce. 1974. *Speculum: De l'autre femme*. Paris: Les Editions de Minuit.
Jacobson, Rolf A. 2004. *"Many Are Saying": The Function of Direct Discourse in the Hebrew Psalter*. LHBOTS 397. London: T&T Clark.
Janowski, Bernd. 2010. "Ein Tempel aus Worten: Zur theologischen Architektur des Psalters." Pages 279–306 in *The Composition of the Book of Psalms*. Edited by Erich Zenger. Leuven: Peeters.
Jobes, Karen H. 1996. *The Alpha-Text of Esther: Its Character and Relationship to Masoretic Text*. SBLDS 153. Atlanta, GA: Scholars Press.
Jobes, Karen H. 1999. *Esther*. The NIV Application Commentary. Grand Rapids, MI: Zondervan.
Kahana, Hanna. 2005. *Esther: Juxtaposition of the Septuagint Translation with the Hebrew Text*. CBET 40. Leuven: Peeters.
Kalimi, Isaac. 2004. "The Book of Esther and the Dead Sea Scrolls' Community." *TZ* 60: 101–6.
Katzin, David. 2004. "The Time of Testing: The Use of Hebrew Scriptures in 4Q171's Pesher of Psalm 37." *HS* 45: 121–62.
Kaufmann, Thomas. 2017. *Luther's Jews: A Journey into Anti-Semitism*. Oxford: Oxford University Press.
Kenshur, Oscar. 2003. "Human Nature," in *The Encyclopedia of Enlightenment*. Volume 2. Edited by Alan Charles Kors. Oxford: Oxford University Press. https://www.oxfordreference.com/view/10.1093/acref/9780195104301.001.0001/acref-9780195104301-e-326 (Accessed January 21, 2022).
Kim, Hee Suk. 2011. "Yhwh Sayings and King Sayings in Proverbs: 10:1–22:16." *Korean Journal of Christian Studies* 75.1: 83–104.
Kinnes, Ian. 1988. "The Cattleship Potemkin: Reflections on the First Neolithic in Britain." Pages 308–11 in *The Archaeology of Context in the Neolithic and Bronze Age: Recent Trends*. Edited by J. C. Barrett and Ian A. Kinnes. Sheffield: University of Sheffield Press.
Kirshenblatt-Gimblett, Barbara. 1973. "Towards a Theory of Proverb Meaning." *Proverbium* 22: 821–7.
Kissling, Paul J. 2013. "Self-Defense and Identity Formation in the Depiction of Battles in Joshua and Esther." Pages 105–20 in *Interested Readers: Essays on the Hebrew Bible*

in Honor of David J. A. Clines. Edited by James K. Aitken, Jeremy M. S. Clines, and Christl M. Maier. Atlanta, GA: SBL Press.

Klein, Lillian R. 1989. *The Triumph of Irony in the Book of Judges*. Sheffield: Almond Press.

Klein, Lillian R. 1993. "A Spectrum of Female Characters." Pages 24–33 in *Judges: A Feminist Companion to the Bible (First Series)*. Edited by Athalya Brenner. Sheffield: Sheffield Academic.

Klein, Lillian R. 1995. 'Honor and Shame in Esther." Pages 149–75 in *A Feminist Companion to Esther, Judith and Susanna*. Edited by Athalya Brenner. Sheffield: Sheffield Academic.

Klein, Ralph W. 2012. *2 Chronicles*. Hermeneia. Minneapolis, MN: Fortress Press.

Kneebone, Emily. 2013. "Josephus' Esther and Diaspora Judaism." Pages 165–82 in *The Romance between Greece and the East*. Edited by Tim Whitmarsh and Stuart Thomson. New York: Cambridge University Press.

Koller, Aaron. 2014. *Esther in Ancient Jewish Thought*. Cambridge: Cambridge University Press.

Krause, Joachim J. 2012. "Vor wem soll die Auskundschaftung Jerichos geheim gehalten werden? Eine Frage zu Josua 2.1." *VT* 62.4: 454–6.

Krause, Joachim J. 2015. "Aesthetics of Production and Aesthetics of Reception in Analyzing Intertextuality: Illustrated with Joshua 2." *Bib* 96.3: 416–27.

Kruger, Paul. 2005. "The Inverse World of Mourning in the Hebrew Bible." *BN* 124: 41–9.

Kugel, James L. 1986. "Two Introductions to Midrash." Pages 77–103 in *Midrash and Literature*. Edited by Geoffrey H. Hartman and Sanford Budick. New Haven, CT: Yale University Press.

Kugel, James L. 1990. *In Potiphar's House: The Interpretive Life of Biblical Texts*. Cambridge, MA: Harvard University Press.

Kynes, Will. 2011. "Beat Your Parodies into Swords and Your Parodied Books into Spears: A New Paradigm for Parody in the Hebrew Bible." *BI* 19: 276–310.

Kynes, Will. 2012. *My Psalm Has Turned into Weeping: Job's Dialogue with the Psalms*. BZAW 437. Berlin: de Gruyter.

Kynes, Will. 2015. "The Modern Scholarly Wisdom Tradition and the Threat of Pan-Sapientialism: A Case Report." Pages 11–38 in *Was There a Wisdom Tradition? New Prospects in Israelite Wisdom Studies*. Edited by Mark Sneed. Atlanta, GA: SBL Press.

Kynes, Will. 2019. *An Obituary for "Wisdom Literature": The Birth, Death, and Intertextual Reintegration of a Biblical Corpus*. Oxford: Oxford University Press.

Lacocque, André. 1999. "The Different Versions of Esther." *BibInt* 7: 301–22.

Laniak, Timothy S. 1998. *Shame and Honor in the Book of Esther*. SBLDS 165. Atlanta, GA: Scholars Press.

Laniak, Timothy S. 2003a. "Esther's *Volkcentrism* and the Reframing of Post-Exilic Judaism." Pages 77–90 in *Book of Esther in Modern Research*. Edited by Sidnie White. Crawford: Leonard J. Greenspoon.

Laniak, Timothy S. 2003b. "Esther." Pages 169–267 in *Ezra, Nehemiah, Esther*. NIBCOT. Edited by Leslie C. Allen and Timothy Laniak. Peabody, MA: Hendrickson.

Lau, Peter H. W. 1998. *Shame and Honor in the Book of Esther*. SBLDS 165. Atlanta, GA: Scholars Press.

Lau, Peter H. W. 2018. *Esther*. Asia Bible Commentary. Carlisle: Langham.

Lee, Sherman A., Laurin B. Roberts, and Jeffrey A. Gibbons. 2013. "When Religion Makes Things Worse: Negative Religious Coping as Associated with Maladaptive Emotional Responding Patterns." *Mental Health, Religion and Culture* 16.3: 291–305.

Leiman, Shnayer Z. 1976. *The Canonization of Hebrew Scripture: The Talmudic and Midrashic Evidence*. Transactions of the Connecticut Academy of Arts and Sciences 47. Hamden, CT: Archon Books.

Lerner, Judith A. 1991. "A Rock Relief of Fath Ali Shah in Shiraz." *ArsOr* 21: 31–44.

Levenson, Jon D. 1976. "The Scroll of Esther in Ecumenical Perspective." *JES* 13: 440–52.

Levenson, Jon D. 1993. *Death and Resurrection of the Beloved Son: The Transformation of Child Sacrifice in Judaism and Christianity*. New Haven, CT: Yale University Press.

Levenson, Jon D. 1997. *Esther: A Commentary*. OTL. Louisville, KY: Westminster John Knox.

Liberman, Saul. 1994. *Greek in Jewish Palestine/Hellenism in Jewish Palestine*. New York: JTS Press.

Lignée, Hubert. 1963. "L'apocryphe de la Genèse." Pages 208–15 in *Les Textes De Qumran: Traduits Et Annotés*. Edited by Jean Carmignac, Édouard Cothenet, and Hubert Lignée. Paris: Éditions Letouzey et Ané.

Loader, James A. 1978. "Esther as a Novel with Different Levels of Meaning." *ZAW* 90: 417–21.

Loader, James A. 1980. *Esther*. POuT. Nijkerk: Callenbach.

Loader, James A. 1992. "Das Buch Ester." Pages 199–280 in *Das Hohelied, Klagelieder, Das Buch Ester*. Edited by Hans-Peter Müller, Otto Kaiser, and James A. Loader. 4th ed. ATD 16.2. Göttingen: Vandenhoeck & Ruprecht.

Lyons-Pardue, Kara J. 2020 "'Little Daughters' and Big Scriptural Allusions: Reading Three of Mark's Stories Featuring Women with Care." Pages 45–69 in *Listening Again to the Text: New Testament Studies in Honor of George Lyons*. Edited by Richard P. Thompson. Claremont, CA: Claremont.

Macchi, Jean-Daniel. 2018. *Esther*. Translated by Carmen Palmer. IECOT. Stuttgart: Kohlhammer.

Maccoby, Hyam. 1999. *Ritual and Morality: The Ritual Purity System and Its Place in Judaism*. Cambridge: Cambridge University Press.

MacDonald, Nathan. 2008. *Not Bread Alone: The Uses of Food in the Old Testament*. Oxford: Oxford University Press.

Machiela, Daniel. 2009. *The Dead Sea Genesis Apocryphon: A New Text and Translation with Introduction and Special Treatment of Columns*. STDJ 79. Leiden: Brill.

Mandolfo, Carleen R. 2007. *Daughter Zion Talks Back to the Prophets: A Dialogic Theology of Lamentations*. SemeiaSt 58. Atlanta, GA: SBL Press.

Marcus, Joel. 1992. *The Way of the Lord: Christological Exegesis of the Old Testament in the Gospel of Mark*. Louisville, KY: Westminster John Knox.

Mason, Steve, ed. 1999. *Flavius Josephus: Translation and Commentary*. 8 vols. Leiden: Brill.

Matthews, Laura T., and Samuel J. Marwit. 2006. "Meaning Reconstruction in the Context of Religious Coping: Rebuilding the Shattered Assumptive World." *Omega* 53.1–2: 87–104.

McAleer, G. J. 2014. "Catholic Ideas about War: Why Does Carol Schmitt Reject Natural Law Justifications of War?" *Touro Law Review* 30.1: 65–76.

McCarter, P. Kyle, Jr. 1980. *1 Samuel*. AB 8. Garden City, NY: Doubleday.

McDowell, Markus. 2006. *Prayers of Jewish Women: Studies of Patterns of Prayer in the Second Temple Period*. WUNT 2.211. Tübingen: Mohr Siebeck.

McGeough, Kevin. 2008. "Esther the Hero: Going beyond 'Wisdom' in Heroic Narratives." *CBQ* 70.1: 44–65.

McKane, William. 1961. "A Note on Esther IX and 1 Samuel XV." *JTS* 12: 260–1.

Meinhold, Arndt. 1975. "Die Gattung der Josephsgeschichte und des Estherbuches: Diasporanovelle." *ZAW* 87: 306–24.

Meinhold, Arndt. 1976. "Die Gattung der Josephgeschichte und des Estherbuches: Diaspora Novella II." *ZAW* 88: 72–93.

Melamed, Abraham. 2012. *Philosopher-King in Medieval and Renaissance Jewish Political Thought*. Edited by Lenn E. Goodman. New York: State University of New York Press.

Melton, Brittany N. 2014. "Solomon, Wisdom, and Love: Intertextual Resonance Between Ecclesiastes and Song of Songs." Pages 130–41 in *Reading Ecclesiastes Intertextually*. Edited by Katharine Dell and Will Kynes. LHBOTS 587. London: Bloomsbury T&T Clark.

Melton, Brittany N. 2018. *Where Is God in the Megilloth? A Dialogue on the Ambiguity of Divine Presence and Absence*. OTS 73. Leiden: Brill.

Melton, Brittany N., and Heath A. Thomas. 2021. "A Sea of Intertexts: Introduction to *Reading Lamentations Intertextually*." Pages 1–13 in *Reading Lamentations Intertextually*. Edited by Brittany N. Melton and Heath A. Thomas. LHBOTS 714. London: Bloomsbury T&T Clark.

Mendels, Doron. 1992. *The Rise and Fall of Jewish Nationalism*. Garden City, NY: Doubleday.

Meyers, Carol. 2005. *Exodus*. New Cambridge Bible Commentary. Cambridge: Cambridge University Press.

Michael, Matthew. 2016. "Daniel at the Beauty Pageant and Esther in the Lion's Den: Literary Intertextuality and Shared Motifs between the Books of Daniel and Esther." *OTE* 29.1: 116–32.

Michaud, H. 1957. "Une livre apocryphe de la Genèse Araméen." *Positions luthériennes* 5: 91–104.

Miles, Johnny. 2015. "Reading Esther as Heroine: Persian Banquets, Ethnic Cleansing, and Identity Crisis." *BTB* 45: 131–43.

Milik, Jozef Tadeusz. 1992. "Les Modèles Araméens du Livre d'Esther dans la Grotte 4 de Qumran." *RevQ* 15: 321–99.

Millar, Suzanna R. 2020. *Genre and Openness in Proverbs 10:1–22:16*. Atlanta, GA: SBL Press.

Miller, David. 2002. "Cosmopolitanism: A Critique." *Critical Review of International Social and Political Philosophy* 5.3: 80–5.

Miller, Geoffrey D. 2011. "Intertextuality in Old Testament Research." *CurBR* 9: 283–309.

Mittleman, Alan L. 2015. *Human Nature and Jewish Thought: Judaism's Case for Why Persons Matter*. Princeton, NJ: Princeton University Press.

Montesquieu, Charles-Louis, II. 1989. *Montesquieu: The Spirit of the Laws-Cambridge Texts in the History of Political Thought*. Edited and Translated by Anne M. Cohler, Basia Carolyn Miller, and Harold Samuel Stone. Cambridge: Cambridge University Press.

Moore, Carey A. 1971. *Esther: A New Translation with Introduction and Commentary*. AB 7B. Garden City, NY: Doubleday.

Moore, Carey A. 1992. "Esther, Book of." Pages 633–43 in *The Anchor Bible Dictionary*. Vol. 2. Edited by David Noel Freedman. Garden City, NY: Doubleday.

Morgenstern, Mira. 2009. *Conceiving a Nation: The Development of Political Discourse in the Hebrew Bible*. University Park: Pennsylvania State University Press.

Morgenthau, Hans J. 1946. *Scientific Man Versus Power Politics*. Chicago: University of Chicago Press.

Morgenthau, Hans J. 1954. *Politics among Nations: The Struggle for Power and Peace.* New York: Knopf.
Morrow, William. 2006. "The Affirmation of Divine Righteousness in Early Penitential Prayers: A Sign of Judaism's Entry into the Axial Age." Pages 101–18 in *The Origins of Penitential Prayer in Second Temple Judaism.* Edited by Mark J. Boda, Daniel K. Falk, and Rodney A. Werline. Vol. 1 of *Seeking the Favor of God.* EJL 21. Atlanta, GA: SBL Press.
Motzo, Bacchisio Raimondo. 1928. "Il testo di Ester in Giuseppe." *SMSR* 4: 4–105.
Müller, Hans-Peter. 1977. "Die weisheitliche Lehrerzählung im Alten Testament und seiner Umwelt." *WO* 9.1: 77–98.
Nagel, Thomas. 2010. "The Problem of Global Justice." *Cosmopolitan Reader* 33.2: 393–413.
Nelson, Richard D. 1997. *Joshua: A Commentary.* OTL. Louisville, KY: Westminster John Knox.
Newsom, Carol. 2003. *The Book of Job: A Contest of Moral Imagination.* Oxford: Oxford University Press.
Niditch, Susan, and Robert Doran. 1977. "The Success Story of the Wise Courtier: A Formal Approach." *JBL* 96.2: 179–93.
Noble, Paul R. 2002. "Esau, Tamar, and Joseph: Criteria for Identifying Inner-Biblical Allusion." *VT* 43: 219–52.
Nodet, Étienne. 2018. *The Hebrew Bible of Josephus: Main Features.* CahRB. Leuven: Peeters.
Nolan Fewell, Danna, ed. 1992. *Reading between Texts: Intertextuality and the Hebrew Bible.* Louisville, KY: Westminster John Knox.
Noth, Martin. 1981. *The Deuteronomistic History.* JSOTSup 15. Sheffield: JSOT Press.
Olyan, Saul M. 2003. *Biblical Mourning: Ritual and Social Dimensions.* Oxford: Oxford University Press.
O'Neill, Patrick. 1983. "The Comedy of Entropy: The Contexts of Black Humour." *Canadian Review of Comparative Literature* 10.2: 145–66.
Ozkirimli, Umut. 2010. *Theories of Nationalism: A Critical Introduction.* Basingstoke: Palgrave.
Paton, Lewis Bayles. 1908. *The Book of Esther.* ICC. Edinburgh: T&T Clark.
Pfeiffer, Robert H. 1948. *Introduction to the Old Testament.* New York: Harper.
Pham, Xuan Huong Thi. 1999. *Mourning in the Ancient Near East and the Hebrew Bible.* JSOTSup 302. Sheffield: Sheffield Academic.
Pierce, Ronald W. 1992. "The Politics of Esther and Mordecai: Courage or Compromise?" *BBR* 2: 75–89.
Poebel, Arno. 1933. "The Acropolis of Susa in the Elamite Inscriptions." *AJSL* 49.2: 125–40.
Polaski, Donald C. 2001. *Authorizing an End: The Isaiah Apocalypse and Intertextuality.* BibInt 50. Leiden: Brill.
Poser, Ruth. 2016. "No Words: The Book of Ezekiel as Trauma Literature and Response to Exile." Pages 27–48 in *Bible through the Lens of Trauma.* Edited by Elizabeth Boase and Christopher G. Frechette. SemeiaSt 86. Atlanta, GA: SBL Press.
Prinsloo, G. T. M. 2013. "Suffering Bodies—Divine Absence: Towards a Spatial Reading of Ancient Near Eastern Laments with Reference to Psalm 13 and An Assyrian Elegy (K 890)." *OTE* 26: 773–803.
Quick, Laura. 2019. "Decorated Women: A Sociological Approach to the Function of Cosmetics in the Books of Esther and Ruth." *BibInt* 27: 354–71.

Rad, Gerhard von. 1953. "Josephsgeschichte und ältere Chokma." Pages 120–7 in *Congress Volume Copenhagen 1953*. Edited by G. W. Andersen, Aage Bentzen, P. A H. de Boer, Millar Burrows Henri Cazzeles, and Martin Noth. VTSup 1. Leiden: Brill
Rad, Gerhard von. 1962–5. *Old Testament Theology*. 2 vols. New York: Harper & Row.
Rajak, Tessa. 2009. *Translation and Survival: The Greek Bible of the Ancient Jewish Diaspora*. Oxford: Oxford University Press.
Raj, P. Prayer Elmo. 2015. "Text/Texts: Interrogating Julia Kristeva's Concept of Intertextuality." *Ars Artium* 3: 77–80.
Reeves, John C. 1986. "What Does Noah Offer in 1QapGen X, 15?" *RevQ* 12.3: 415–19.
Ricoeur, Paul. 1976. *Interpretation Theory: Discourse and the Surplus of Meaning*. Fort Worth, TX: Texas Christian University Press.
Ricoeur, Paul. 1981. *Hermeneutics and the Human Sciences*. Edited and translated by John B. Thompson. Cambridge: Cambridge University Press.
Rindge, Matthew S. 2010. "Jewish Identity under Foreign Rule: Daniel 2 as a Reconfiguration of Joseph 41." *JBL* 129.1: 85–104.
Ringgren, Helmer. 1962. "Das Buch Esther." Pages 370–404 in *Sprüche, Prediger, Das Hohe Lied, Klagelieder, Das Buch Esther*. Edited by Helmer Ringgren, Artur Weiser, and Walther Zimmerli. ATD 16. Göttingen: Vandenhoeck & Ruprecht.
Rodgers, Zuleika. 2012. "Josephus's Biblical Interpretation." Pages 436–64 in *A Companion to Biblical Interpretation in Early Judaism*. Edited by Matthias Henze. Grand Rapids, MI: Eerdmans.
Rodriguez, Angel Manuel. 1995. *Esther: A Theological Approach*. Berrien Springs, MI: Andrews University Press.
Roese, Herbert E. 1982. "Some Aspects of Topographical Locations of Neolithic and Bronze Age Monuments in Wales." *Bulletin of the Board of Celtic Studies* 29.1: 763–5.
Römer, Thomas. 2007. *The So-Called Deuteronomistic History*. New York: T&T Clark.
Rosenthal, Ludwig A. 1895. "Die Josephgeschichte, mit den Büchern Ester und Daniel verglichen." *ZAW* 15: 278–84.
Rousseau, Jean-Jacques. 2002. *The Social Contract; and the First and Second Discourses*. Edited by Susan Dunn. New Haven, CT: Yale University Press.
Ruiz-Ortiz, Francisco-Javier. 2017. *The Dynamics of Violence and Revenge in the Hebrew Book of Esther*. VTSup 175. Leiden: Brill.
Said, Edward W. 2003. *Orientalism*. Reprinted with a new preface. London: Penguin.
Schäfer, Peter. 1997. *Judeophobia: Attitudes toward Jews in the Ancient World*. Cambridge, MA: Harvard University Press.
Scharfstein, Ben-Ami. 1995. *Amoral Politics: The Persistent Truth of Machiavellism*. New York: State University of New York Press.
Schieffelin, Edward, ed. 1976. *The Sorrow of the Lonely and the Burning of the Dancers*. New York: St. Martin's.
Schiffman, Lawrence H. 1994. "The *Temple Scroll* and the Nature of Its Law: The Status of the Question." Pages 37–55 in *The Community of the Renewed Covenant: The Notre Dame Symposium on the Dead Sea Scrolls*. Edited by Eugene Ulrich and James C. VanderKam. Notre Dame, IN: University of Notre Dame Press.
Schleiermacher, Friedrich. 1998. *Hermeneutics and Criticism and Other Writings*. Edited by Andrew Bowie. Cambridge: Cambridge University Press.
Schmid, Wolf. 2010. *Narratology: An Introduction*. Berlin: de Gruyter.
Schmitt, Carl. 1996. *The Leviathan in the State Theory of Thomas Hobbes: Meaning and Failure of a Political Symbol*. Westport, CT: Greenwood Press.

Schmitt, Carl. 2007. *The Concept of the Political*. Translated by George Schwab. Chicago: University of Chicago Press.
Schmitt, Carl. 2008. *Constitutional Theory*. Durham, NC: Duke University Press.
Schmitt, Rüdiger. 1999. "On Two Xerxes Inscriptions." *BSOAS* 62.2: 323–5.
Scott, James M., Ralph G. Carter, and A. Cooper Drury. 2019. *IR: International, Economic, and Human Security in a Changing World*. 3rd ed. Los Angeles: CQ Press.
Segal, Michael. 2009. "Joseph to Daniel: The Literary Development of the Narrative in Daniel 2." *VT* 59: 123–49.
Seitz, Christopher. 2016. *Joel*. ITC. London: Bloomsbury T&T Clark.
Seyberlich, R. M. 1964. "Esther in der Septuaginta und bei Flavius Josephus." Pages 363–6 in *Neue Beiträge zur Geschichte der Alten Welt, vol 1: Alter Orient und Griechenland*. Edited Elisabeth Charlotte Welskopf. Berlin: Akademie-Verlag.
Seybold, Klaus. 1996. *Die Psalmen*. Tübingen: Mohr Siebeck.
Sharvit, Shimon. 2008. *Studies in Mishnaic Hebrew*. Jerusalem: Bialik (Hebrew).
Sneed, Mark. 2011. "Is the 'Wisdom Tradition' a Tradition?" *CBQ* 73.1: 50–71.
Speiser, Ephraim Avigdor. 1960. "'People' and 'Nation' of Israel." *JBL* 79.2: 157–63.
Spilsbury, Paul. 1998. *The Image of the Jew in Flavius Josephus' Paraphrase of the Bible*. TSAJ 69. Tübingen: Mohr Siebeck.
Spilsbury, Paul. 2003. "Flavius Josephus on the Rise and Fall of the Roman Empire." *JTS* 54: 1–24.
Spilsbury, Paul. 2016. "Josephus and the Bible." Pages 123–34 in *A Companion to Josephus*. Edited by Honora Howell Chapman and Zuleika Rodgers. Chichester, UK: Wiley.
Spilsbury, Paul, and Chris Seeman. 2017. *Judean Antiquities 11: Translation and Commentary*. Edited Steve Mason. Vol. 6 of *Flavius Josephus: Translation and Commentary*. Leiden: Brill.
Spoelstra, Joshua Joel. 2014. "The Function of the משתה יין in the Book of Esther." *OTE* 27: 285–301.
Stead, Mark R. 2012. "Intertextuality and Innerbiblical Interpretation." Pages 355–64 in *Dictionary of the Old Testament Prophets*. Edited by Mark J. Boda and J. Gordon McConville. Downers Grove, IL: InterVarsity Press.
Stern, Elsie R. 2010. "Esther and the Politics of Diaspora." *JQR* 100.1: 25–53.
Sternberg, Meir. 1978. *Expositional Modes and Temporal Ordering in Fiction*. Baltimore, MD: Johns Hopkins University Press.
Stewart, Anne. 2014. "Esther (Book and Person)." Pages 10–54 in vol. 8 of *Encyclopedia of the Bible and Its Reception*. Edited by Dale C. Allison, Christine Helmer, Volker Leppin, Choon-Leong Seow, Hermann Spieckermann, Barry Dov Walfish, and Eric Ziolkowsk. Berlin: de Gruyter.
Stone, Meredith J. 2018. *Empire and Gender in LXX Esther*. Atlanta, GA: SBL Press.
Strawn, Brent A. 2005. *What Is Stronger Than a Lion? Leonine Imagery and Metaphor in the Hebrew Bible and the Ancient Near East*. Göttingen: Vandenhoeck & Ruprecht.
Suetonius. *Lives of the Caesars, Volume II: Claudius. Nero. Galba, Otho, and Vitellius. Vespasian. Titus, Domitian. Lives of Illustrious Men: Grammarians and Rhetoricians. Poets (Terence. Virgil. Horace. Tibullus. Persius. Lucan). Lives of Pliny the Elder and Passienus Crispus*. Translated by J. C. Rolfe. LCL 38. Cambridge, MA: Harvard University Press, 1914.
Sun, Chloe T. 2021. *Conspicuous in His Absence: Studies in the Song of Songs and Esther*. Downers Grove, IL: InterVarsity Press.
Swart, G. J. 2006. "Rahab and Esther in Josephus—An Intertextual Approach." *Acta Patristica et Byzantina* 17: 50–65.

Sweeney, Marvin A. 2000. "Absence of God and Human Responsibility in the Book of Esther." Pages 264–75 in *Exegetical and Theological Studies*. Vol. 2 of *Reading the Hebrew Bible for a New Millennium: Form, Concept, and Theological Perspective*. Edited by Wonil Kim, Deborah Ellens, Michael Floyd, and Marvin A. Sweeney. Harrisburg, PA: Trinity Press International.

Sweeney, Marvin A. 2007. *1 and 2 Kings: A Commentary*. OTL. Louisville, KY: Westminster John Knox.

Sweeney, Marvin A. 2008. *Reading the Hebrew Bible after the Shoah: Engaging Holocaust Theology*. Minneapolis, MN: Fortress.

Sweeney, Marvin A. 2011. "The Question of Theodicy in the Historical Books: Contrasting Views Concerning the Destruction of Jerusalem according to the DtrH and ChrH." *Journal of the Institute of Biblical Studies* 5: 7–37.

Sweeney, Marvin A. 2012. *Tanak: A Theological and Critical Introduction to the Jewish Bible*. Minneapolis, MN: Fortress.

Tabory, Joseph, and Arnon Atzmon. 2014. *Midrash Esther Rabbah: Critical Edition Based on Manuscripts*. Jerusalem: Leshon Limudim.

Talmon, Shemaryahu. 1963. "'Wisdom' in the Book of Esther." *VT* 13: 419–55.

Talmon, Shemaryahu. 1995. "Was the Book of Esther Known At Qumran?" *DSD* 2: 249–68.

Tan, Nancy Nam Hoon. 2008. *The "Foreignness" of the Foreign Woman in Proverbs 1–9: A Study of the Origin and Development of a Biblical Motif*. Berlin: de Gruyter.

Thackeray, Henry S. J., and Ralph Marcus, eds. 1926–65. *Josephus*. 10 vols. LCL. Cambridge, MA: Harvard University Press.

Thiessen, Matthew. 2018. "Protecting the Holy Race and Holy Space: Judith's Reenactment of the Slaughter of Shechem." *JSJ* 49: 165–88.

Thomas, Heath A. 2013. *Poetry and Theology in the Book of Lamentations*. Hebrew Bible Monographs 47. Sheffield: Sheffield Phoenix.

Thomas, Heath A. 2018. *Habakkuk*. Two Horizons Old Testament Commentary. Grand Rapids, MI: Eerdmans.

Thomas, Heath, and Craig Bartholomew. Forthcoming. *Old Testament Minor Prophets: A Theological Introduction*. Downers Grove, IL: IVP Academic.

Thomsen, Jacob Als. 1997. "Carl Schmitt—The Hobbesian of the 20th Century?" *Social Thought & Research* 20.1/2: 5–28.

Tigay, Jeffrey. 1996. *Deuteronomy*. Jewish Publication Society Torah Commentary. Philadelphia, PA: Jewish Publication Society of America.

Tomasino, Anthony. 2019. "Interpreting Esther from the Inside Out: Hermeneutical Implications of the Chiastic Structure of the Book of Esther." *JBL* 138: 101–20.

Tov, Emanuel. 1998. "The Significance of the Judean Desert for the History of the Text of the Hebrew Bible: A New Synthesis." Pages 277–309 in *Qumran Between the Old and the New Testaments*. Edited by Frederick H. Cryer and Thomas L. Thompson. Sheffield: Sheffield Academic.

Tsumura, David Toshio. 2007. *The First Book of Samuel*. NICOT. Grand Rapids, MI: Eerdmans.

Tull, Patricia. 2000. "Intertextuality and the Hebrew Bible." *CurBS* 8: 59–90.

Uchelen, N. A. van 1974 "A Chokmatic Theme in the Book of Esther: A Study in the Structure of the Story." Pages 132–40 in *Verkenningen in Een Stroomgebild: Proeven Ven Oudtestamentisch Onderzoek*. Edited by M. Boertien, A. G. van Daalen, F. J Hoogewoud, and E. H. Plantenga. Amsterdam: University of Amsterdam Press.

Van der Walt, Larry C. P. 2007. "A Literary Comparison between the Prayers of Esther (LXX) and Judith." *Ekklesiastikos Pharos* 89.18: 307–21.
Van der Walt, Larry C. P. 2008. "The Prayers of Esther (LXX) and Judith against their Social Backgrounds—Evidence of a Possible Common Grundlage?" *JSem* 17.1: 194–206.
Vermes, Geza. 1973. *Scripture and Tradition*. 2nd rev. ed. Studia Post-Biblica 4. Leiden: Brill.
Vesco, Jean-Luc. 2006. *Le psautier de David: traduit et commenté*. Paris: Cerf.
Vogelsang, Willem J. 1998. "Medes, Scythians and Persians: The Rise of Darius in a North-South Perspective." *IrAnt* 33: 195–224.
Wahl, Harald Martin. 2009. *Das Buch Esther: Übersetzung und Kommentar*. Berlin: de Gruyter.
Walfish, Barry Dov. 1993. *Esther in Medieval Garb*. Albany: State University of New York Press.
Watts, Rikki E. 1997. *Isaiah's New Exodus in Mark*. Grand Rapids, MI: Baker.
Wechsler, Michael G. 2000. "Two Para-biblical Novellae From Qumran Cave 4: A Reevaluation of 4Q550." *DSD* 7: 130–72.
Westermann, Claus. 1981. *Praise and Lament in the Psalms*. Atlanta, GA: John Knox.
Whedbee, J. William. 1998. *The Bible and the Comic Vision*. Cambridge: Cambridge University Press.
Whitcomb, John C. 1979. *The Triumph of God's Sovereignty*. Chicago: Moody Press.
Whybray, Roger Norman. 1968. *The Succession Narrative*. London: SCM Press.
Wills, Lawrence. 1990. *The Jew in the Court of the Foreign King: Ancient Jewish Court Legends*. Minneapolis, MN: Fortress.
Wilson, Gerald H. 1985. *The Editing of the Hebrew Psalter*. SBLDS 76. Chico, CA: Scholars Press.
Wilson, Gerald H. 2005. "The Structure of the Psalter." Pages 229–46 in *Interpreting the Psalms*. Edited by Philip S. Johnston and David G. Firth. Nottingham: Apollos.
Wilson, Lindsay. 1990. "The Place of Wisdom in Old Testament Theology." *RTR* 49: 60–9.
Winitzer, Abraham. 2011. "The Reversal of Fortune Theme in Esther: Israelite Historiography in Its Ancient Near Eastern Context." *JANER* 11: 170–218.
Wolde, Ellen van. 1997. "Texts in Dialogue with Texts: Intertextuality in the Ruth and Tamar Narratives." *BibInt* 5: 1–28.
Zakovitch, Yair. 1995. *Through the Looking Glass: Reflection Stories in the Bible*. Tel Aviv: Hakibbutz Hameuchad (Hebrew).

AUTHOR INDEX

Abernethy, A. 75
Adelman, R. E. 62
Aletti, J.-N. 115, 116
Alexander, P. S. 148
Anderson, B. W. 195
Anderson, G. A. 85, 86
Aronowicz, A. 188
Atzmon, A. 170, 171, 173–5

Bachmann, V. 169
Bal, M. 47
Balentine, S. E. 105, 106, 123, 196
Barclay, J. M. G. 157
Bardtke, H. 27, 195
Barthes, R. 73
Bartholomew, C. 87
Barton, J. 4
Beal, T. K. 48, 54, 55, 57, 59, 62, 90, 110, 111, 195
Bechtel, T. K. 28
Ben-Dov, J. 142
Berg, S. B. 12, 32, 57, 62, 66, 74, 90
Berger, Y. 2, 11, 58–61
Berkovits, E. 196
Berlin, A. 1, 3, 11, 42, 47, 49, 53, 54, 58, 64, 83, 115, 116, 118, 176, 195
Berman, J. 40
Bickerman, E. J. 149
Block, D. I. 53, 170
Boase, E. 132
Boda, M. J. 85, 94, 126
Börner-Klein, D. 73
Botha, P. J. 105, 188
Braiterman, Z. 196
Briant, P. 77
Brown, J. K. 91
Brown, W. P. 112
Bruns, G. L. 169
Burnett, J. S. 99, 103
Bush, F. 188

Cameron, G. G. 186, 188
Camp, C. V. 116
Campbell, A. F. 198
Carruthers, J. 1
Carter, R. G. 187
Cassuto, U. 177
Cataldo, J. W. 53
Chalupa, P. 150, 155
Chapman, C. R. 63, 147
Cho, P. K.-K. 78
Clines, D. J. A. 1, 24, 29, 31, 57, 99
Coats, G. 198
Coetzee, J. H. 105
Collins, J. J. 12
Coote, R. B. 38
Craghan, J. F. 25
Craig, K. 11, 195
Crawford, S. W. 25, 57, 59, 62, 139, 141, 142
Creach, J. F. D. 100
Crenshaw, J. L. 109

Davies, P. 61
Davis, B. 132
Day, L. 41, 89
De Troyer, K. 1, 99, 136, 139, 145
Dell, K. 1, 4
Dickson, C. R. 188
Douglas, M. 127, 129
Doyle, B. 99
Dozeman, T. B. 198
Drury, A. C. 187
Dunne, J. A. 135
Durkheim, E. 187
Duvall, J. S. 108

Edenburg, C. 72
Efthimiadis-Keith, H. 123, 128–31
Ego, B. 123, 124
Eichrodt, W. 195

Eisenman, R. H. 135
Enenkel, K. A. E. 188
Epstein, I. 188

Fackenheim, E. 195
Falk, D. K. 94
Feinstein, E. 188
Feldman, L. H. 86, 147, 149, 151
Finkel, J. 136, 137
Firth, D. G. 1–3, 37, 40, 42, 58, 65, 66, 100, 187
Fishbane, M. 169
Fitzmyer, J. A. 138
Flesher, L. S. 129, 131
Foer, J. S. 187
Fox, M. V. 1, 17, 24, 27, 31, 38, 57, 61, 63, 109–11, 116, 118, 188, 195
Frechette, C. G. 132
Frei, P. 189
Frenkel, Y. 169
Frilingos, C. A. 155
Fu, J. 78

Gan, M. 12
Garrett, D. A. 4
Gera, D. L. 123, 124, 128
Gerleman, G. 30, 175
Gibbons, J. A. 132
Gilat, Y. D. 180
Gilmour, R. 60
Glickman, E. R. 188
Goitein, S. 25
Goldingay, J. 86, 87
Goodman, M. 157
Gordis, R. 169
Gottlieb, I. B. 176
Grohmann, M. 83
Grossman, J. 1, 11, 28–30, 38, 57, 60, 63, 67, 93, 94, 169, 170, 172, 175, 180
Gruen, E. S. 148

Hagelia, H. 77
Hamley, I. 50, 52
Hammond, M. 156
Hartenstein, F. 101
Harvey, C. D. 118, 188
Hatton, P. 110
Hayek, F. A. 184, 185, 189, 191–3
Hays, C. B. 78

Hays, J. D. 108
Hays, R. B. 4, 38, 58, 159
Hazony, Y. 89, 91, 92, 135, 195
Heinemann, I. 169, 172, 173
Herrmann, G. 186
Ho, P. C. 102
Hobbes, T. 183, 189, 190
Hollender, E. 73
Holm, T. 15, 16
Hornung, G. 12
Hoschander, J. 30
Humphreys, W. L. 16, 31, 45, 63

Irigiray, L. 51

Jacobson, R. A. 100, 102, 104
Janowski, B. 101
Jobes, K. H. 1, 84, 90, 91

Kahana, H. 94
Kalimi, I. 135
Katzin, D. 143
Kaufmann, T. 195
Kenshur, O. 192
Kim, H. C. P. 83
Kim, H. S. 113
Kirschenblatt-Gimblett, B. 110
Kissling, P. J. 37, 43
Klein, L. R. 50, 62, 63
Klein, R. W. 202, 203
Kneebone, E. 149, 150, 155
Koller, A. 1, 57, 62, 63, 65, 66, 135
Krause, J. J. 39
Kruger, P. 86
Kugel, J. L. 73
Kynes, W. 1, 4, 63, 64, 109

Lacocque, A. 1
Laniak, T. S. 25, 30, 54
Lau, P. H. W. 37
Lee, S. A. 132
Leiman, S. Z. 145
Lerner, J. A. 186
Levenson, J. D. 25–7, 31, 33, 57, 59, 65, 72, 80, 176, 195
Liberman, S. 180
Lignée, H. 138
Loader, J. A. 31, 57, 89, 109, 175
Lyons-Perdue, K. J. 167

Macchi, J.-D. 83, 89
Maccoby, H. 127
MacDonald, N. 76
Machiela, D. 138
Mandolfo, C. R. 196
Marcus, J. 159, 165
Marwitt, S. J. 132
Mason, S. 147
Matthews, L. T. 132
McAleer, G. J. 190
McCarter, P. K., Jr. 198
McDowell, M. 125
McGeough, K. 112
McKane, W. 58
Meinhold, A. 11, 24
Melamed, A. 191
Melton, B. N. 1, 4, 57, 73, 79, 99, 106, 108
Mendels, D. 187
Meyers, C. 176, 198
Michael, M. 2, 3
Michaud, H. 138
Miles, J. 75
Milik, J. T. 138–40
Millar, S. R. 110, 112, 117
Miller, D. 192
Miller, G. D. 71, 171
Montesquieu, C.-L., II 190, 192
Moore, C. A. 12, 93, 197
Morgenstern, M. 47
Morgenthau, H. J. 183
Morrow, W. 126
Motzo, B. R. 149

Nagel, T. 192
Nelson, R. D. 39
Newsom, C. 196
Noble, P. R. 173
Nodet, E. 149
Noth, M. 200

O'Neill, P. 118
Olyan, S. M. 84–9
Ozkirimli, U. 187

Paton, L. 196
Payne, D. 86, 87
Pfeiffer, R. H. 188, 195
Pham, X. H. T. 85, 86
Pierce, R. W. 135

Poebel, A. 186
Polaski, D. C. 80
Poser, R. 132
Prinsloo, G. T. M. 104

Quick, L. 114

Rad, G. von 17, 109, 195
Raj, P. P. E. 4
Rajak, T. 149, 154
Reeves, J. C. 138
Ricoeur, P. 73
Rindge, M. S. 20
Ringgren, H. 89
Roberts, L. B. 132
Rodgers, Z. 147
Rodriguez, A. M. 30, 32, 33
Römer, T. 200
Rosenthal, L. A. 11
Ruiz-Ortiz, F.-J. 75, 78

Said, E. 114
Sasson, G. 169
Schäfer, P. 157, 197
Schiffman, L. H. 145
Schleiermacher, F. 73
Schmid, W. 4
Schmitt, C. 184, 190, 191
Schmitt, R. 186
Scott, J. M. 187
Seeman, C. 147, 149, 152–4
Segal, M. 20
Seitz, C. 84
Seyberlich, R. M. 149
Seybold, K. 100, 103
Sharvit, S. 179
Sneed, M. 109
Speiser, E. A. 170, 186
Spilsbury, P. 147–9, 152–4
Spoelstra, J. J. 75
Stead, M. R. 72
Stern, E. R. 180
Sternberg, M. 174
Stewart, A. 195
Stone, M. 161, 162, 166
Strawn, B. A. 113
Sun, C. T. 99
Swart, G. J. 149, 150
Sweeney, M. A. 57, 63, 195, 201–4

Tabory, J. 170, 171, 173–5
Talmon, S. 16, 17, 31, 57, 109–13, 116, 135, 136, 138, 141–3, 169
Tan, N. N. H. 114
Thackeray, H. S. J. 147
Thiessen, M. 126, 129–31
Thomas, H. A. 4, 73, 85, 86, 88, 93
Thomsen, J. A. 185
Tigay, J. 198
Tomasino, A. 57, 59
Tov, E. 135
Tsumura, D. T. 198
Tull, P. 171

Uchelen, N. A. von 109

Van der Walt, L. C. P. 123, 126
Vermes, G. 148

Vesco, J.-L. 101, 103, 104
Vogelsgang, W. J. 188

Walfish, B. D. 195
Watts, R. E. 159
Wechsler, M. G. 139
Werline, R. A. 94
Westermann, C. 125
Whedbee, J. W. 188
Whitcomb, J. C. 30
Whybray, R. N. 109
Wills, L. 12
Wilson, G. H. 100, 101
Wilson, L. 109
Winitzer, A. 150
Wise, M. O. 135
Wolde, E. van 72, 73

Zakovitch, Y. 172

BIBLICAL AND OTHER ANCIENT SOURCES INDEX

Genesis		44:3	13
11:27-32	24	44:4-6	13
11:30	13	44:18-34	13
12	137	44:34	3
12:2	13	45:1	19
18:9-15	13	46:27	26
21:12	13	47:11	14
22:10	13	49:33	13
22:11-12	13	50:2-7	14
25:23	13	50:3	12, 14
25:34	171	50:4-6	14
34	128, 129		
34:13	128, 129	Exodus	
34:17	129	1:8-22	27, 159
34:22	129	2:25	174
34:40	129	3:1	174
36:12	171	5:1-9	159
37–50	11, 23	5:2	27
37:20	13	5:15-19	159
37:24	13	7:5-10	18
37:33-35	13	8:1-2	18
37:35	85	11	177
38	114	11:3	176
39:9	24	12	28
39:10	3, 172	12:36	27
40	173	12:42	3
40:20	77	14:3	189
41	20	17	196, 198
41:10	173	17:8-16	196, 198, 199
41:16	24	24:3-8	28
41:25-32	20	28	27
41:34-37	3	28:5	27
41:38-46	13		
41:41-42	20	Leviticus	
41:42-43	3	23:5	26
41:42	172	23:6	26
41:43	173		
41:45	20	Numbers	
41:47-49	13	12:3	175, 177
41:50-52	20	25:1-5	39
42:6	16		
43:1	13	Deuteronomy	
43:14	3	4:5	175
43:26	13, 16	6:12	28
44:2	13	6:20-25	28

7:1-2	40	19:3-9	52
12:12	28	19:5	48
12:18	28	19:6	48
14:22-29	28	19:8	48
16:11-12	28	19:9	48
16:11	28	19:12	53
16:14	28	19:22	48
17:14-20	191	19:30	53, 54
25	196, 198	20	54
25:17-19	196, 198, 199	20:3-11	51
26:14	86	21:10	55
32	72	21:25	48
32:1	72		
		Ruth	
Joshua		3	114
1:5	38, 43		
2	38-40	1 Samuel	
2:3-4	42	1–15	196
2:9-11	40	2:3	66
2:9	40	2:4-8	66
2:12	39, 40	2:7	66
2:14	39	8	66, 159
6	38	8:11-17	191
6:17	40	8:22	174
6:22-23	40	9:1	3, 58, 59, 174, 197
6:25	40	9:2	59, 60
7	40, 42	10:16	60
7:4-5	44	10:17-24	60
7:6	92	10:27	60
8:2	44	11	60
8:27	44	15	3, 58, 59, 64, 196–9
8:29	145	15:2	198
9:1-2	43	15:10	65
10–11	43	15:15	64
10:1-5	43	15:19	58
11:1-5	43	15:21	58
11:14	41	15:23	65
11:20	41	15:24	64
21:44	38, 44	15:26	65
23:9	38, 44	15:28	171
23:15	41	15:29	31
		15:32	58
Judges		16	65
3:15-30	49	16:1-13	61
4	52	16:1	65
4:1	24	16:7	66
4:3	174	16:12	60, 114
4:4	174	17:11	174
9	52	17:12	174
9:2	26	25:36-37	3
9:4	26	30:1-3	61
17:6	48	30:4	87
19	47, 48, 53	30:17	61
19:1	51		

Biblical and Other Ancient Sources Index 229

2 Samuel
1:1-16   3
1:12   90
1:15   61
3:31   86
12:1-15   159
12:16-20   89
13:19   87
13:28   3
14:2   86
16:5-13   58
19:16-23   58
19:16   58
19:18   58
21:21   61

1 Kings
1:5   3
1:16   3
3:15   77
12:2   202
21:27   92

2 Kings
19:1   92
19:15-19   89
22–23   203
22:11   92
24:11-15   3

1 Chronicles
1:1   202
12:33   171
16   203
29:1   65
29:19   65

2 Chronicles
10:2   202
11:1-12   203
20:6-12   89
32:1-8   203
33   203
34–35   203
34:19   92
35   203
35:20-27   203
36   203
36:14   204
36:20-21   204
36:22-23   204

Ezra
9   83, 95

9:3   87
9:5   87
10:6   87

Nehemiah
1:4   87
1:5-11   89
9   83, 95

Esther
1–9   112
1   26
1:1-12   3
1:1-9   106
1:1-4   26
1:3-8   17
1:3-4   74
1:3   76, 77, 80, 164
1:4   65, 77
1:5-8   74
1:5   76, 77, 80
1:6   77, 138
1:7   77
1:8   49, 77
1:9-12   161
1:9   74, 76, 171
1:10-12   59, 161, 165
1:10   3
1:11   149
1:12   14, 77
1:13-22   51, 161, 189
1:13-20   59
1:13-14   185
1:13   171
1:15   162
1:17-22   161
1:19-22   163
1:19-21   163
1:19   43, 59, 151, 162, 163
1:20   14
1:21-22   59, 65
1:21   49, 163
1:22   143
2   38-42, 115
2:1-18   3, 106
2:1-4   174
2:1   163
2:2-4   14, 162
2:2   168
2:3-4   3
2:4   39, 49, 161, 163, 174
2:5-7   174, 186
2:5-6   63, 141, 197

2:5	48, 58, 59, 113, 139, 144	3:15	48, 74, 124, 188
		4–7	26
2:6	3, 61	4	42, 78, 83, 87–95, 111
2:7	60, 106, 111, 149, 168, 197	4:1-4	29
		4:1-2	89
2:8	111	4:1	15, 88, 92–4, 124
2:9	39, 40, 163	4:3-4	124
2:10-11	60, 186	4:3	78, 86, 88–91, 143, 164
2:10	41, 111, 113, 156, 162		
2:11	143, 170	4:4-17	93
2:12-15	15	4:4-5	94
2:12	12, 14, 114, 143, 149, 168	4:7-8	124
		4:8	111, 112
2:13	52	4:8	24
2:14	114, 162	4:9-17	25, 164, 166
2:15-17	114	4:10-17	162
2:15	111, 114, 149	4:10-11	124
2:16-17	163	4:11-23	50
2:17	15, 39, 41, 60, 65, 114, 137, 149, 162, 163	4:11	112, 113, 143, 161, 164
		4:12-17	199
2:18	74-7, 80	4:12-16	89
2:19-20	24	4:13-14	93, 124
2:20	62, 111, 113, 156	4:13	42
2:21	143	4:14	29, 31, 42, 57, 60, 88, 90–2, 116, 199
3–5	26		
3	41	4:15-17	112
3:1-15	3	4:15-16	99
3:1-6	3, 124	4:15	124
3:1-2	16, 124	4:16	3, 19, 25, 26, 78, 88, 89, 113, 117
3:1	3, 15, 16, 58, 153, 197		
3:2-3	124	4:17	42
3:2	17	4:28-30	50
3:3	59	5–10	90
3:4	3, 113, 143, 172	5	29
3:5	17	5:1	26, 29
3:6	41, 107, 164, 171	5:3	3, 141, 161, 162
3:7	26, 124, 142	5:4-8	74
3:8-33	161	5:4	26, 62, 76, 124, 163
3:8-12	124	5:5-8	75
3:8-9	59, 113, 186	5:6-7	112
3:8	17, 25, 153	5:6	141, 162, 164
3:9	163	5:7	115
3:10-11	59	5:8	26, 62, 76, 115, 124
3:10	3, 199	5:9-10	16
3:11	49, 65, 163	5:9	3, 17
3:12-15	26	5:10	140
3:12-14	41	5:13-14	163
3:12	17, 143	5:13	112
3:13	55, 118	5:14	107, 163
3:14-15	163	6	28
3:14	143	6:1	3, 140, 141

Biblical and Other Ancient Sources Index 231

6:1	24	8:11	55, 113, 143
6:1-14	3	8:12	27
6:1-2	117	8:13	143
6:3	66	8:15–9:11	124
6:4	117	8:15-17	26, 27
6:6-11	27	8:15	27, 78, 124, 137,
6:6-10	19		138, 173
6:6	48, 101	8:16-17	78, 80
6:9	173	8:16	79, 144
6:10	17, 65	8:17	33, 43, 74, 75, 79,
6:11	3, 62, 117, 173		107, 125, 143
6:13	107	9	38, 63, 78
6:14–7:9	74, 75	9:1-19	43, 44
6:21	143	9:1-10	44
6:22	163	9:1	44, 99
7	29, 118	9:2-3	125
7:1-6	124	9:2	38, 43, 44
7:2	26, 115, 141, 161,	9:3-4	176
	162, 164	9:5-16	58
7:3-6	42	9:5-10	27
7:3-4	116	9:5	49
7:3	62, 115, 163	9:6-16	166
7:4	116	9:10	44, 199
7:5-10	19	9:11-15	44
7:6	29, 48, 107, 116, 199	9:12-15	124
7:7-10	116	9:12	162
7:7	58, 66	9:13-14	27, 163
7:8	29, 117, 118	9:13	59, 145
7:9	118	9:16-19	27, 80
7:10	26, 117, 118	9:16-17	28
7:17-19	124	9:16	44, 107, 118, 166
7:22-23	124	9:17-18	79
7:24-28	130	9:17	79, 107
7:25	130	9:18-19	78
7:28	130	9:18	75, 79
8	42	9:19	79, 107
8:1-2	166	9:20-23	28
8:1	199	9:20-22	80
8:2	3, 124, 172	9:20	79
8:3-12	166	9:21	143
8:3-8	163	9:22	28, 74, 75, 79,
8:3	3		107, 144
8:5-12	124		
8:5-8	163	9:23	28, 73
8:5-6	62	9:24-28	166
8:5	3, 49, 163	9:24	3
8:6	3	9:27	33, 143
8:8	43, 137, 163	9:28	143
8:9-15	26	9:29-32	112
8:9-12	26, 33, 164	9:29-31	124
8:9-10	65	9:30	175
8:9	143	9:31	78
8:11-12	43, 166	10:1-3	53, 166
		10:3	170, 175, 178

10:4-13	24	15:5	103
10:17-19	28	30	100
3:9+11	163	30:11	85
9:181	74	33	102
		53	105
Psalms		75:9	77
1–2	101, 102	77	99
1	103, 108	78:54-55	100
1:6	108	79	100
3–14	101, 102	90:10	26
3–7	101	105	179
3	101	105:11	100
7:3	113	106	178–80
8	101	106:6	178
8:6	103	106:19-23	178
9–14	7, 100–2, 106–8	106:23	175, 178
9–10	101–5	106:24	179
9	101, 107	106:40-44	180
9:14	103	116:13	100
9:18	107	145:3	65
9:19	102	145:11-12	65
9:20	103, 107		
9:21	102	Proverbs	
10	103, 106	1:4	111
10:1-11	102–4, 106	1:26-28	118
10:1	102	1:32	111
10:4	102, 103	2:3	114
10:5	103, 106	2:7	114
10:6	103	2:16	114, 116
10:7-9	107	3:2	112
10:11	103, 106	3:8-11	112
10:12	103	3:15	114
10:15	107	3:17	118
10:18	103, 108	3:31	118
11–12	105, 107	4:1-5	111
11	103, 104	4:8	115
11:1-3	102	4:11	112
11:2-3	104	4:16	112
11:2	107	5:3	116
11:3	104	5:4	118
11:4	104	5:19	115
11:5	104, 107	5:20	115
11:7	104, 105	6:17-19	111
12	104	6:19	118
12:4	107	6:24	114, 116
12:5	102, 107	6:25	114
13	104, 105, 107	6:27	118
13:2	105	7	114
13:3	107	7:1-5	111
13:5	102, 105, 107	7:5	114, 116
14	101–3, 105, 106	7:6-23	111
14:1	102	7:9	114
14:4	105–7	7:16-17	114
14:7	107	7:17	114

7:18	114, 115	31	112
7:21	116	31:1-9	112
7:23	118	31:3-5	115
8:30	111	31:10-31	112
9:4	116	31:30	114
9:6	116	45:8	114
9:16	116		
9:17-18	116	Ecclesiastes	
9:18	116	7:2	86
10:2	116	7:4	86
10:8	111		
10:19	111	Song of Songs	
11:4	116	1:13	114
11:6	116, 119	5:5	114
11:12	111	5:13	114
11:16	114, 118		
12:6	116	Isaiah	
12:17-19	111	1–39	86
12:17	118	1	72
12:23	111	1:2	72, 171
12:26	111	3:26	85
13:1	111	5:29	113
13:3	111	19:8	85
14:5	118	24	76
14:15	111	24:4	85
15:5	111	24:7	77, 85
16:9	117, 119	24:9	77
16:10-15	113	24:23	76
16:14	112, 113, 119	25	71, 76–8, 81
16:15	113	25:1-5	80
16:29	111, 118	25:4	80
17:4	111	25:6-10	74–6, 78, 79
17:27-28	110	25:6-8	75–7, 80, 81
17:27	111	25:6-7	80
19:5	118	25:6	75–7, 79, 80
20:1	115	25:7-8	76, 78
20:2	112, 113, 119	25:7	80
20:22	118	25:8	76, 78, 80
20:24	117	25:9-10	75, 76, 78
21:7	118	25:9	78, 79
21:28	118	32:12	85
22:11	116	33:9	85
23:3	116	37	92, 93, 95
23:20-21	115	37:1	91–3
23:23	175	37:2-35	93
23:27	114	37:14-20	93
23:29-35	115	37:21-35	93
24:1-2	118	37:36-37	93
24:28	118	40:1-2	87
24:29	118	40:1	86
25:15	116	40:2	86
26:4-5	110	47:10	101
26:27	118	55:13	73
28:15	113	56	33

56:3	33	24:16	85
56:6	33	24:23	85
57:18	85	26:16	85
58	93–5	26:17	85
58:5	29, 91–5	27:2	85
60:20	85	27:31	86
61:2-3	85	27:32	85
61:3	87	28:12	85
66:10	85	32:2	85
		32:16	85

Jeremiah
4:8	85	Daniel	
4:28	85	1–6	3, 11, 12, 23
6:16	85	1	23
6:26	85	1:8-16	3
7:29	85	2	20, 23
9:9	85	2:1	3
9:19	85	2:13	20
12:4	85	2:15-24	20
14:2	85	2:27-28	20
16:4-6	85	2:29-45	20
16:7	85	2:46	20
22:18	85	2:47	20
23:10	85	2:48-49	20
25:33	85	3	16, 18, 19, 23
29:10	26	3:1-30	3
31	144	3:1-5	17
31:13	85, 87, 144	3:4-6	17
34:5	85	3:7	17
47:5	86	3:12	17
49:3	85	3:13-15	18
50:17	113	3:16-18	19
		3:24-25	18

Lamentations
1:1	105	3:28	18
1:2	86	3:29	18
1:7	86	5:1-4	3
1:9	86	6	24
1:16	86	6:1-24	3
1:17	86	6:2	172
1:21	86	6:18	3
2:1	105	9	83, 95
3:55-66	105	9:4-19	89
3:60-61	105		
4:1	105	Hosea	
5:20	105	4:3	85
		10:5	85

Ezekiel
2:10	85	Joel	
7:12	85	1–2	87
7:27	85	1:6	113
16:15	114	1:9-10	85
19:1	85	1:13-14	87
19:14	85	1:13	85, 87
		1:14	87

Biblical and Other Ancient Sources Index 235

2	89-92, 94	4:26	168
2:12-14	29	4:41	167
2:12	86, 87, 90	5:21-43	167
2:14	29, 87, 90	5:22-24	160, 167
2:15-16	91	5:23	165
2:17	87–9	5:34	167, 168
2:18-27	88, 90	5:35-43	160, 167
2:26-27	88	5:41-42	164
		6:3	160
Amos		6:14-29	160
5:1	85	6:14-16	160
5:16	85	6:17-29	161, 164
8:8	85	6:17-19	165
8:10	85, 86	6:18-20	164
9:5	85	6:19	165
		6:20	161, 163, 165
Jonah		6:21	164
2:4	87	6:22-23	161, 165
2:7	87	6:22	161–4
3	92	6:23	161, 162, 165
3:5-9	91	6:24	165
3:5-8	89	6:25-34	160
3:9	90, 91, 94	6:25	165
		6:26	166
Micah		6:28	161, 165, 166
1:2	88	6:30-52	167
1:3-7	88	6:30	168
1:8	85, 86	6:34	167
1:16	86	7:24-30	160, 167
		7:25-30	167
Zechariah		7:25	160, 165
7:5	85	7:27	167
8:23	144	7:29	168
12:10	85	7:30	160
12:12	85	8:2	167
		9:1	168
NEW TESTAMENT		9:17-29	167
Matthew		9:23	167
14:1	161	9:36-37	167
		9:47	168
Mark		10:2	160
1:14-15	168	10:4	160
1:30-31	160	10:7	160
1:35-39	167	10:13-16	167
1:37-38	167	10:14-15	168
1:41	167	10:23-25	168
2:5	167	10:24	167
3:31-35	160	10:29-30	160
3:31	160	11:10	168
3:32	160	12:19-23	160
3:33	160	12:34	168
3:34	160	12:40	160
3:35	160	12:42-44	160
4:11	168	12:43-44	168

13:17	160	9:2	125, 128, 129
14:3-9	160	9:3	128, 129
14:6	168	9:4	125, 128, 129
14:9	160	9:5-11	124
14:25	168	9:5-6	125, 130
14:66	160	9:7-24	129
14:69	160	9:7-14	129
14:72	160	9:7-10	128
15:2	168	9:7	125, 129
15:9	168	9:8-10	125
15:12	168	9:8	129
15:18	168	9:9-10	129
15:26	168	9:10	129
15:32	168	9:11	125, 129
15:40	160	9:12-13	125
15:47	160	9:13-14	128
16:1	160	9:13	129
30	168	9:14	125
		10:1-5	24
Luke		10:1-4	124
3:19	161	10:4	129
9:7	161	11:1-23	130
		11:12-19	124
APOCRYPHA		12:1-9	25
Tobit		12:10–13:11	124
2:2	28	13:12–16:20	125
		13:16	25
Judith		15:1-3	125
5:7	24	15:10	125
5:17-18	24	16:25	125
6:18	130		
7:19	130	Additions to Esther	
7:23-31	124	11–12	28
7:23	130	B:4-5	124
7:26	131	C:2-10	127
7:28	131	C:7-13	124
7:30-31	131	C:7	151
8:1	124	C:14-30	123
8:9	124	C:14b	125, 126
8:10-36	124	C:14c-15	125, 126, 128
8:11-17	24	C:14c-d	126
8:12	131	C:16	125, 126
8:14	131	C:17-18a	126
8:15	131	C:17-18	125, 126
8:16	131	C:18b	126
8:17	131	C:19-21	125, 126
8:19	131	C:19-20	152
8:20	131	C:22-25b	125, 126
8:24-27	131	C:22	150
8:27	131	C:23-25b	128
9:1	130	C:23	152
9:2-14	123, 128	C:25c-26	126, 127
9:2-6	129	C:25c-29	125, 126
9:2-4	125	C:26	152

C:27	152	4Q524		
C:30a-b	126	f1 4:3	145	
C:30a-c	125, 128			
C:30d	125, 128	4Q550		
D:3	124	f1	139	
D:7	124	f1:3-5	140	
D:8-9	151	f2:4	140	
D:12-15	124	f2:7	139	
E:1-24	154	f4:1-2	139	
E:19	154	f5+5a:3-4	141	
		f5+5a:5	140	
DEAD SEA SCROLLS				
1Q20		11Q5		
20:1-34	136	24:4	144	
20:6-7	137			
20:30	137	CD		
20:31	137	14:10-11	143	
1QM		JOSEPHUS		
17:7	144	Jewish Antiquities		
		1.5	155	
1QS		1.10-12	147	
6:10-11	143	1.14	148, 150	
9:12	143	1.17	147	
		3.91-294	147	
4Q166		4.196-301	147	
2:17	144	8.251	154	
		9.122	154	
4Q171		10	155	
ii 18-19	143	11	147, 155, 156	
		11.120-33	155	
4Q177		11.133	156	
f1 4:11	143	11.159-67	155	
		11.173	156	
4Q259		11.184-296	147	
3:8	143	11.184	155	
		11.185	156	
4Q300		11.188	151	
8:8	144	11.190	149	
		11.191	150	
4Q333		11.195	149, 151	
f2:1	144	11.200	149	
		11.202	149	
4Q416		11.203	156	
f1:5	143	11.204	150	
		11.205	151	
4Q418		11.209	153	
11	143	11.210	153	
		11.211	153	
4Q427		11.212	153	
f7 2:4	144	11.214	152	
		11.217	150, 153	
4Q431		11.227	57, 152	
f2:3	144	11.228	151	

11.229	152	13b	173, 188
11.230	151		
11.231	151	Sanhedrin	
11.232	151, 152	100a	136
11.234	152		
11.237	151, 152	Sukkah	
11.238	151	43b	180
11.247	150		
11.257	150	MIDRASH	
11.259	152	Esther Rabbah	
11.265	150	1:8	171
11.268	150	3:2	153
11.273-83	154	4:1	171
11.276	154	4:9	59, 171
11.279	152–5	5:4	60, 174
11.280	152	6:2	175
11.281	154	6:8	170
11.282	152, 156	6:13	173
11.286	150	7:4	153, 171
11.289	152	7:10	171
11.294	152		
11.295-96	155	Genesis Rabbah	
11.296	155	87:6	173
11.33-63	155		
14.185-267	154	CLASSICAL AND ANCIENT CHRISTIAN	
14.305-22	154	WRITINGS	
16.160-78	154	Cicero	
16.174	154	Pro Flacco	
		67	154
Against Apion		69	154
1.40	148		
1.42	147	Diodorus Siculus	
1.73-91	154	40.3.4	154
1.227-50	154		
2.148	154	Juvenal	
2.178	155	Satires	
		14.103-104	154
Jewish War			
7.41-111	156	Martin Luther	
7.110	157	47.156	195
MIDRASH		Suetonius	
Midrash Esther		Nero	
9 Meg. 10A, B	73	34	166
TARGUMIC TEXTS		Tacitus	
Targum Sheni		Histories	
Esther 4.13	199	5.5.1	154
BABYLONIAN TALMUD		OTHER	
Megillah		AT	
7a	136	4:22	152
12b	149	4:23	150
13a	153, 199	4:25	152

4:26	152	4:15	151
5:8-9	151		
5:11	99	Proto-AT	
7:22-32	154	iv:5-6	24
7:29	154	viii:33-38	24

www.ingramcontent.com/pod-product-compliance
Lightning Source LLC
Chambersburg PA
CBHW062136300426
44115CB00012BA/1948